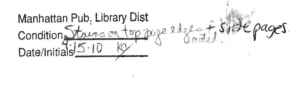

3D GAME
PROGRAMMING
FOR TEENS,
SECOND EDITION

MANEESH SETHI

Course Technology PTR

A part of Cengage Learning

D1405337

COURSE TECHNOLOGY
CENGAGE Learning

Australia • Brazil • Japan • Korea • Mexico • Singapore • Spain • United Kingdom • United States

COURSE TECHNOLOGY
CENGAGE Learning™

**3D Game Programming for Teens,
Second Edition**
Maneesh Sethi

Publisher and General Manager, Course Technology PTR: Stacy L. Hiquet

Associate Director of Marketing: Sarah Panella

Manager of Editorial Services: Heather Talbot

Marketing Manager: Jordan Casey

Senior Acquisitions Editor: Emi Smith

Project Editor: Jenny Davidson

Technical Reviewer: David Rivers

PTR Editorial Services Coordinator: Jen Blaney

Interior Layout Tech: Macmillan Publishing Solutions

Cover Designer: Mike Tanamachi

CD-ROM Producer: Brandon Penticuff

Indexer: Larry Sweazy

Proofreader: Laura Gabler

For product information and technology assistance, contact us at
Cengage Learning Customer & Sales Support, 1-800-354-9706

For permission to use material from this text or product, submit all requests online at **www.cengage.com/permissions**
Further permissions questions can be emailed to
permissionrequest@cengage.com

Blitz3D is a trademark of Blitz Research Ltd. Corel-DRAW/PHOTO-PAINT are trademarks or registered trademarks of Corel Corporation and/or its subsidiaries in Canada, the United States, and/or other countries. Autodesk 3ds Max is a registered trademark of Autodesk, Inc.

All other trademarks are the property of their respective owners.

Library of Congress Control Number: 2008939940

ISBN-13: 978-1-59863-843-1

ISBN-10: 1-59863-843-2

Course Technology, a part of Cengage Learning
20 Channel Center Street
Boston, MA 02210
USA

Cengage Learning is a leading provider of customized learning solutions with office locations around the globe, including Singapore, the United Kingdom, Australia, Mexico, Brazil, and Japan. Locate your local office at:
international.cengage.com/region

Cengage Learning products are represented in Canada by Nelson Education, Ltd.

For your lifelong learning solutions, visit **courseptr.com**

Visit our corporate website at **cengage.com**

Printed in the United States of America
1 2 3 4 5 6 7 11 10 09

3 8001 00089 6484

For Rachita Sethi. Forse un giorno, leggerai questo libro.

Acknowledgments

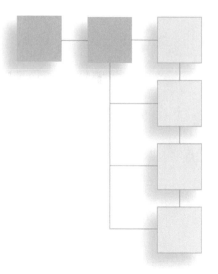

Jeez, there are so many people to thank. This feels like I'm accepting an Oscar: I'm afraid the band will start playing and usher me off the stage. Thanks, first of all, to everyone who worked with me on this book—Emi Smith, for being an awesome editor, and everyone else at Course Technology PTR.

To all of my brothers and sisters: Rachi, who offered her help even though she was across an ocean; Nagina, whose love and support (and numerous phone calls) helped carry me through; and Ramit, who has always been a source of motivation. Thanks for being here and giving me support when I needed it. To my mom Neelam and my dad Prabhjot: I couldn't have done this without you. I love you so much.

And to everyone whose name I forgot, you know who you are. Thanks!

About the Author

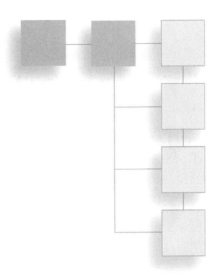

Maneesh Sethi is a Stanford student, freelance web developer, game developer, best-selling author, blogger, programmer, arm wrestling champion, original iPod Sock developer (Google iPod superCase), and much more. Maneesh was the founder and head designer of Standard Design, a website design company; the team leader of Cold Vector Games, a game programming team; and currently runs a freelance web development company. Additionally, he blogs about freelance programming at www.freelancenomad.com. Maneesh has taught game programming on TechTV's "Call for Help" and at game programming conferences across the country. He is the author of *Game Programming for Teens, Web Design for Teens,* and *PHP for Teens,* all published by Course Technology PTR, and *How to Succeed as a Lazy Student.* His books have been translated and have been best-sellers in several countries.

Besides game programming, Maneesh enjoys playing games (of course), sports, such as tennis and basketball, and of course, sleep. Learn more about Maneesh, as well as his award-winning T-shirts and iPod Sock case at www.maneeshsethi .com. Maneesh is currently living in Buenos Aires, Argentina.

Contents

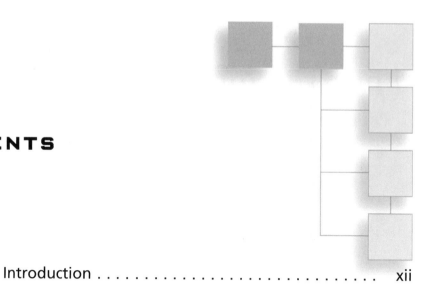

INTRODUCTION

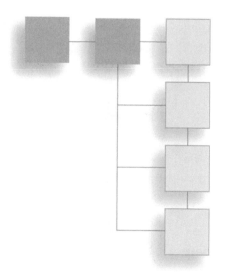

Congratulations on taking your first step to becoming a 3D game programmer by buying this book! If you are looking at this introduction online or are flipping through the pages while standing in a bookstore... What are you waiting for? It's time for the adventure to begin.

Unfortunately, I don't have a crystal ball or great psychic ability, so I can't say for certain exactly who you are, but I think I have a few good guesses. You might be a teenager who is interested in getting started in 3D game programming, and you're looking for a great resource to get started. If so, you've come to the right place. Or, you might be the parent of a teenager or young adult who is looking for a good resource for your child to start 3D game programming. Again, if so, you've come to the right place. My final guess is that you may not be a teenager or the parent of a teenager at all, but you may just be someone who is interested in getting into 3D game programming, and you're looking for a great resource for beginners that isn't intimidating and won't get you lost in a wilderness of heavy technical jargon and difficult math computations. Don't let the title of this book restrict you from diving right in; this book is designed specifically for *anyone* who is interested in starting the journey to 3D game programming.

Here's what I'm assuming: You love games, but you have little or no programming experience. The good news is that you don't need any experience. You just need the will to learn and some time. The only tool that you need to use this book properly is a computer with a CD drive. I'll provide you with everything else. Our journey will involve the use of three different programs: one for programming (Blitz3D), one for graphic design (CorelDRAW/PHOTO-PAINT), and one for 3D modeling (Autodesk 3ds Max), all of which are included on the accompanying CD or can be downloaded free of charge from the Internet.

What's in the Book?

This book is meant to be a guide to teach any beginner how to design and develop games. Inside the book you will find a wealth of knowledge all written to help you reach the goal of making a game. Each chapter builds on the previous chapters and makes the book seem like a staircase—you move up step by step. The last chapter helps use all of your culminated knowledge in the production of a final game.

Part I discusses the Blitz3D language. During this time, the book does not discuss graphical programs, but instead uses text-based programs to get the language points across.

Part II teaches you all about graphics within games. This part teaches the majority of the 3D concepts you need to make awesome games.

Part III examines other related parts of game programming. You can learn how to use sounds, gravity, timers, and everything else you need to develop a game. This part also creates the final game that the book has been leading up to.

A handy appendix is included at the end of the book. Here, you will find all of the scan codes (for handling input).

What Do You Need to Know?

There are literally very few requirements. All you really need is a basic knowledge of math, like addition, subtraction, multiplication, and division. If you know those techniques, you are pretty much set! I use some rudimentary algebra, but those instances are few and far between, and should be easy to comprehend.

You don't need to have any knowledge of other programming languages. Not that it won't help if you do, of course. If you do know any other languages, you can learn from this book as well. But, *3D Game Programming for Teens* teaches the language of game programming along with the ability to actually implement games.

If you are the parent of a child you want to learn programming, this book is the way to go. General programming is a long and boring subject, but game programming allows your child to create things that are *fun*. Help your child with programming while he or she reads this book. Not only will you both learn programming, but who knows, it may strengthen the bond between parent and child (this comes from my psychologist side).

Who Am I?

Hey everybody, I am Maneesh Sethi. I am a student at Stanford University, and the reason I am writing this book is because I believe that, because I am a basically a teenager myself, I would be the best one to help other teens learn about programming. I began programming in 1999 in C and C++. I wrote a book on BlitzBasic, entitled *Game Programming for Teens*, which eventually became an international best-seller.

Blitz3D seems to be the easiest way for any novice to begin writing 3D games, and I want to help you progress as fast as possible. The website for this book is located on www.maneeshsethi.com, and you can e-mail me with any questions (before or after you buy the book) at maneesh@maneeshsethi.com. I love to get e-mails!

The CD

The CD included with the book includes demo software and the source for all of the code in the book.

Let's Get Ready to Rumble

If you are still browsing this book in the bookstore, now would be the time to take it home. The bookstore would probably appreciate it if you buy it first (so would I!).

The first part quickly teaches you all of the intricacies of the Blitz3D programming language.

And so we begin. . .

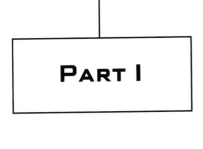

PART I

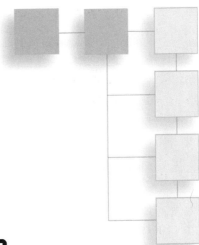

THE BASICS OF BASIC

CHAPTER 1

GETTING STARTED

Welcome to the amazing world of game programming! This book will show you the ins and outs of video games and teach you to develop your own. Game programming is a huge topic, however, and we are going to hurry through the boring material in order to get to the fun stuff. In other words, let's start right away!

If you have read my book *Game Programming for Teens*, you might notice that the first four chapters of this book are awfully similar to the introduction of that book. There is a reason why: The BASIC language, taught in both books, is exactly the same, and the first part of the book is a time-tested tutorial of the language. So, if you've already read my other book, go ahead and skip to Part II, where we start learning about 3D graphics!

The easiest language for learning programming (at least in my opinion) is BASIC. BASIC stands for **B**eginner's **A**ll Purpose **S**ymbolic **I**nstruction **C**ode, but that's not really important. BASIC is very easy to write and understand, and it's modeled after human language (it uses words instead of just numbers), so if you can speak English, you shouldn't have a hard time with BASIC.

We will be using a program called Blitz3D in this book. Blitz3D is built to use a modified version of BASIC in its programming. We begin with a short history of BASIC, just to get the ball rolling on the language.

A Brief History of BASIC

The language of BASIC was first developed in 1964 by J. Kemeny and T. Kurtz at Dartmouth College. It was designed to be a very easy language to understand, translate, and write. It was also meant to be the first step toward writing programs for tougher languages.

In the 1970s, two people, Paul Allen and Bill Gates, decided to develop a BASIC language for the new Altair Personal Computer. The developers of the Altair showed a lot of interest in the BASIC language, and Gates and Allen licensed it.

Bill Gates and Paul Allen put BASIC onto other types of computers. By 1980, BASIC was moved to Atari, Commodore, and Apple computers as well as the Altair. Bill Gates developed an operating system called DOS (Disk Operating System) with a BASIC interpreter. This allowed any user that owned DOS to write programs in BASIC.

Eventually Microsoft, which was headed by Gates, realized how popular BASIC was and decided to write a compiler for it that did not require DOS. QuickBasic, the first standalone BASIC compiler, was born. Soon after, Microsoft decided to focus on graphics and developed Visual Basic, which created graphical programs using BASIC as a core language.

Blitz3D, the program we are using in this book, was developed by Mark Sibly and is geared toward the game developer. Blitz3D is very easy to learn and understand due to its BASIC nature, and it is a good way to learn game programming without having to worry about extra code that has almost nothing to do with the actual game itself.

Installing Blitz3D

We need to get Blitz3D onto our computers so that we can start writing games as soon as possible. Blitz3D is a compiler, so it takes your code and turns it into a program that any computer can run. However, the demo version that is included on the CD does not include the compiler, but only the interpreter. Unlike a compiler, an interpreter does not create an executable file that can be run on any computer; instead, it only runs from within the compiler. In other words, the programs you write will only be able to be run from the compiler on your computer. If you want to compile the program into a standalone executable, you can purchase the full Blitz3D package from http://www.blitzbasic.com. Just go to the Product tab at the top of the page. The Blitz3D installer is shown in Figure 1.1.

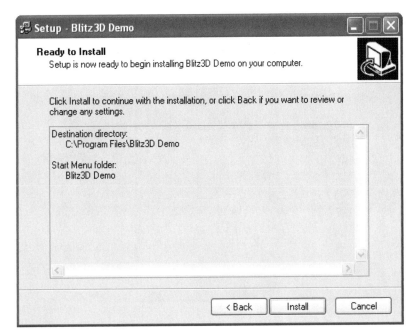

Figure 1.1
Blitz3D installer.

Okay, first things first. To install this program, put the CD into your CD-ROM drive, and run Blitz3DDemo.exe. Blitz3D will ask you where you want to install the program. Choose a directory (the default one is a good choice), and press install. When the installation finishes, click OK, launch the program, and you're done! You now have a full BASIC interpreter on your computer.

Understanding the IDE

Blitz3D can seem a little daunting at first. The program has a lot of menus and icons, but you can master them with a little effort. The first thing you see when you open the program is the documentation window, pictured in Figure 1.2. If you need to find tutorials or sample programs, this is the place to do it. After you have read through anything that interests you, open a new document by selecting File > New or the New button on the main toolbar.

Note

The > (arrow) symbol means a selection from a menu. In other words, File > New instructs you to open the File menu and select New. You can access the menus at the top of the program, right above the main toolbar.

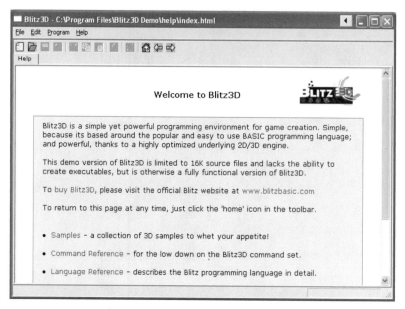

Figure 1.2
The documentation window.

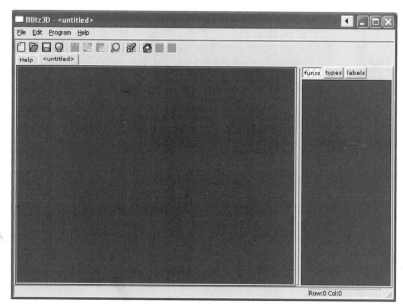

Figure 1.3
The Blitz3D IDE.

What you see now, as in Figure 1.3, is considered the IDE. IDE means Integrated Development Environment, and it is an area in which you can write and compile your programs in the same workspace.

Each of the windows, toolbars, and menus is necessary for game programming, so a good explanation of each might be helpful.

Windows and Panels

The main window takes up most of the program space and it is the most important part of Blitz3D. This window is where the actual code from the game is typed. The keywords and important parts of your program will be highlighted when you type in this area. If you want to see an example, type the word **End**, so that your screen looks like the one pictured in Figure 1.4. You will notice that as soon as you complete the word and press the spacebar, it becomes a different color. This highlight feature helps in reading and understanding your program.

Take a look to the right of the screen. Although not pictured in the previous figure, the only visible panel located on the right is under buttons labeled *funcs, types,* and *labels.* Each of these buttons displays separate info on the panel. Funcs shows which functions you have created, types shows your defined types, and labels shows any existing labels. These descriptions probably don't mean much to you now, but by the end of this book, you will understand what they do.

Toolbars

The main toolbar (shown in Figure 1.5) is simply a set of shortcut icons. It allows you to perform actions quickly without having to search through the menus for the command. Table 1.1 briefly describes each icon going from left to right.

Figure 1.4
Highlighted code.

Figure 1.5
The main toolbar.

Table 1.1 Main Toolbar Shortcut Icons

Icon	Description
New	Opens a new blank Blitz3D file.
Open	Allows you to open an existing file from the disk.
Save	If your program has been saved previously, the Save icon quick-saves the open file; if not, Save asks for a file name and a location to save the file to.
Close	Closes a single file.
Cut, Copy, and Paste	The Cut command saves highlighted text to the clipboard but deletes the highlighted text, the Copy command saves the highlighted text to the clipboard but leaves the highlighted text untouched, and Paste places saved text in the clipboard in the file.
Find	Allows you to search for a certain word or certain words in an opened file.
Run	Compiles and runs an open file.
Home, Back, Forward	All three commands allow you to navigate through the Blitz3D documentation. Unless you are in the documentation window, Back and Forward will be grayed out.

File   Edit   Program   Help

Figure 1.6
Blitz3D menus.

Table 1.2 Blitz3D Menu Commands

Command	Description
Program > Check for errors	This command allows you to error-check your code without compiling and running it.
Program > Debug Enabled?	If this feature is enabled, you will be able to run your program in a small window (instead of the program taking the entire screen) and debugging your program becomes much easier.

Menus

The menu bar allows you to exercise the full power of Blitz3D. The menu bar is pictured in Figure 1.6. Buried within each menu are many helpful and useful commands. Table 1.2 shows the most important.

Table 1.3 Keys Used in Jumping Cone

Key	Action
Up Arrow	Speed up cone
Down Arrow	Slow down cone
Escape	Exit game

The First Program: Jumping Cone!

All right, now you will be able to see what a simple 3D program can do! Basically, this program is just a simple cone that jumps up and down. To play, either run demo01-01.exe from the CD or compile the code.

To compile the code yourself, you need to find demo01-01.bb on the CD. After finding it, copy it to your computer and open it through the Blitz3D compiler. To open it, find the File menu on the top of the compiler and choose Open. Navigate to demo01-01.bb and press Enter. The code should now appear inside your compiler.

To actually compile, find the Program menu in Blitz3D. Select Program > Run Program, and the game will compile and run! If you get a window asking you to save the file, choose a directory to save it in or just press Cancel, and the program will run. You have just compiled your first program!

Feel free to examine the code; although it may seem very weird and hard to understand now, you will soon be able to figure out this code easily.

Table 1.3 lists the keys you will use for this game.

Okay, let's actually take a look at the code. Read it, but don't worry if some of it is hard to understand. This is the first program you have seen, and it isn't easy. You will learn how to actually write this code throughout the book.

The First Program: Jumping Cone

```
;demo01-01.bb - Jumping Cone, your first program!
;--------------------------------------------------

;Set up the graphics
Graphics3D 640, 480
```

```
SetBuffer BackBuffer()
;Define constants
Const ESC_KEY   = 1
Const UP_KEY    = 200
Const DOWN_KEY  = 208

;Define variables
camdistance = 10
type_player = 1
type_ground = 2

;track the position and jump of the cone
velocity#   = 0
```

This is the end of the declaration section of the code. This part sets up the important variables for the program as well as some constants. (Don't worry; you will be introduced to all of this as the book progresses.)

After the declaration, we begin the initialization. Initialization is the process of setting up everything that will be used in the program—in this section, the initialization section sets up the shapes and objects on the screen.

```
;Create the camera, which is what the user sees
camera=CreateCamera()
RotateEntity camera, 45, 0, 0

;Create the light, so the user can see!
light=CreateLight()

;Create a plane and texture, the actual objects on the screen
;Create texture
grid_text = CreateTexture(32, 32, 8)
ScaleTexture(grid_text, 10, 10)

;Draw the texture, and reset the drawing back to the main screen
SetBuffer TextureBuffer(grid_text)

;Create two rectangles
Color 0,0,64
Rect 0,0,32,32
Color 0,0,255
Rect 0,0,32,32
```

```
SetBuffer BackBuffer()

;Create the plane
grid_plane = CreatePlane()


CreateMirror()

HandleEntities(grid_plane, grid_text)

;Create a cone
cone = CreateCone(64)
EntityType cone, type_player
PositionEntity cone, 0, 1, 5
ScaleEntity cone, 0.4, 0.4, 0.4
EntityRadius cone, 0.5

;Create texture for the cone
texture = CreateTexture(16,16):SetBuffer TextureBuffer(texture)
ClsColor 256, 6, 56
Cls
;assign a color for the texture
Color 12, 126, 256
Rect 0, 0, 8, 8, 1
Rect 8, 8, 8, 8, 1
ScaleTexture texture, .2, .2
;put the texture on the cone
EntityTexture cone, texture
```

The initialization section sets up some important variables for the game, such as the score and the player variables. These variables keep track of where the cone is located and how fast it's jumping.

After initialization, the actual loop begins:

```
;MAIN LOOP
While Not KeyDown(ESC_KEY)

     ;Handle User Input
     If KeyDown(UP_KEY)
          velocity = velocity - .001
     EndIf
     If KeyDown(DOWN_KEY)
```

```
        velocity = velocity + 0.001
     EndIf
     ;Move the cone and camera around to see everything
     MoveEntity cone, 0, velocity, 0
     TranslateEntity cone, 0, -0.03, 0
     PositionEntity camera, EntityX(cone), 0, EntityZ(cone)
     MoveEntity camera, 0, 0, -5

     ;Test for collisions so things can't go through walls
     Collisions type_player, type_ground, 2, 2
     Collisions type_ground, type_player, 2, 2

     UpdateWorld
     RenderWorld
     Flip

     Wend ;END MAIN LOOPS

End ;End of the program
```

What Is a Frame?

I am about to reference the word *frame* a bunch of times in a few moments, and you should know what it means. A frame is the screen at any given moment. A game can be compared to an animated film—both are made up of a bunch of different pictures that, when put together, create animation. The frames blend together so quickly that the objects on the screen appear to be moving. An average game runs at 30 frames per second, which means 30 pictures on the screen are blended together each and every second.

This is the end of the main loop. To put it bluntly, the main loop is the entire game. Every frame of a game is a single iteration of the main loop. By the way, a loop causes some code to be repeated over and over until some condition becomes false. Here, the condition is that the Esc key has not been pressed. Usually, the main loop is a *while* loop, shown here in the line

```
While Not KeyDown(ESC_KEY)
```

At this point, the actual game loop has been completed, so we must now define the functions. A function is called with its name followed by parentheses; for example, HandleEntities(). Functions are like little helpers that perform specific activities that we want to do over and over. If you look at the main loop, you will see that most of these functions are called from there, and some others are called from within other functions.

```
;FUNCTIONS

;Function HandleEntities() - this function assigns the texture to the grid plane
and deals with Entities
Function HandleEntities(grid_plane, grid_text)
     ;Make texture and plane appear on screen
     EntityTexture grid_plane, grid_text
     EntityBlend grid_plane, 1
     EntityAlpha grid_plane, .6
     EntityFX grid_plane, 1
     EntityType grid_plane, type_ground

End Function
```

This function simply makes the ground become the ground—it sets the texture color and makes it look pretty.

Figure 1.7 shows the Jumping Cone program!

Figure 1.7
The Jumping Cone!

Compiling the Code

Compiling the code is a very simple procedure. Just open the file (demo01-01.bb) off the CD in Blitz3D (or type it into the workspace), save the file (File > Save) onto your computer, and select Program > Run Program.

Well, that isn't what you would call a full game. I did not add any special effects or sounds because they aren't very important at this point. The idea is to get a feel for what code looks like and how it is written. You will notice that the meanings of most of the functions are easy to understand because of the function names. This helps in understanding the program.

Let me summarize the main parts of a game. The game consists of:

- The initialization section

- The main loop

- The shutdown

Initialization sets up variables and functions that are used throughout the game. Declaration is part of initialization and is used to set up variables that will be used later in the program. The game loop is what you see on the screen. Each *iteration* (an iteration is each time the program runs through the loop) of the loop is one frame of the game. Usually, there are at least 30 frames, or iterations, per second.

The shutdown sequence is the final part of the game, and it runs just before and during the end of the game. It closes all open files, deletes any running variables, and quits the game.

Of course, there are a few other important parts to any game, but I will go over them with you when learning about them is necessary. For now, read over the commented code (on the CD) and try to understand what in heck is going on. If you follow the functions, it shouldn't be too hard.

Summary

We have certainly covered a lot of ground in this chapter! So far, we have learned about the history of BASIC, we have installed Blitz3D, we have learned the important features of the program, and we have written, read, and played our first game. One important thing: *Do not* be disheartened by the length or complexity of the sample code. This game is not a tough one, and although it seems long now, it will be relatively simple to write by the time you finish this book.

In this chapter, we covered the following concepts:

- The history of BASIC

- Installing the Blitz3D program

- Creating our first game

- Compiling our first game

The next chapter will introduce you to the fundamentals of BASIC; it will discuss common operators and operations. If you've made it this far, the next chapter should be a cinch.

Just sit back, relax, and enjoy the ride.

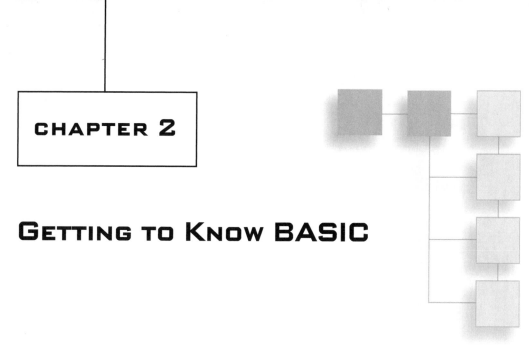

CHAPTER 2

GETTING TO KNOW BASIC

This chapter examines the simple and fundamental aspects of the BASIC language. There will be very few graphical programs in this chapter, so everything we will make will be mostly text.

I suggest taking what you learn about general BASIC programming from this chapter and writing your own sample programs. Although you will not be able to make graphical programs, you will be able to make simple text-based programs. Sample programs help cement ideas that you learn into your mind, so it will be much easier to remember them. The next chapters build heavily on the concepts you learn here, so make sure you understand the fundamentals explained in this chapter before moving on to the next chapters.

In this chapter, you will learn how to use variables, input, and conditionals. Ready?

Hello, World!

Okay, before you go any further, you're going to write your first program. This is a common one for first-time programmers to write in any computer programming language, most likely because it is so simple. This program simply displays the text Hello, World! on the screen. That's right, no graphics, no special effects, just pure, hard-core text.

Let's go over how to compile the following code. Type what follows into your Blitz3D compiler or open demo02-01.bb (see Figure 2.1). Next, select Program > Run Program and watch the magic.

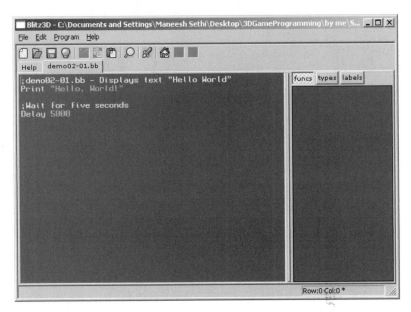

Figure 2.1
The Hello World program in Blitz3D.

If you decide to type the code into the compiler, make sure that the workspace into which you are typing is blank first. Only the code should be displayed in the main window of the Blitz3D compiler.

If you don't want to compile the code, you can also run this program from the CD. Figure 2.2 shows the executed Hello World program.

```
;demo02-01.bb - Displays text "Hello World"
Print "Hello, World!"

;Wait for five seconds
Delay 5000
```

Although this program may seem very simple, you have just crossed a big hurdle. You just created a file, typed in the code, compiled it, and ran it as a program. Congratulations!

Let's analyze this program a bit (although there isn't much to analyze). First of all, the line

```
;demo02-01.bb - Displays text "Hello, World!"
```

is a comment. A comment is any text that is written after a semicolon (;). The comment ends at the end of the line. A comment does not have to occupy

Figure 2.2
The executed Hello World program.

its own line; it can be written after some actual program code. For example, this line

```
Print "This is code" ;This is a comment.
```

consists of two parts: a line of code and a comment. Comments are used to help you understand the code; the compiler does not understand or care about information in comments. The compiler automatically ignores any comments. Figure 2.3 demonstrates how comments look inside a compiler.

Tip

You might be wondering, "If it's my code, why would I need a comment to understand it? I wrote it, so I understand it!" The problem with this assumption is twofold: one, you may decide to share the code with someone after you write the program, and two, you could forget how your program works and spend a lot of time trying to figure out what some parts do. I remember once, at an old coding job, I had to rewrite some old code. "Who wrote this crappy code?!" I asked my boss, because it was taking hours to rewrite. He looked up the logs—guess who had written it? Me, a few months before. I had forgotten not only what the code did, but also that it was I who had written it in the first place. Anyway, the moral of the story is *always comment your code*.

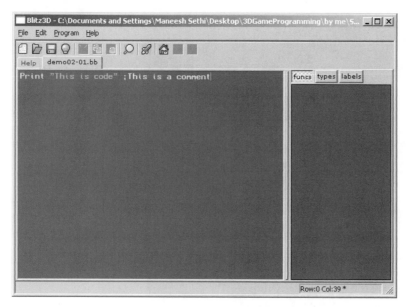

Figure 2.3
Comments in a compiler.

The next line of code is the meat of the program.

```
Print "Hello, World!"
```

This line prints the text string "Hello, World!" on the screen (a text string is simply a set of characters) and begins a new line. To see what I mean by new line, add another Print command to the code. You will see that the new text is written below the old text.

Note the quotes around "Hello, World!" Quotes are necessary around any part of a string. The quotes identify to the program that what is being typed is a set of letters and numbers, not a variable name. If you leave off the quotes, you will get an error.

I usually like to provide the function declaration for easy reference when calling functions. A *function declaration* describes any parameters taken in by the function as well as the function name. The function declaration for Print is:

```
Print [string$]
```

Note

Notice the square brackets ([]) on the left and right of the [string$] variable. These brackets mean that the variable is optional. If the variable is required but omitted, you will receive an error and not be able to compile your code.

Table 2.1 Parameters for Print

Parameter	Description
string$	A text string followed by a new line that will be displayed onscreen. If string$ is omitted, only a new line will be printed.

As you can see, the function's name is Print and the only parameter is [string$]. A string is just a series of characters put together; you can think of a sentence as a string. The string would be the entire sentence lined up together, including the spaces and punctuation.

First of all, Print is a function. Functions (which are described in more detail later) come in two flavors: user-defined and compiler-defined. User-defined functions are written by the programmer, and compiler-defined functions are embedded in the compiler and are available for use in a program. Print is an example of a compiler-defined function.

See Table 2.1 for a description of the Print parameters.

The final line calls the function Delay.

```
Delay millisecs%
```

This function simply pauses for the given amount of time before proceeding. In this program, I had the program pause for 5000 milliseconds, or five seconds. If you remove this line from the program, the program will end before the user can read Hello, World!.

One question remains: What are that dollar sign and the percent sign doing after the parameters to the functions? That brings you to the next topic, variables.

Variables

Variables are intrinsic to almost every program written. A variable is just that: "variable." This means that the value of a variable can change. For example, say you were running a program that uses a high score that is stored in a variable. When the high score changes, the high score variable changes to reflect the new score.

Table 2.2 Description of Variable Types

Parameter	Description
integer%	Fixed-point variables with no decimal places.
float#	Floating-point variables with decimal places allowed.
string$	A text string.

Declaring Variables

Variables are very easy to use because they can be used as regular numbers. However, unlike numbers, variables must first be declared. When a variable is declared, the program knows that the variable exists, and you can use it in your program.

There are three types of variables in BASIC: integer variables, floating-point variables, and string variables. See Table 2.2 for a description of the types of variables.

Note

When variables are created, they are automatically assumed to be integers, or whole numbers in other words. Therefore, the percent sign on all integer variables is unnecessary and from now on, they will mostly be omitted from the code.

Each type of variable is defined in a similar way. Simply type the name of the variable you want to define followed by the type symbol (%, #, or $). For example,

```
highscore% = 100
pi# = 3.14159
myname$ = "Maneesh Sethi"
```

Using Variables

You are now ready to write a few programs using variables. These programs should demonstrate a few important points about variables.

```
;demo02-02.bb - Adds two cool numbers

;VARIABLES
favnum = 314
```

```
coolnum = 13

;Print the two variables
Print "I like " + favnum + " And I like " + coolnum
;Print the variables added together
Print "These numbers added together are " + (favnum + coolnum)
;Delay for 5 seconds
Delay 5000
```

The output is shown in Figure 2.4.

Well, this is certainly interesting. Let's check it out. First, a comment is written to describe the program. This is good practice and should be used on most programs. Next, I initialized two variables: `favnum` and `coolnum`. Then, I called the `Print` function. The string variable begins with the static text `"I like"` and then displays `favnum`. To display `favnum`, you use the concatenation operator (+). The concatenation operator links separate strings together; in this case, it displays the variable `favnum`. It finishes out the first `Print` statement by displaying `"And I like"` + the variable `coolnum`.

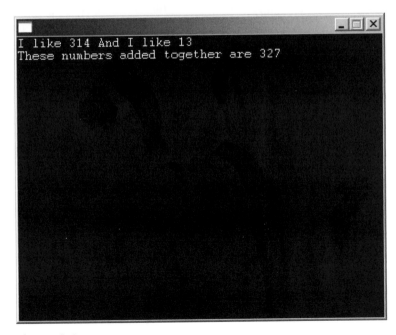

Figure 2.4
The demo02-02.bb program.

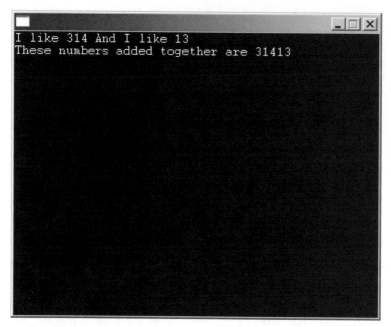

Figure 2.5
Demo02-02.bb without parentheses.

The next `Print` statement displays `"These numbers added together are"` and shows 327, which is equal to 314 + 13. However, try removing the parentheses around `favnum` and `coolnum`. A strange answer comes up when these parentheses are removed: 31413! (See Figure 2.5.)

The reason for this strange answer is that without the parentheses, the addition operator (+) is interpreted as the concatenation operator due to the context in which it is used. Because there are no parentheses, the operator simply adds the string "13" to the end of the string "314" and displays it as a string rather than an integer. The only way to fix this problem is to use parentheses.

Here is an example using only string variables.

```
;demo02-03.bb - adds strings together
string1$ = "I "
string2$ = "like "
string3$ = "programming!"
;concatenate the strings
completestring$ = string1$ + string2$ + string3$
;print 'em out
Print completestring$
Delay 5000
```

Figure 2.6
The demo02-03.bb program.

In this program, a set of single words are created and joined together in the `completestring$` variable using the concatenation operator. As you can see in Figure 2.6, `"I " + "like " + "programming!"` becomes `"I like programming!"`.

Input

Finally, you understand how variables work. Now, let's use those variables to get input from the user of the program. Using input, you can recognize what keys the user presses, or you might have the user answer a question. Either way, most input is stored in a variable. Figure 2.7 shows the output of this program.

```
;demo02-04.bb asks user's name and shows it
;get the user's name
name$ = Input$("Hi! May I know your name please? ")
Print "Hi " + name$ + "."

;Wait five seconds
Delay 5000
```

The first line is a comment that tells what the program does. The second line takes in the input, and the third and final line displays what the user entered.

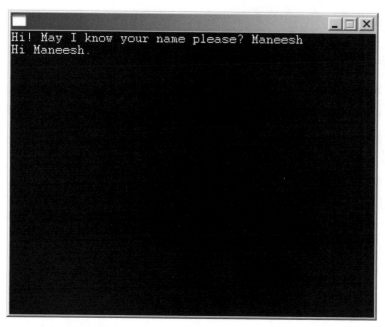

Figure 2.7
The demo02-04.bb program.

Table 2.3 Parameters for Input$()

Parameter	Description
prompt$	The string displayed to the user before allowing the user to enter an input value.

Input$ is declared as this:

Input$(prompt$)

Table 2.3 describes Input$'s parameters.

Caution

Notice that the function name, Input$, has a $ sign attached to the end. This symbol signifies the return type of the function. Because it is a string, the function only returns strings. What this means is that if you request the user to put in numbers to add together, such as 2 + 2, the value returned will be "2 + 2", NOT 4. Of course, if the user typed in 4, the function would return 4.

Input$ is the name of the function. Table 2.3 explains that prompt$ is a string that is displayed to the computer before taking the input value. prompt$ is usually used to ask the user to provide you with the info you want so that the user will know what to tell the program. Notice that there are parentheses around `prompt$` in the function. Parentheses are required; if you fail to place them in the program, the program will not compile. Also, notice that there are no brackets around `prompt$`. This means that the variable is required. If you want to have a blank `prompt$`, use "" (two quotation marks) as your prompt.

In the previous program, `name$` is set equal to the `Input$` command. When the `Input$` command receives an answer from the user, it is stored in the `name$` variable. If you left this line looking like this:

```
Input$("Hi! May I know your name please? ")
```

without including a variable, the response that the user made would be simply thrown away. Using `Input$` without a variable is not a good idea.

`Input$` only returns strings (that's why a $ is added to the function name). However, if the variable you use to retrieve the user input is an integer instead of a string, the value will be interpreted as an integer. Therefore, if you ask the user "How old are you?" and the variable you use to retrieve the value is an integer, the variable will contain whatever the user types in.

Okay, you now have the basics of input down. However, this input function isn't very useful so far. Who wants a program that tells him his own name? This brings me to the next topic: conditionals.

Conditionals

Conditionals are a very important part of any program. Conditionals allow your program to think. With conditionals, any program can make choices and decisions. Before you can fully understand conditionals, however, you must first learn about the Blitz3D idea of truth and falsehood.

Truth and Falsehood

Blitz3D has a different idea about what is true and what is false than we humans do. To a human, some things may be partly true, but to a computer, any expression is either true or false. Although parts of an expression can be different from the rest, the entire expression is only evaluated as one or the other.

Table 2.4 Relational and Logical Operators

Operator	
Relational Operators	
>	Greater than
>=	Greater than or equal to
<	Less than
<=	Less than or equal to
=	Equal to
<>	Not equal to
Logical Operators	
And	
Or	
Not	

Blitz3D (and computers in general) believes that zero is false and any other value (nonzero value) is true, although the true value is usually one. This makes programming a much easier job.

To determine whether something is true or false, you use the relational and logical operators. These operators check one statement against another to see whether the aspect of their relationship that is being checked is true or false. Table 2.4 lists all of the relational and logical operators.

Using Table 2.4 as a guide, you can see that if, say, variable A is equal to 14 and variable B is equal to 12, A>B will return True, because 14 is a larger number than 12.

If...Then

The first conditional you will learn is the If statement. The If statement has a very basic declaration:

```
If
```

The idea of an If statement is that it allows your program to make choices. You pass an expression into the If statement by following the If command with the expression:

```
If expression is true Then
;Do something
Endif
```

As you can see, the If statement is followed by an expression. If the expression is true, the code between the If and EndIf commands is executed. If not, nothing happens.

```
;demo02-05.bb - Tests if you are old enough to vote

;Find out how old the user is
age = Input$("How old are you? ")
;if older than or equal to 18, print out confirmation that user is allowed to vote.
If age >= 18 Then
    Print "You are legally allowed to vote!"
EndIf
;Wait five seconds
Delay 5000
```

This program simply asks how old you are, tests it against the age 18, and then prints "You are legally allowed to vote!" if you are 18 years or older. But what if you want to tell the user something else, even if they aren't over 18? As you can see from the code, this program does nothing if the user is younger than 18. The program then waits for the user to press a key for the program to exit. Figure 2.8 shows the program running.

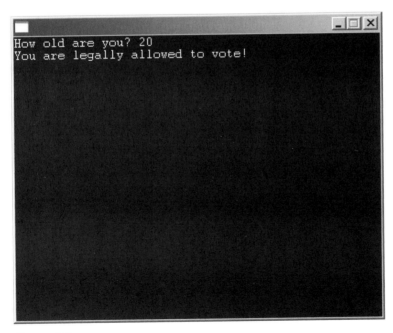

Figure 2.8
The demo02-05.bb program.

You may not understand what the EndIf command does. The EndIf command signifies the end of the If...Then test. When the program reaches the EndIf, it resumes normal processing of commands instead of only executing the commands when the condition tested in the If statement is met.

If...Then...Else

Perhaps you want the program to test if the user is younger than 18. You could rewrite the program by adding another If statement to check if the user is younger than 18, but there is another easier (and better) way: Use the Else statement.

```
;demo02-06.bb - Tests if you are old enough to vote

;Ask how old the user is
age = Input$("How old are you? ")

;if older than or equal to 18 then let them vote
If age >= 18 Then
    Print "You are legally allowed to vote!"

;if younger than 18, do not let them vote

Else Print "Sorry, you need To be a few years older."
EndIf

;Wait five seconds
Delay 5000
```

Figure 2.9 shows the output.

This time, the program tests the user's age, but if it is less than 18, it prints out the sentence under the Else statement.

There is also one other effective use of the If...Else conditional. You can combine the two to create Else If.

```
;demo02-07.bb Tests if you are old enough to vote
age = Input$("How old are you? ")
If age = 18 Then
    Print "You can now vote."
Else If age > 18
    Print "You've been able to vote for a while."
```

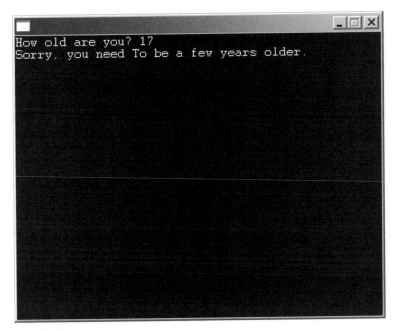

Figure 2.9
The demo02-06.bb program.

```
Else If age ≤ 18
     Print "Sorry, you will have to wait a few years to vote."
EndIf
WaitKey
```

Figure 2.10 shows the output.

Caution

This program will only work if the user enters an integer. If the user enters a string, the variable will always be zero. You can fix this problem using a loop, which will be explained soon.

Notice the new function WaitKey. Instead of delaying for five seconds, WaitKey just waits for the user to press any key before continuing on with the program.

This program tests all three user possibilities.

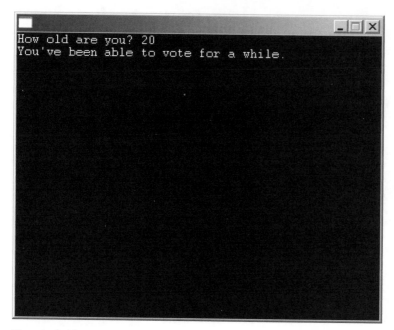

Figure 2.10
The demo02-07.bb program.

Sometimes, you might want to test a large number of possibilities, and using If...Then can be awkward. A conditional statement was made to fix this problem: Select...Case

Select...Case

Select...Case makes working with a large number of values much easier. The best way to demonstrate is with an example.

```
;demo02-08.bb - tests the keys pressed

x = Input$("Enter 1 to say hi, or 0 to quit. ")

Select x
    Case 1
        Print "Hi!"
    Case 0
        End
    Default
        Print "Huh?"
```

```
End Select

;Wait five seconds
Delay 5000
```

In this listing, the program asks the user to enter either one or zero. It then either writes "Hi!" or quits the program. The default case is a catch-all command; if the user enters neither one nor zero, the default code is displayed.

Note

> If you haven't observed it already, notice that I have been indenting my code in a very easy to understand and logical manner. This makes reading and understanding code much easier, and I highly recommend that you do the same.

In this case, Select...Case isn't very necessary. Because there are only two cases, it is just as easy to use an If...Else. However, when the programs get more complex, Select...Case becomes a more useful tool.

By the way, the declaration for Select...Case is

```
Select variable
```

Easy enough, huh?

Logical Operators

Logical operators are a base for expressions and conditional statements. You can view all of the Blitz3D logical operators in Table 2.5. It lists all of the conditions that make the logical operators true and false.

The AND operator is true only if both its parameters are true; the OR operator is true if one or more of its parameters are true; and the NOT operator is true only if its parameter is false. On the next page is an example of the AND operator.

Table 2.5 Logical Operator Truth Table

P	Q	P AND Q	P OR Q	NOT P
0	0	0	0	1
0	1	0	1	1
1	1	1	1	0
1	0	0	1	0

```
;demo02-09.bb - Shows use of the And operator

;find out how old the user is
age = Input$("How old are you? ")
;find out if the user lives in america
location = Input$("Do you live in America? (1 For yes, 2 For no) ")

;Write out the proper string depending on the user's age and location
If age >= 18 And location = 1 Then
     Print "Congrats, you are eligible to vote!"
Else
     Print "Sorry, you can't vote."
EndIf

;Wait five seconds
Delay 5000
```

The output is shown in Figure 2.11.

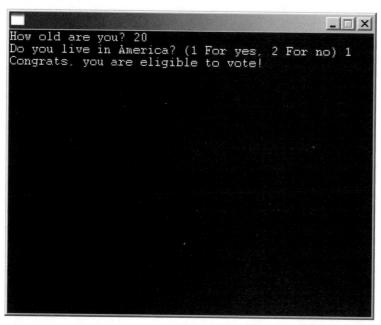

Figure 2.11
The demo02-09.bb program.

The NOT Operator

The NOT operator is a little bit different from the other two logical operators. Instead of two operands, it only takes one. And instead of returning a value based on the other two operands, it only returns the opposite of the operand it is working on.

Remember that because false is zero and true is one, the only value NOT will return is one or zero. If you write

```
Not 0
```

your answer will be one, and conversely if you write

```
Not 1
```

your answer will be zero.

The Goto Command

Before writing a full-fledged game, I want to introduce you to the concept of Goto. Goto is a very simple command, but it can be misused very easily, so I recommend using Goto as sparingly as possible. Almost always, if something can be done by using Goto, it can be done in another way.

Goto works like this: you add a label somewhere in your code, and Goto jumps to that label. (See Figure 2.12.) The best illustration of this is a sample program.

```
;demo02-10.bb Demonstrates use of Goto
.label
Print "Hello"
selection = Input("Enter 1 if you want me to repeat 'Hello' = => ")
If (selection = 1)
        Goto label
EndIf
End
```

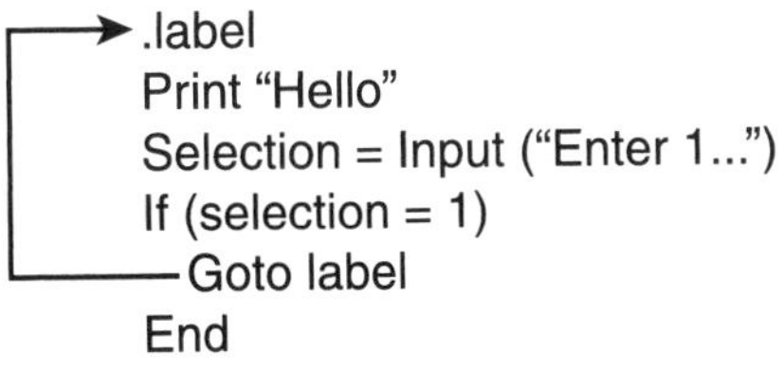

```
.label
Print "Hello"
Selection = Input ("Enter 1...")
If (selection = 1)
Goto label
End
```

Figure 2.12
Using Goto.

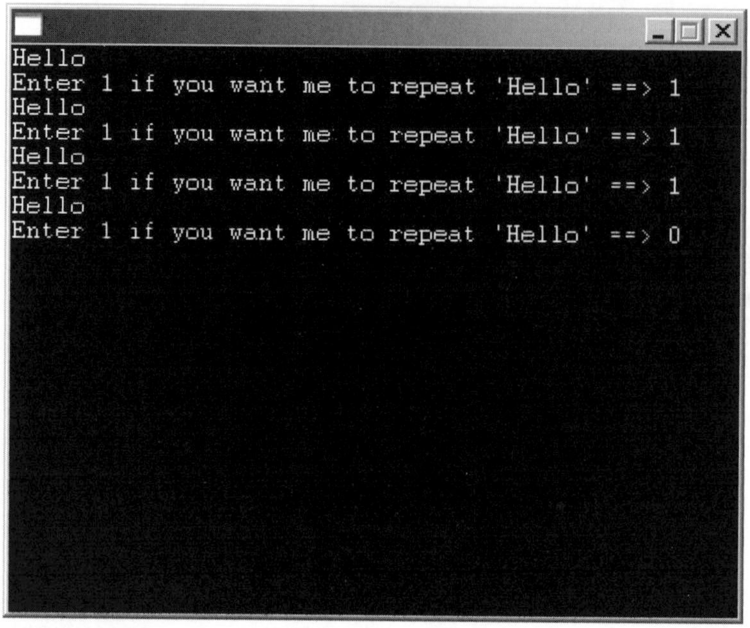

Figure 2.13
The demo02-10.bb program.

The output is shown in Figure 2.13.

N o t e

Notice that I did not include WaitKey in this program. Because the program repeats and then ends with an End command, the WaitKey is not necessary.

As you can see in Figure 2.12, calling Goto starts the program back at the top. This is accomplished by putting .label at the top of the program. You can make Goto move anywhere by simply moving the line .label. Notice that when you define the label, you put a period (.) before it. When you call it from Goto, however, you discard the period.

A Text-Based Guessing Game

Now, let's put together all of what you learned in this chapter and create your first guessing game! Basically, the users enter a number, and you will tell them if they are too high or too low. You will allow the users to guess until they figure it out. In order to make this game work, you will be using a loop in this game. If you cannot understand what the loop's function is, it is explained in the next chapter.

First you need to create an initialization section. It will look something like this.

```
;demo02-11.bb - Try to guess the number
Print "Welcome to the Guessing Game!"
AppTitle "Guessing Game!"
;Seed the random generator...don't worry, it will be explained later
SeedRnd MilliSecs()

;Pick a number between 1 and 100
numbertoguess = Rand(1,100)

;The num of guesses the user has used
numofguesses = 0
```

The first line, after Print, calls the function AppTitle. This changes the name in the heading bar, so that instead of the program being named "Blitz Runtime Window," it will be named "Guessing Game!".

The randomizer works like this: numbertoguess is assigned to a random number, which is returned by Rand. Rand returns a number between what is given; here, it returns a number between 1 and 100. This section prints out introduction text, sets up the guessing number, and declares some variables.

Next you set up the loop and the test to make sure the player guessed a number between 1 and 100.

```
;set the beginning of loop label
.loopbegin
        ;Find out the user's guess
        guess = Input$("Guess a number ")

        ;If player guesses outside of range, tell him to guess again
        If guess > 100 Or guess < 1
                Print "Pick a number between 1 and 100, silly!"
                ;Go back to the beginning
                Goto loopbegin

        EndIf
```

The first line of this code sets up a label to go back to the loop later. Next, the loop begins, the player is asked for input, and the number is tested to see if it is within the correct range. If not, the player is sent back to the beginning of the loop.

Now, you insert the code to see if the player has guessed correctly.

```
;Add a guess to the guess counter
numofguesses = numofguesses + 1

;If the guess is too low, go back to beginning
If guess < numbertoguess Then

Print "The number was too low."
      Goto loopbegin
;If guess is too high, go back to the beginning
Else If guess > numbertoguess Then
      Print "The number was too high."
Goto loopbegin
EndIf
```

The first line adds one to the user's number of guesses. Then, the code is tested to see if the user has guessed too high, too low, or just right. If the player has guessed just right, the code just continues through to the end of the program without going back to the beginning of the loop.

Finally, you enter the last section of code.

```
Print "You guessed the number " + numbertoguess + " in " + numofguesses   + " tries!"

;Wait five seconds
Delay 5000
```

This program can be run off the CD. It is named demo02-11.bb. Figure 2.14 shows the output of the complete Guessing Game.

Summary

This was a tough chapter. I hope that you remember most of what I have told you so far. I suggest you write a few sample programs using everything taught in this program before you head on to the next chapter; it will help solidify the information in your head.

This chapter covered the following concepts:

- The Hello, World! program

- Variables

- Input

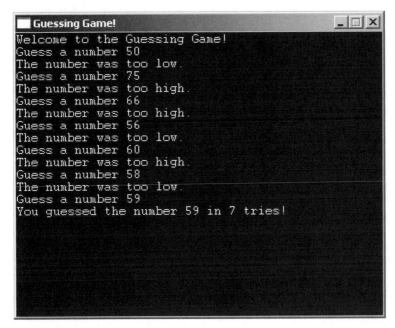

Figure 2.14
The complete Guessing Game.

■ Conditionals

The next chapter discusses loops, functions, arrays, and types. I hope you're ready!

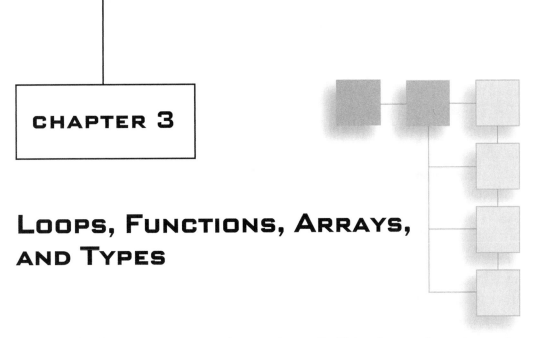

CHAPTER 3

Loops, Functions, Arrays, and Types

We are finally moving up to the tough stuff. This chapter introduces the important and interesting subjects of loops, functions, arrays, and types. All of these are essential to any computer game program.

In this chapter, I'm going to explain each of the processes separately and then create a simple game that incorporates them all. By the time you get there, you will know how to use loops, functions, arrays, and types.

Understanding Loops

A *loop* is a block of code that is repeated over and over until a condition is met. For example, the main game loop is repeated over and over until the player quits or wins the game. We can use goto, a command that we learned in the previous chapter, as a loop. If you remember the demo02-10.bb program, a set of commands was repeated until the user wanted them to stop. Loops work exactly like this: a set of commands is repeated over, and over, and over, until a condition is met—either the user wants to exit the loop or the loop is executed a specific number of times. Figure 3.1 shows a sketch of a loop.

Loops are used for many repetitive tasks in computer programs. In a space shooter game, for example, we have to use a loop to check every bullet against the enemy ships. We will also use loops to update the artificial intelligence (AI) for each of the ships.

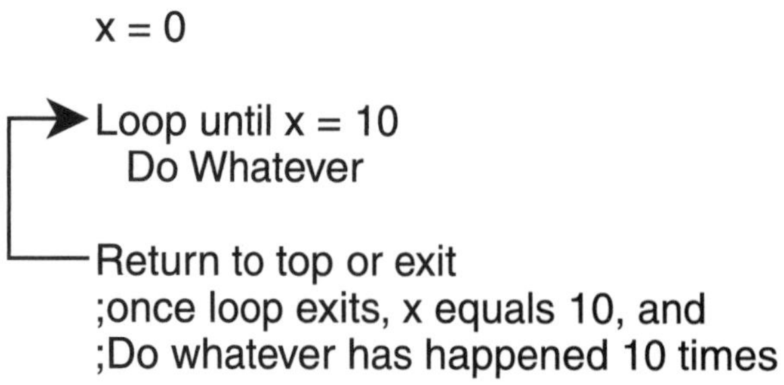

x = 0

Loop until x = 10
   Do Whatever

Return to top or exit
;once loop exits, x equals 10, and
;Do whatever has happened 10 times

Figure 3.1
The loop.

There are three types of loops, and although they are somewhat interchangeable, each has a specific style and it is best if they are used in the proper situation. The three types of loops are

- For... Next

- While... Wend

- Repeat... Until

For...Next

The For...Next loop steps through a block of code a set number of times. In other words, you use it when you know how many times the loop should iterate. You might use this loop when you want the player to move up exactly 10 spaces. Because you know the number of times you want the player to move up, you might have each iteration of the loop move the player up one space and have the loop go through its commands ten times. This loop also can update the info of a set of types (types are explained later in this chapter).

Note

Before we move on, I want to discuss the concept of iterations. As you know, a loop processes a number of commands over and over again, starting at the top, going to the bottom, and moving back to the top again. An *iteration* occurs when all of the commands have been processed one full time. When the loop finishes the last statement of the loop, but has not returned to the top of the loop, it has completed one iteration. When it returns to the top, the second iteration begins, and so on.

For...Next loops are always used as follows:

```
For variable = beginning_number To
ending_number [Step step_amount]
      ;Perform actions
Next
```

As you can see, a For...Next loop begins with For and ends with Next. The To command defines how many times the loop performs its actions. Step_amount, which is optional, defines how much is added to beginning_number each time. If you omit Step, beginning_number is incremented by 1 each time the loop is traversed.

Let's examine a code example:

```
;demo03-01.bb - counts from 1 to 10
;start counter at one and loop till 10
For counter = 1 To 10
     ;Print whatever counter is equal to
     Print counter
Next

;Delay for five seconds
Delay 5000
```

Figure 3.2 shows the output.

This program simply prints the numbers 1 to 10 on the screen. The first line after the entry comment begins the For...Next loop. It declares counter and initializes

Figure 3.2
The demo03-01.bb program.

it to 1. The To command tells the compiler how many iterations the loop will go through. Here, it says it will count from one to ten.

The next line simply prints the value of counter, which adds one to its count every iteration of the loop. The final line of the loop returns the code to the beginning of the loop and raises counter by one.

You can change the step amount of the loop if you want. The step amount is how much is added to the variable on each iteration of the loop. By default, the step amount is 1.

To change the step amount, simply add the command Step after the To command like this:

```
;demo03-02.bb - Counts backwards using step amounts
;start counter at 5 and loop till 0 by -1.2
For counter# = 5.0 To 0.0 Step -1.2
        ;Print value of counter
        Print counter
Next

;Delay for five seconds
Delay 5000
```

The output is shown in Figure 3.3.

Caution

Make sure to double-check your loops to ensure you did not make them never-ending. If this program had been written with the step value as 1.2 (as opposed to -1.2), the program would have looped forever and never ended. Fortunately, Blitz3D normally catches this error and simply skips the loop.

This program might seem a little strange, but I wrote it as such in order to make a few points. First, the counter variable is a floating-point variable (a variable with decimal places). The starting value is 5.0 and the ending value is 0.0. The step value is −1.2.

The step value causes the program to count down instead of counting up. On the first iteration of the loop, the counter variable is 5.0. Then it decreases to 3.8, and so on.

Let's look at the values for this loop. Table 3.1 explains the values of the counter variable, the step amount, and the output throughout the program. As you can see,

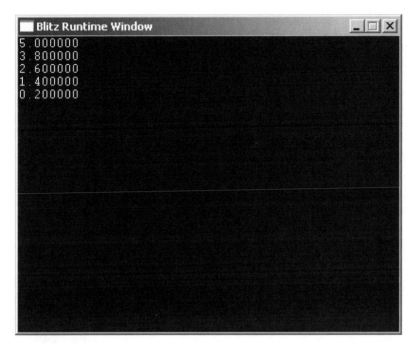

Figure 3.3
The demo03-02.bb program.

Table 3.1 Demo03-02.bb's Variable Values

Iteration	Counter#/Output	Step
1	5.0	–1.2
2	3.8	–1.2
3	2.6	–1.2
4	1.4	–1.2
5	0.2	–1.2

the first iteration of the For...Next loop does not decrease the Step amount; instead, the Step amount begins being subtracted beginning with the second iteration.

Now is a good time to introduce *float trimming*. If you look at the output of the demo03-02.bb sample (see Figure 3.3), you will notice that there are six digits after the decimal place. Six digits after the decimal is the default value. Because only one of the digits is significant, why leave the extra five sitting there? Trimming in this context is removing the trailing zeroes from a float value.

In order to trim the trailing zeroes, we have to follow two steps. First, we must convert the floating variable (which has decimal places) into a string. Next, we remove all the unnecessary digits. Then, we are free to display the string.

Let's try it:

```
;demo03-03.bb - Counts using step amounts
;loop backwards, from 5.0 to 0.0 by -1.2
For counter# = 5.0 To 0.0 Step -1.2
    ;print out 3 digits of counter, so 5.000000 becomes 5.0 - decimal is a digit
        Print Left$( Str counter, 3)
Next

;Delay for five seconds
Delay 5000
```

Figure 3.4 shows the output.

Note

Notice that this example uses 3 as the length variable. The reason is because the number is converted to a string, and the decimal is part of it. The example keeps the number before the decimal, the decimal, and one number after the decimal.

Figure 3.4
The demo03-03.bb program.

Table 3.2 Parameters for Left$

Parameter	Description
string$	The string you want to trim
length	The number of letters you want to include

This program begins the same way as the previous program did: it creates a For-Next loop that begins with 5.0 and decreases by 1.2 until it reaches 0.0. The next line prints the newly trimmed version of counter's value. Let's examine this statement.

The Print statement writes out each float value with one digit after the decimal place. The first thing it does is call the Left$() function. Left$() is declared as

```
Left$ (string$, length)
```

In this case, the string$ variable was

```
Str counter
```

The Str function takes an integer or a float and converts it to a string. It then returns the created string. Because the return value is a string, we can use it in place of the string$ variable. The length variable is set to 3 to include the number and only one decimal point. Table 3.2 describes the parameters.

While...Wend

The next type of loop is the While...Wend loop. This loop is very much like the For...Next loop, but it is normally used to test variable conditions. In other words, the While...Wend loop is normally used when you aren't sure when to exit the loop.

While loops are the most common main loops in games. The main loop (also known as the *game* loop) is a loop that runs over and over until the game is over. Because it cannot be determined *exactly* when to end a game, the While...Wend loop is a perfect choice.

```
;demo03-04.bb - Waits for a key and then exits
Graphics 640,480
Text 0,0, "This program is worthless."
Text 0,12,"Press escape to exit."
Flip
;Wait until user presses 1 to Escape
While Not KeyDown(1)
Wend
End
```

Note

You might notice some strange functions in this program, such as Flip and Graphics. To check for KeyDown(), you have to be in graphics mode, and the Graphics command does that. You will learn more about this in Part II; for now, just pretend it isn't there.

Figure 3.5 shows the output of this program.

This program simply displays some text and asks you to quit. Almost a waste of time, huh? Well, at least it demonstrates While...Wend and it introduces a new function, KeyDown().

The While...Wend loop begins like this:

```
While Not KeyDown(1)
```

This line of code sets up a While loop that exits only when the user presses the Esc key. The loop continues until the user presses the Esc key. KeyDown(), which is declared as

```
KeyDown(scancode)
```

and determines whether Esc has been pressed.

Figure 3.5
The demo03-04.bb program.

Here, the number 1 is used as the scan code. A *scan code* is a code generated by pressing any key on a keyboard. Each key has its own separate scan code. Esc has the scan code of 1. You can see a list of all of the scan codes in Appendix A.

KeyDown returns 1 (true) if the key has been pressed and 0 (false) if the key has not been pressed. Because we want the While...Wend loop to continue until the key has been pressed, we invert the return value by including NOT. Therefore, if the player does not press Esc, the KeyDown returns 0. The NOT command inverts this to a 1, and the While...Wend loop continues to the next iteration.

Now is a good time to introduce the basic game loop. This loop only ends when the user presses Esc. If the user loses, a function is called that will end the program. Note that this code *will not* work. It will only call functions that don't exist (functions are introduced later in this chapter).

```
;Basic Game loop
While Not KeyDown(1)
     PerformLogic()
     Animation()
     If playerlost Then
        GameOver()
     EndIf
Wend
```

This game loop is basically the most simplified version possible. Unless the player loses or presses Esc, the loop continues to iterate. The PerformLogic() function probably updates the AI for the game and Animation() probably draws and animates everything onscreen. If the playerlost variable is set to 1 (most likely by the PerformLogic() function), the GameOver() function is called and the game is over.

You should always strive to keep your main loop as simple as possible. It should not perform more operations than necessary. You will learn how to delegate operations to smaller and more efficient functions soon in this chapter.

Repeat...Until

The final Blitz3D loop is the Repeat...Until loop. This loop is almost exactly like the While...Wend loop, except that the condition is written after the closing statement (Until) instead of the opening statement (Repeat).

Doesn't seem like a big difference, huh? The only time you use this type of loop is when you know for sure that the loop should be executed at least once. This is evident in situations that involve displaying menus and testing for keys.

```
;demo03-05.bb - Closes program after player presses ESC.
Graphics 640,480
Text 0,0, "Why did you open this program?"
Flip
;y is the variable that judges the location of the text
y=12
Repeat
     ;Print text
     Text 0,y, "Press Esc to exit."
     ;wait a sec
     Delay 1000
     Flip

     ;Move next line of text down
     y=y+12

;repeat until user hits esc
Until KeyHit(1)
Text 0,y, "Program is ending."
Flip
```

The output is shown in Figure 3.6.

Figure 3.6
The demo03-05.bb program.

This program simply writes "Press Esc to exit" to the screen until the user presses Esc. It introduces two main functions: Delay and KeyHit().

Delay pauses the program's execution for a set number of milliseconds. Delay is declared as

Delay milliseconds

where milliseconds is the number of milliseconds you want to delay the program for. This program delays the execution for one second (1000 milliseconds).

The other new function introduced is KeyHit()

KeyHit(scancode)

scancode is the code for the key that might be pressed. This function determines if the key was pressed. If the key was pressed, it returns true; if not, it returns false.

The y variable tracks the location of the Text command. Each time, the y variable is incremented by 12, moving the text down one line.

The reason that the text is moved down 12 pixels is because the font size of the text is size 12. Moving the text down 12 pixels is equivalent to making a new line in the program. The condition for exiting the Repeat...Until loop is the opposite of While...Wend and For...Next loops. Instead of continuing to iterate the loop only as long as the condition is true, the Repeat...Until loop continues only when the condition is false. Take extra precautions to make sure you do not create a never-ending loop.

Note

> You might wonder about the difference between the new function KeyHit() and the previously introduced function KeyDown(). The fact is, there is very little difference. KeyDown() determines if the button is down at the time of the test, whereas KeyHit() determines if it has been down since the last KeyHit() was checked. You can see the difference in any game. If you use KeyDown(), you can hold down a key to make it work repeatedly; if you use KeyHit(), you have to press the button every time you use it.

Because the program used Repeat...Until, the "Press Esc to exit" line will always be shown, even if you press Esc before the loop begins. If you ever write a program that utilizes menus (most RPG [*Role-Playing Game*] games do), you should use a Repeat...Until loop.

Okay, I have now thoroughly discussed each of the loops. I hope that you are now an expert on how, as well as when, to use all three of the types of loops. Now on to an extremely important subject: functions.

Understanding Functions

Functions are integral to any program. Even in the programs you have been writing so far, you have used functions such as Print and Delay, and you have even written your own implicit main function. This section teaches you how to write your own functions that will make understanding and writing your program much easier and simpler.

Functions are small snippets of code that usually perform a single task. All programs consist of at least one function: main. Although main isn't actually defined, it still exists within the program.

Every line of code written so far (with the exception of the ones in Chapter 1) has been written in the function main. This function is the starting point and ending point of every Blitz3D program. Figure 3.7 shows an example of the main function in action. Because the main function is never formally declared, I always write a comment telling myself where it begins. I suggest you do the same.

Main calls two types of programs to do its work: user-defined and program-defined functions. *User-defined functions* are those that are written by the programmer. All of these functions must be defined before they are used. *Program-defined functions* are defined within the compiler, like the function Print. All of these have already been written; all you have to do is call them with the proper parameters.

A parameter is a piece of information sent to the function to tell it what to do. For example, the string$ variable is a parameter to the Print function. This variable tells Print what you want printed to the screen.

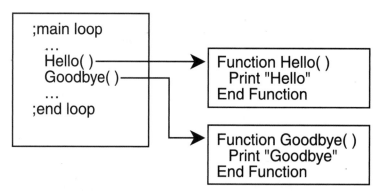

Figure 3.7
A function example.

You can send parameters to your own functions as well, but make sure that you declare the parameters in advance. If your function is called with an extra parameter, your code will not compile.

To use any function, you first must declare it. The function declaration is usually written directly before the function code.

```
Function functionname([parameter variable,])
```

Looks kind of complex, huh? Let's make this easy. First type **Function**. This is required for every function declaration. Now, pick a function name (make sure it describes what the function does; for example, if it counts, call it *Count*). Now, add an open parenthesis. Add as many parameter variables as you need, each separated by a comma. Finally, add an ending parenthesis.

Here is an example

```
Function ConvertFtoC (fvalue)
```

This function most likely converts a Fahrenheit value to a Celsius value. You can see that by looking at the function's name. Make sure yours are easy to understand too.

Next, you write the actual function code.

```
Return (5.0/9.0 * (fvalue - 32))
```

Remember that the * sign means multiplication and the / sign means division. This code returns the Celsius value of the variable sent. A return value is any number or string returned by a called function. For example, on the KeyHit() function, either a one or a zero is returned. Here, the returned value is the Celsius equivalent to the Fahrenheit number.

Finally, we end the function.

```
End Function
```

We now need a main function call to actually use this function.

```
Print "Welcome to our FtoC converter"
fvalue = Input$("What Fahrenheit value do you wish to convert?")
cvalue = ConvertFtoC(fvalue)
Print fvalue + " Fahrenheit = " + cvalue + " Celsius."
```

This section of code is the actual main program. It starts off by introducing the program and receiving the Fahrenheit value to convert. Next it calls ConvertFtoC() and stores its value in the variable cvalue. Finally it prints the results.

Let's put all these parts together now.

```
;demo03-06.bb - Converts Fahrenheit to Celsius

;MAIN PROGRAM
Print "Welcome to our FtoC converter"
;get Fahrenheit and put it in fvalue
fvalue = Input$("What Fahrenheit value do you wish to convert? ")

;Convert fvalue to Celsius
cvalue = ConvertFtoC(fvalue)

;print results
Print fvalue + " Fahrenheit = " + cvalue + " Celsius."

;Delay for five seconds
Delay 5000

;END OF MAIN PROGRAM

Function ConvertFtoC(fvalue)
      ;convert value and return it
      Return 5.0/9.0 * (fvalue - 32)
End Function
```

Figure 3.8 shows the output of this program.

And that's all there is to functions. Well, almost . . .

Scope Considerations

There are two possible scopes in Blitz3D: global and local. *Global variables* are visible throughout the program, in every function and every line of code. *Local variables* are valid only in the function in which they are defined. This means that a variable defined within one function is not valid in another.

What Is Scope?

Scope is kind of hard to understand, so to help, I went to http://www.dictionary.com and looked up scope. Here is what it said:

"The scope of an identifier is the region of a program source within which it represents a certain thing. This usually extends from the place where it is declared to the end of the smallest enclosing block (begin/end or procedure/function body). An inner block may contain a redeclaration of the same identifier, in which case the scope of the outer declaration does not include (is "shadowed" or "occluded" by) the scope of the inner."

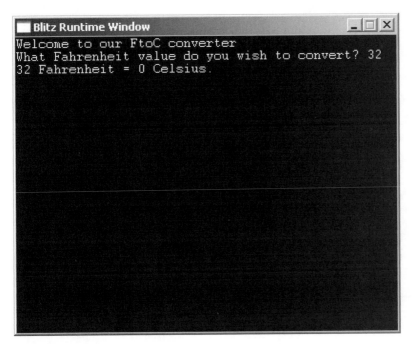

Figure 3.8
The demo03-06.bb program.

What? If you finished reading that (20 bucks says you gave up after "program source within which it represents a certain thing"), you are probably as lost as you were before.

Scope is a range of operation from where variables can be referenced. The fact that there are two kinds of scopes allows programmers to create programs that have two or more variables with the same name. You can have one variable with the name `variablex` in the global scope (otherwise known as the main program) and another variable named `variablex` in the function `HiIAmAFunction()`. Even though every other part of the program, including other functions, will use the global scope's version of `variablex`, `HiIAmAFunction()` will use its separate, more specialized, version of `variablex`.

By the way, Scope is also a mouthwash.

Let me show you an example of scoping. Note that this code will not work. It is only used to demonstrate scope problems.

```
;CallMe() - Broken
CallMe()
Print x

Function CallMe()
      x = 314
End Function
```

Figure 3.9
The broken CallMe() program.

The example output is shown in Figure 3.9.

As you can see, this program calls CallMe() and x is assigned to 314. Then it tries to print x, but it ends up printing 0! What gives?

You guessed it—scope. This function calls CallMe() and has x assigned to 314. But when it returns back to main, the 314 has been flushed from memory. Although x is equal to 314 in CallMe(), it is equal to 0 in main.

There are a few ways to fix this. One way is to have CallMe() return a value like this:

```
CallMe()
Print "x is equal to " + CallMe()

Function CallMe()
      x = 314
      Return x
End Function
```

In this example, CallMe() returns the x value, which is printed by main.

The other way to solve this problem is to use global variables. Global variables have global scope and are visible throughout the program. This means that the scope of x in CallMe() will be the same as the scope of x in main.

To create a global variable, simply precede the variable with the Global command.

```
;demo03-07.bb - Fixed CallMe()
Global x
CallMe()
Print "x is equal to " + x

;Delay five seconds
Delay 5000

Function CallMe()
        x = 314
End Function
```

The example output is shown in Figure 3.10.

Figure 3.10
The fixed CallMe() program.

Note

Notice that I wrote Global x in the main program rather than the function CallMe(). This is because you can only create global variables in the main program. If you want to use global scope, you must create the variable in the main program. By the way, the act of creating a variable without actually setting the variable is called *declaring*. Making the variable equal to something is called *defining* it.

This time, we make x global. Then, when we assign 314 to x, x is equal to 314 in every function, and not just in CallMe()

What Is Portable Code?

Porting is an important concept, because in the long run, it can save you a lot of time. In English, for something to be portable, it must be able to easily move around. Think of that *Game Boy Advance* you saw at Walmart a few days ago. Portable code is easy to move around. Portable code is independent code that doesn't rely upon global variables for information. This allows you to cut and paste functions from one program to another. Take the demo03-06.bb, the Fahrenheit-to-Celsius calculator. That is a very portable function because you can rip that program right out and use it in another program, if the need ever arises. Because the function does not rely on any global variables, you have nothing more to set up. When the function does rely on global variables, it is extremely hard to cut and paste code from one program to another, simply because global variables usually do not exist in two different programs.

Global variables are common in games, but you should try to use them as little as possible for a few reasons. First, because every function has access to them, it is very easy to change the variable by accident. Second, using global variables makes functions less portable. If a function only uses parameters and local variables, it can be ported to other programs by just copying and pasting. If it uses global variables, you have to go through the code and change any references to global variables that don't exist in the new program. Although it doesn't seem like a big deal now, it can be a big pain to have to search through functions when you decide to add them to a new program.

By the way, another way to create a local variable is to add the keyword Local before a variable, such as:

```
Local x
```

If you add the Local keyword to x in the previous program

```
x = 314
```

the x variable in main will once again equal zero. This is because the local scope takes precedence over the global scope. Therefore, the local version of x is initialized to 314, while the global version is left unaffected.

There is no difference between

`Local variable`

and

`variable`

if there is no declared global variable. In other words, when you declare a local variable, you can omit the `Local` keyword (although you might want to keep it just for clarity and style).

When to Use Functions

Functions are necessary to programming. You know that you have to use them, but when should you do so?

Use functions whenever you have to perform a task. I know that this is a vague statement to make, but you should have at least a few functions for anything but the most trivial of programs.

Usually, the main function should do little, if any, work. The tasks should be handed to functions. If the task can be subdivided into two or more tasks, be sure to create the extra functions. You can always call functions from within another function.

Here is an example: say you are creating a spaceship game and you have a function to draw everything onscreen. You should probably make separate functions for drawing each part of the game: a separate function for drawing the ships and the bullets. It is possible to subdivide those even more. If you wanted to, you could create separate functions for drawing the bullets from the player and bullets from the enemy. Two more functions would draw the player and the enemy ships.

Basically, if you see a place where a function could be useful, write it. It takes hardly any more code than just putting the task in the `main` function and it makes your code much more portable, not to mention readable.

Understanding Arrays

One large problem in programming is the creation of a large number of variables. Think about how long it would take to create 10 variables of the same type right now. It might look something like this:

```
variable 0 = 314
variable 1 = 314
variable 2 = 314
```

```
variable 3 = 314
variable 4 = 314
variable 5 = 314
variable 6 = 314
variable 7 = 314
variable 8 = 314
variable 9 = 314
```

Seems like a waste of time, huh? But imagine if you had to create a thousand variables. That might take forever!

As you might have guessed, Blitz3D has a way to remedy this problem. The solution is to use a feature called an *array*. Arrays are basically sets of variables with almost the same name. An array looks like any other variable, except it appends a subscript (a number within parentheses) to the end of the variable name.

Imagine an array as a single-column box that contains separate places to place jars (see Figure 3.11). Each jar contains a number. In this case, each jar contains the number 314, but you can change these numbers. You can access the number through the array counter, which looks like `variable(0)` or `variable(1)`. Basically, each jar is independent of the other jars, but they are all packaged in the same box. In arrays, the box represents the array, the jars are the individual array variables, and the numbers are the variable data.

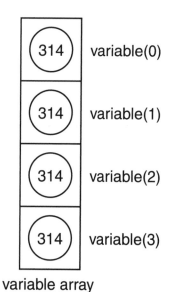

variable array

Figure 3.11
Box to array comparison.

Any variable that is part of an array is written something like this:

```
variablename(subscript#)
```

Here, the name of the array is `variablename` and the `subscript#` (it is always an integer, never a string) is equal to the number of array variables you want to generate.

Now we actually have to create the array. Let's use the variables from the previous example.

```
Dim variable(10) ;Declare array

variable(0) = 314
variable(1) = 314
variable(2) = 314
variable(3) = 314
variable(4) = 314
variable(5) = 314
variable(6) = 314
variable(7) = 314
variable(8) = 314
variable(9) = 314
```

Doesn't seem any simpler, does it? That's because I created the array in the longer way. However, using a `For...Next` loop, we can condense this into a much shorter procedure.

Note

You might be wondering what the `Dim` command means. `Dim` literally means "dimension," and it simply creates memory space that will be used later. You must use the `Dim` command to declare arrays before using them.

```
;demo03-08.bb - initializes 10 vars to 314
Dim variable(10) ;Declare array

For i=0 To 10
        variable(i) = 314
        Print variable(i)
Next
WaitKey
```

The output is shown in Figure 3.12.

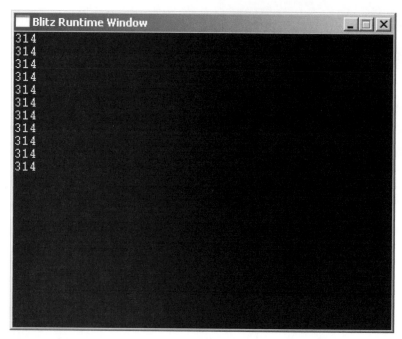

Figure 3.12
The demo03-08.bb program.

This does the same thing and more (it prints out the variable as well), but it is a heck of a lot shorter! This time, the array is declared just as in the previous example. Next, a For...Next loop iterates through each variable and sets it equal to 314! Easy, huh?

Note

Make sure you notice that all of the variables begin with 0. Computers count differently from humans because they start counting with 0 rather than 1. In other words, the 10th variable in declaration of array(10) is array(9). In other words, when you declare an array, you are telling the computer how many elements the array should have, plus one. However, because computers always count from 0, you access the array elements beginning with 0 and ending with *n*, where *n* is equal to the size of the array. For example, if you take an array declared as array(5), the array would contain the elements array(0), array(1), array(2), array(3), array(4), and array(5). So an array that had five elements would be accessed with the numbers; 0, 1, 2, 3, 4, and 5—no more, no less. I often use less than the maximum amount of units, however, so I use 0—4 on an array(5) declaration.

To see how the box and jar example fits in with this program, see Figure 3.13.

All right, how about one more example of functions? This program will set a series of variables to an increasing number. From there, the user can choose to add, subtract, multiply, or divide two of the numbers. It's sort of like a mini calculator.

Figure 3.13
Demo03-08.bb box and jar example.

```
;demo03-09.bb - Allows user to perform math operations of 1-100

;op1 and op2 are global so they can be accessed from all functions
;op1 contains first operand, op2 contains second
Global op1
Global op2
Dim array(100) ;0 - 100
InitializeArray()

;continue is 1 as long as program is running
continue = 1

While continue ;as long as the computer wants to play
        ;Get the first operand
        op1 = Input("What is the first number? ")
        ;Get the second operand
        op2 = Input("And the second? ")

        ; what does the user want to do?
        operator$ = Input("Enter +, -, *, or / ")
        ;Print the answer
        PrintAnswer(operator$)
```

ouch !
0 - 99

```
        ;Find out if user wants to continue
        continue = Input("Enter 1 to continue or 0 to quit ")

        ;Insert a new line
        Print ""
Wend
End
```

This ends the initialization and the main loop sections of the calculator program. The program begins by creating two global variables: op1 and op2. These are the two numbers that will be added together. For example, in the expression 3 + 14, 3 represents op1 and 14 represents op2.

Next, it creates the array. The array has 101 elements, and therefore, it goes from array(0) to array(100) (remember that arrays begin counting from 0). After the array declaration, InitializeArray() is called.

The continue variable is then created. This variable determines whether the program is still running. As long as continue is not equal to 0, the game loop continues to run.

The main loop begins next. First, it receives the variables op1 and op2 from the user. After that, it asks for operator. operator gives the users a choice of what operation they want to perform (addition, subtraction, multiplication, or division).

The loop then calls PrintAnswer() to print the answer. Finally, the loop asks the users if they would like to go through the program again. If the user chooses yes, continue remains as 1 and the game loop starts from the top. If not, the program exits.

This program has two user-defined functions: PrintAnswer() and InitializeArray(). Let's take a look at each of them.

```
;This Function sets up the array
Function InitializeArray()
For i=0 To 100
        array(i) = i
Next
End Function
```

This function simply creates the array that is used in the following calculations. Each array element contains its respective number. Therefore, the 14th element (array(13)) is equal to 13. After the numbers 0 through 100 have been initialized, they are all sent back to the main loop to go through the rest of the input.

The next user-defined function is `PrintAnswer()`.

```
;This function prints the answer to the expression
Function PrintAnswer(operator$)
Print op1 + " " + operator$ + " " + op2 +
    " is equal to " + FindAnswer(operator$)
End Function
```

This function simply writes out what the user wants to do. If the user wants to add 13 and 31, this function writes out "13 + 31 is equal to 44." You might be wondering how it gets the answer. That is accomplished by the final user-defined function: `FindAnswer()`.

```
;This function performs the math based on the user input
Function FindAnswer(operator$)
      Select operator
            Case "+"
                  Return array(op1) + array(op2)
            Case "-"
                  Return array(op1) - array(op2)
            Case "*"
                  Return array(op1) * array(op2)
            Case "/"
                  Return array(op1) / array(op2)

      End Select
End Function
```

Note that if op1 or op2 is larger than 100 or less than 0, the program will not function.

The output is shown in Figure 3.14.

By the way, one thing about this program. The program will crash if op2 is set to 0 and operator$ is division. This is because it is impossible to divide any number by 0. As you can see, this function begins with a `Select` statement. The `Select` command chooses an action based on which operator is being used. If the user chooses to multiply something, the function returns op1 times op2. The return value is then printed to the screen in the `PrintAnswer()` function.

Note

If you happen to try dividing two numbers that aren't evenly divisible, you will get the correct number, but the decimal place will be missing. That is because this program uses integers. Try modifying this program so it uses floating-point variables instead.

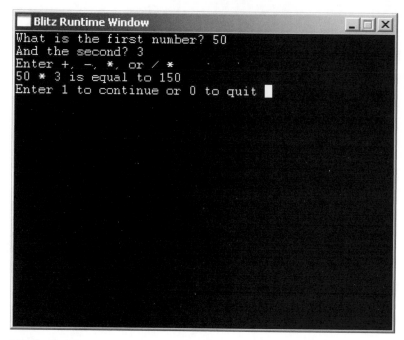

Figure 3.14
The demo03-09.bb calculator program.

Figures 3.15 and 3.16 portray the array as a box and demonstrate how two numbers are added.

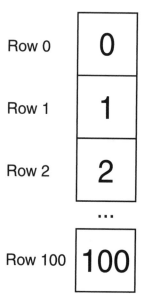

Figure 3.15
The array box.

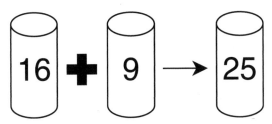

Figure 3.16
Adding two jars.

Multi-Dimensional Arrays

Multi-dimensional arrays are very similar to regular arrays, except that, well, they have more than one dimension. In essence, the main difference is that a multi-dimensional array has more than one subscript. An easy way to visualize a multi-dimensional array is to use the box example again. However, instead of only having one column, it has two or more, as shown in Figure 3.17.

Multi-dimensional arrays are used in situations in which you need sets of variables within the array set. For example, you might create an array of bullets. You could then create an array with two dimensions and place the bullets shot by the player in one dimension and the bullets shot by the enemy in the other. This is demonstrated in Figure 3.18.

Okay, let's make a multi-dimensional array. This process is very similar to making a single-dimensional array; you only have to add another subscript into the declaration.

```
Dim bullets(2,100)
```

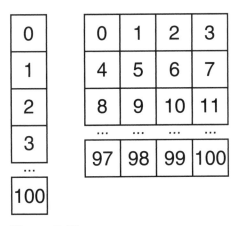

Figure 3.17
Single and multi-dimensional arrays.

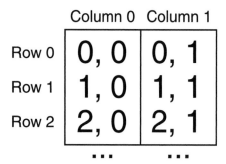

Figure 3.18
The two-dimensional bullet array.

This command creates an array of bullets with two parts. The first part determines who shot the bullet and the second part determines which bullet it was. Each column contains 100 bullets.

Now, to actually use the array, you only have to add the second subscript to the variable call like this:

```
bullets(0,23)
```

This command calls the 24th bullet from the player. Remember, because the computer begins counting at 0, the subscript 23 is the 24th element of the array.

All right, let's make a program. This simply draws out 25 asterisks (*) and 25 plus signs (+). It doesn't do much, but you will understand how you can use arrays when you learn about types in the next section. Figure 3.19 portrays the info in a table.

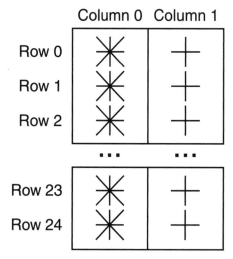

Figure 3.19
The starsplusses$ array.

```
;demo03-10.bb - Draws out 25 '*'s and 25 '+'s

;create the array
Dim starsplusses$(2,24)

;initialize the array. The first dimension will contain *'s and
the second will contain +'s
For rows = 0 To 1
    For columns=0 To 24
            Assign either + or *, depending on the return value of FindChar$()
            starsplusses$(rows,columns) =
            FindChar$(rows)
    Next
Next
```

This first fragment begins by creating the starsplusses$ array. Because its subscript is (2,25), it will contain a total of 50 objects. How did I get this number? I simply multiplied the first subscript by the second subscript: 2*25 = 50.

The next section of the code initializes the array. It runs two for loops within each other. In multi-dimensional arrays, two for loops are commonly used. The first loop runs throughout the first subscript and the second loop runs throughout the second subscript. The outer loop, For i = 0 To 1, counts from 0 to 1. The second for loop counts from 0 to 24. The line

```
starsplusses$(rows,columns) = FindChar$(rows)
```

determines what each element is set equal to with the help of the FindChar$() function.

FindChar$() is a user-defined function. It looks like this:

```
;FUNCTION FINDCHAR$(i)
;returns * or +
Function FindChar$(i)
        If i = 0
                Return "*"
        Else If i = 1
                Return "+"
        EndIf
End Function
```

If the initialization loop calls this function with the row number being 0, the array element becomes an asterisk (star). If the function is called with the row being 1, the array element is a plus sign. Therefore, the array has two rows of 25 characters—one row is made up of stars, the other is made up of plusses.

Next, you have to display the array.

```
;display the array
For rows = 0 To 1
        For columns = 0 To 24
                ;Write each value to the screen
                Write
                starsplusses$(rows,columns)
        Next
        ;write a new line after each row
        Print ""
Next
;Delay five seconds
Delay 5000
```

Once again, this function has two for loops running within each other. The outer loop counts by rows and the inner loop counts by columns. Every element is drawn to the screen. When the loop gets to the end of the first row, a new line is printed so it can print out the next row.

A new function, Write, is introduced here. Write has the same prototype as Print:

```
Write string$
```

In fact, these two functions are extremely similar. The only difference between Write and Print is that Write, unlike Print, does not automatically print out a new line after the line is written. This is extremely useful when trying to write out the contents of the array because you don't want a new line after each element. Figure 3.20 shows what demo03-10.bb looks like when Write is substituted for Print.

Figure 3.21 shows the demo03-10.bb program.

Using Types

The entire chapter has been leading up to *types*, because they are a very important and useful part of the Blitz3D language. Types are simply a set of related data. That might sound a lot like the definition of an array, but with types, you can have different names for each of the variables, as well as different data types (string, integer, and floating point).

Figure 3.20
Demo03-10 without `Write`.

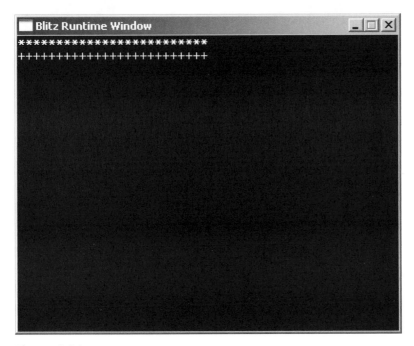

Figure 3.21
The demo03-10.bb program.

Here is an example. Imagine you have a player ship. The computer needs to know where to put the ship. For this example, we are going to put the ship at the coordinates 100, 100 (if you don't understand coordinates, they will be explained soon). You could do something like this:

```
playerx = 100
playery = 100
```

Seems pretty easy, eh? What if you wanted to add a hit counter? You have to create another variable.

```
playerhits = 3
```

That's three variables. If you wanted to make it possible for the ship to move up and down, you would need two more variables. That's a total of five variables!

The best way to remedy this problem is to use types. A type can take all of these unorganized variables and attach them to a single type name, like in Figure 3.22. Here is the creation of a ship type:

```
Type Ship
        Field x,y ;the ship's location
        Field hits ;ship's hit points
End Type
```

To create a new type, add the keyword `Type` before the name of the type. Next, create the individual fields. Each field is a separate variable that is part of the type. Each `Field` variable can be an integer, a floating point, or a string.

Now you have declared the type, and you have to create a variable that can hold this new data type. The procedure to do this is a little different from defining a variable with one of the built-in types (strings, integers, and floats are the built-in types). To create this new variable, or *instance*, use the syntax shown on the next page.

Unattached	Attached Type player
Player x	x
Player y	y
Player hits	hits
Player x = 0	Player\x = 0
Player y = 0	Player\y = 0
Player hits = 0	Player\hits = 0

Figure 3.22
Unattached and attached variables.

```
player.ship = New ship
```

REDUNDANT CODE DESIGN

Wow, that looks bizarre. Let's break it down piece by piece. The first thing that you see is the word player to the left of the decimal point. This word refers to the name of the variable you are creating. After the decimal point, you see the word ship. This is the type you want the variable associated with. This variable will now have all of the same fields as the ship type, declared previously. To finish off the process, we provide the proper fields by setting player.ship equal to New ship.

This creates the new player ship. You could create an enemy ship by simply changing the name of player to enemy. Creation of a new type almost always uses this base:

```
instancename.typename = New typename
```

Now that we have organized all the loose variables by putting them in a type and creating an instance of the type, we can set the field variables.

```
player\x = 100
player\y = 100
player\hits = 3
```

Not too bad, huh? To access one of the variables, just use this formula:

```
instancename\variablename
```

Now you can create, define, and access types. Let's get to an example and see how this baby works. To write this program, I am going to use the function Text, which is declared as

```
Text x,y,string$,[centerx],[centery]
```

Refer to Table 3.3 to see what each parameter means. Text allows you to draw text on the screen, just like Print, but it also provides the capability for the programmer to choose the exact coordinate position that will appear.

Table 3.3 Parameters of Text

Parameter	Description
x	The x coordinate of the text
y	The y coordinate of the text
string$	The string you want printed
[centerx]	Set to true if you want the text horizontally centered
[centery]	Set to true if you want the text vertically centered

Table 3.4 Demo03-11.bb's Keys

Key	Function
Left arrow	Moves the ship left
Right arrow	Moves the ship right
Up arrow	Moves the ship up
Down arrow	Moves the ship down
Spacebar	Decreases the ship's hit points by one
Esc	Exits the game

This program uses Text to draw the players on the screen and to show their hit points. You will also be able to decrease the player's hit points and move them around. This is a pretty basic and simple game. Also, the ship will be represented by the characters <-*->. Table 3.4 describes the keys used in this game.

```
;demo03-11.bb - Draw a ship which can be moved and killed

Graphics 400,300

;CONSTANTS
Const STARTHITPOINTS = 3
Const SHIP$ = "<-*->"
Const ESCKEY = 1, SPACEBAR = 57, UPKEY = 200,
    LEFTKEY = 203, DOWNKEY = 208, RIGHTKEY = 205
Const STARTX = 200, STARTY = 150
```

This is the first part of the program. It begins by setting the graphics mode. Next, it designates which variables are constants. *Constants*, as you remember, are variables whose values don't change throughout the game. If you want to make a change to any of these variables, feel free to do so. The difference will be reflected throughout the entire program. It probably isn't a good idea to change the key constants (such as ESCKEY, SPACEBAR, and so on) because doing so just causes some problems—you will have to search for the correct key.

All of the constants are listed in Table 3.5.

Okay, let's keep going.

```
;TYPES
Type Ship
        Field x,y
        Field hitpoints
```

Table 3.5 demo03-11.bb's Constants

Constant	Default Value	Description
STARTHITPOINTS	3	The number of times you can decrease the hit points (by pressing spacebar) before the game ends.
SHIP$	"<-*->"	The characters that make up the player. Because there are no images, the player is simply a text string. Change this value to change how the player looks.
ESCKEY	1	The key code for Esc.
SPACEBAR	57	The key code for the spacebar.
UPKEY	200	The key code for the up arrow.
LEFTKEY	203	The key code for the left arrow.
DOWNKEY	208	The key code for the down arrow.
RIGHTKEY	205	The key code for the right arrow.
STARTX	200	The starting x position for the ship.
STARTY	150	The starting y position for the ship.

```
    Field shipstring$
End Type
```

This section defines all of the types used in the program. Here, only one is defined—Ship. The Ship type groups all of the variables necessary to draw the ship on the screen. Table 3.6 lists all of the fields of the Ship type.

Next we move to the initialization of the program.

```
;INITIALIZATION SECTION
Global cont = 1
Global player.ship = New ship
player\x = STARTX
player\y = STARTY
player\hitpoints = STARTHITPOINTS
player\shipstring = SHIP$
```

Table 3.6 demo03-11.bb's Types

Field	Description
x	The x coordinate of the ship. The field is first initialized to the x value given in STARTX.
y	The y coordinate of the ship. The field is first initialized to the y value given in STARTY.
hitpoints	The number of hit points remaining on the ship. The field is first initialized to the hit point value given in STARTHITPOINTS.
shipstring$	The actual look of the ship. This field is first initialized to the string value SHIP$.

The initialization section defines all of the variables that will be used in the program. It also initializes the fields of the Ship type. The first variable, cont, is used in the game loop as the variable that determines whether the game continues playing. As long as the user wants to continue, cont is equal to 1.

The line

```
Global player.ship = New ship
```

creates an instance of the Ship type with the name player. Therefore, any fields that are in the ship type can now be accessed via player. The rest of the initialization section sets up the player type by assigning its fields to their respective constants.

Caution

Be careful to not confuse the "/" operator and the "\" operator. A forward slash "/" indicates division. A backward slash "\" indicates that you are accessing something from a type.

Next, move on to the game loop.

```
;Game loop
While cont = 1
      Cls
      Text player\x, player\y, player\shipstring$

      TestInput()
      DrawHUD()
Wend
;End of loop
```

The game loop is short, as it should be. It begins by testing the cont variable. If cont is equal to 1, the game runs; if not, the game exits. After that, the loop clears the screen by calling Cls. Without calling Cls, the screen would exhibit streaks, like in Figure 3.23. After that, the player is drawn to the screen at the given position. The loop then tests the input by calling TestInput() and draws the HUD by calling DrawHUD(). The HUD is the *heads-up display*, or the area of the screen that explains some values that are being used in the game.

```
;TestInput() changes the direction or hit points of the player
Function TestInput()
;If player presses left, move him left.
If KeyHit(LEFTKEY)
```

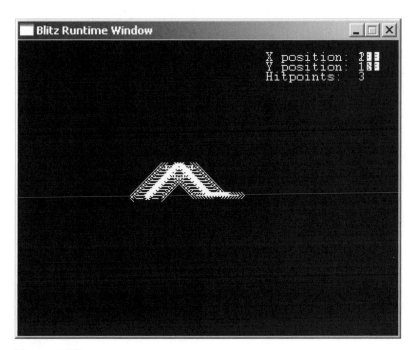

Figure 3.23
The main loop without `Cls`.

```
        player\x = player\x - 3
        If player\x <= 0
                player\x = 10
        EndIf
EndIf

;If player presses right, move him right.
If KeyHit(RIGHTKEY)
        player\x = player\x + 3

        If player\x >= 385
                player\x = 380
        EndIf
EndIf

;If player presses up, move him up.
If KeyHit(UPKEY)

        player\y = player\y - 3
        If player\y <= 0
                player\y = 10
        EndIf
```

```
EndIf

;If player presses down, move him down.
If KeyHit(DOWNKEY)

        player\y = player\y + 3
        If player\y >= 285
                player\y = 280
        EndIf
EndIf

;If player presses spacebar, remove a hit point

If KeyHit(SPACEBAR)

        player\hitpoints = player\hitpoints - 1
        If player\hitpoints <= 0
                cont = 0
        EndIf

EndIf

;If player presses Esc, set cont to 0, and exit the game
If KeyHit(ESCKEY)
        cont = 0
EndIf
```

The TestInput() function is very long, but also very simple. It simply tests the keys that the user has pressed and updates the variables based on the input. Starting from the top, if the user presses the left arrow, the character moves three pixels to the left. If the user happens to move the character too far (off the screen), the ship's position is moved back to the right. If the user presses the right arrow, the character moves left a little. The same happens if the user moves the ship too far up or down—the ship is repositioned back on the screen.

If the user presses the spacebar, the hit point counter decreases by one. The program then tests the counter to determine if the player has 0 hit points. If so, cont is set to 0, and the game is exited on the next frame.

The last test determines if the user pressed Esc. If so, cont is set to 0, and the game exits on the next frame.

```
;DrawHUD() draws user's info in top Right of the screen
Function DrawHUD()
        Text 260, 10, "X position: " + player\x
        Text 260, 20, "Y position: " + player\y
        Text 260, 30, "Hitpoints: " + player\hitpoints
End Function
```

The final function in the program, DrawHUD(), simply writes out the ship's information to the screen. The x and y coordinate positions and remaining hit points are drawn in the top-right section of the screen.

Note

> You might notice a major slowdown on your computer when you run this program. That is because we are running a mini-game without using page flipping. Don't worry, I will teach you how to fix this problem in Part II of this book.

Figure 3.24 shows how the loop works and Figure 3.25 is a screenshot of the actual program.

Coordinate Systems

I'm going to leave the concept of types for a moment to talk about coordinate points. Coordinates explain where on the screen something is. They are shown in the format of x, y. For example, something that is at coordinate 314, 13 has an x position of 314 and a y position of 13. The coordinate plane looks like Figure 3.26.

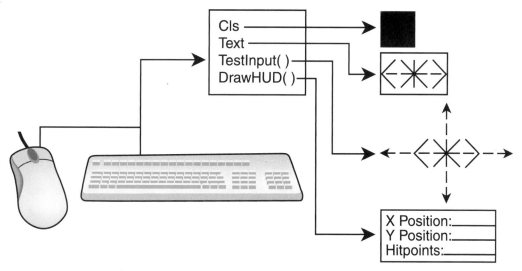

Figure 3.24
The main game loop.

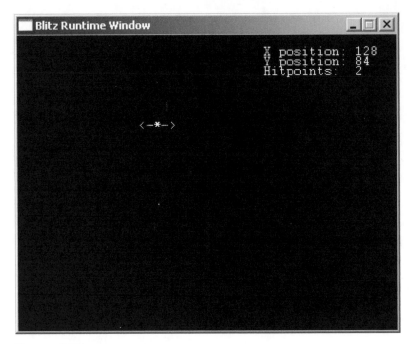

Figure 3.25
The demo03-11.bb program.

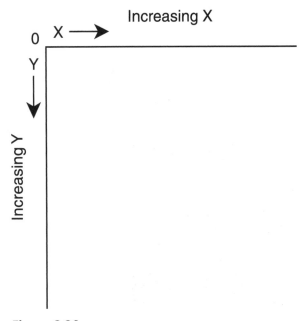

Figure 3.26
A coordinate system.

The origin, or 0 value of both the x and y direction, is at the top-left part of the screen. X increases from the origin right, and y increases from the origin down. When you want to get to coordinate position 314, 13, for example, you move from the origin 314 spaces to the right and 13 spaces down.

Each position is a single pixel on the screen. A *pixel* is the smallest measurement of a computer screen. Each pixel is a different color, and the pixels fitted together create an image. To see the size of a single pixel on your machine, run demo03-12.bb (see Figure 3.27). The tiny white dot in the center is a single pixel. Small, huh?

When you want to plot an object to the screen, you plot it to a certain pixel position. Usually the top-left corner of the object is drawn to that pixel position. So, as in Figure 3.28, if you want to write some text to a certain position, the top left of the text is at the selected pixel. If you write with the Text command, you can also center the text.

For...Each...Next

Types have been specifically designed to work well with loops. In fact, there is a new kind of loop that only works with types. It is called the For...Each...Next loop.

Figure 3.27
A single pixel.

Text 100, 100, "Hello"

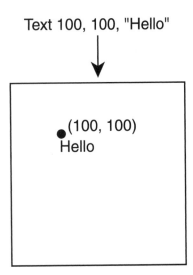

Figure 3.28
Drawing objects at pixel locations.

The For...Each...Next loop allows you to create sets of types and perform actions on them as a whole. For example, using a For...Each...Next loop, you could create a set of enemy ships from one call. Using the type

```
Type ship
    Field x,y
    Field hitpoints
End Type
```

you now create a bunch of enemy ships—say, 100:

```
SeedRnd MilliSecs()
For enemycounter = 0 To 99 ;100 new ships
            enemy.ship = New ship
            enemy\x = Rand(1,640)
            ememy\y = Rand (1,480)
            ememy\hitpoints = 3
Next
```

Well, we have just created 100 different enemy ships. Now, to test all of the enemies, we need to use the For...Each...Next loop. This loop tests every member of a certain type; this makes it easy to create a bunch of copies of an enemy and get rid of them when you're done. Refer to Figure 3.29 to see how the For...Each...Next loop looks in memory. This specific loop tests each enemy's hit points to make sure they are really alive. If not, the program deletes the enemy.

For **enemyships**.ship = Each ship

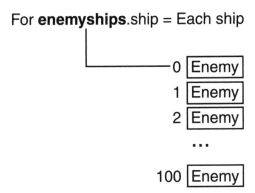

Figure 3.29
The enemyships in memory.

```
For enemyships.ship = Each ship
        If hitpoints <= 0
                Delete enemyships
        EndIf
Next
```

Pretty easy, if I do say so myself! This code snippet tests every one of the ships and deletes them if their hit point counter is equal to or less than 0. To see how the For...Each...Next loop works in memory, check out Figure 3.30.

For enemyship.ship = Each ship

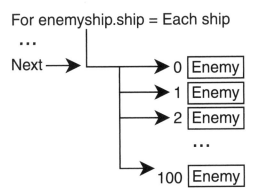

Figure 3.30
The enemyships loop in memory.

Tip

You might wonder why the program determines if the hit point count is equal to *or less than* 0. Because the ship is always deleted at 0, why test for less than 0? The reason is, sometimes a tiny error leaks through, and a ship could be assigned a –1 hit point count (this might happen if the ship was hit twice in the same frame). In cases like these, it's better to be safe than sorry. The moral: always test for unlikely conditions.

You can easily change this loop to interact with the enemy ship's x and y values. For example, if you add an x or y direction, you can make the enemies move randomly. You might update the type to look something like this:

```
Type ship
        Field x,y
        Field directionx, directiony
        Field hitpoints
End Type
```

Next, inside the initialization loop, you randomize the direction values (a positive number for directionx moves the enemy right, and a positive number for directiony moves the enemy down).

```
enemy\directionx = Rand(-3,3)
enemy\directiony = Rand(-3,3)
```

And finally, you would add code in the final loop to move the enemy around:

```
enemy\x = enemy\x + enemy\directionx
enemy\y = enemy\y + enemy\directiony
```

Note

If you put all this code in a program and watch the enemy ships, you might notice that the ships leave streaks behind them. This is because their previous position was not deleted. If you want to fix this problem, simply add the command Cls, clear screen, to the beginning of the game loop.

Congratulations, you have created animation!

Putting It All Together: Textanoid!

Okay, now, using all we have learned, you can put it together and make a game. This game is a simple text-based copy of *Arkanoid* that uses all of the processes discussed in this long chapter.

Because we will be using text, the basic game commands are run by the Text and KeyDown commands. Basically, the idea of the game is to get rid of all the blocks by hitting them with the ball. The player controls a paddle, which can move left or right. The player attempts to keep the ball from hitting the bottom wall of the game board. Each time the player clears the field of blocks, the player will reach a new level. Theoretically, you can go on to an infinite level (because the difficulty never increases), but I'm betting the player will get bored before then.

The full source of the game can be found on the CD under the name demo03-13.bb. This game might be hard to understand for a beginning programmer; however, I am going to help you through the tough parts of the code. Let's start off with the defined types.

```
;TYPES
Type paddle ;the player type
        Field x,y ;coordinates
End Type

Type ball
        Field x,y
        Field directionx, directiony
End Type
```

The output is shown in Figure 3.31.

These types define the player and the ball in the game. The x and y coordinates are simply the position of each object on the screen, but the directionx and directiony variables might seem strange.

Note

Notice that I decided not to make a block type. I felt that it would be easier to create it as an array. For an exercise, try to make and use a block type in the program.

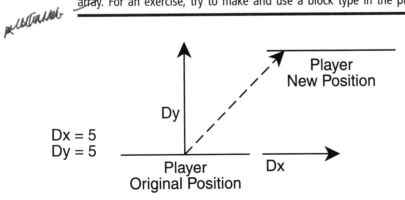

Figure 3.31
How DirectionX and DirectionY work.

The *direction* variables define how the ball moves—the directionx variable defines the left and right movement and the directiony variable defines the up and down movement. Referring to Figure 3.31, you can see that as directionx moves the paddle left, directiony moves the paddle up. The end result is a new position that is above and to the left of the original position.

Next up is the constants section:

```
;Constants
Const BLOCKSTRING$ = "XXXXXXX"
Const PADDLESTRING$ = "--------"
Const BALLSTRING$ = "O"
Const BLOCKROWS = 3
Const BLOCKCOLUMNS = 6
Const BLOCKXGAP = 85
Const BLOCKYGAP = 32
Const BLOCKXORIGIN = 16
Const BLOCKYORIGIN = 8
Global BLOCKHEIGHT = FontHeight()
Global BLOCKWIDTH = Len(BLOCKSTRING$) * FontWidth()
Global PADDLEHEIGHT = FontHeight()
Global PADDLEWIDTH = Len(PADDLESTRING$) * FontWidth()
Global BALLHEIGHT = FontHeight()
Global BALLWIDTH = Len(BALLSTRING$) * FontWidth()
Const STARTX = 300
Const STARTY= 340
Const ESCKEY = 1, LEFTKEY = 203, RIGHTKEY = 205
```

Refer to Table 3.7 to see what each constant means. By the way, the function FontHeight() (which is used in each of the height variables) returns the height in pixels of the selected font (you will learn how to change the font later). The FontWidth() function returns the width of one character of the selected font. The Len function returns the number of characters in a string. Figure 3.32 shows what FontWidth() and Len would return on a sample string. Note that FontWidth() does not take any parameters; it simply tells what the width of the currently used font is.

Note

You might be wondering why the HEIGHT and WIDTH variables are global and not constant. The reason is that a constant value can never be variable. The FontHeight() function can return a different value, and therefore it is variable. Because I need to use the HEIGHT and WIDTH variables throughout the program, I made them global.

Table 3.7 Textanoid!'s Constants

Variable	Description
BLOCKSTRING	Defines what each block looks like
PADDLESTRING	Defines what the paddle looks like
BALLSTRING	Defines what the ball looks like
BLOCKROWS	The number of rows of blocks
BLOCKCOLUMNS	The number of columns of blocks
BLOCKXGAP	The number of pixels between each column
BLOCKYGAP	The number of pixels between each row
BLOCKXORIGIN	The number of pixels from the top-left corner of the window to the first column
BLOCKYORIGIN	The number of pixels from the top-left corner of the window to the first row
BLOCKHEIGHT	The height of each block
BLOCKWIDTH	The width of each block
PADDLEHEIGHT	The height of the paddle
PADDLEWIDTH	The width of the paddle
BALLHEIGHT	The height of the ball
BALLWIDTH	The width of the ball
STARTX	The starting x coordinate of the player
STARTY	The starting y coordinate of the player
ESCKEY	The key code for the Esc button
LEFTKEY	The key code for the left arrow
RIGHTKEY	The key code for the right arrow

Okay, next is the initialization section.

```
;Initialization
SeedRnd MilliSecs()
Global score = 0
Global blockhits = 0
Global level = 1
Dim blocks(BLOCKROWS, BLOCKCOLUMNS)

Global ball.ball = New ball
Global player.paddle = New paddle
NewLevel()
```

Let's discuss this section. First the SeedRnd command seeds the random generator. Next, this section creates the score, blockhits, and level variables. score is the points the player has accumulated, blockhits tells how many times the player has hit a block, and level shows the players what level they are on. All of these variables are used in the function DrawHUD().

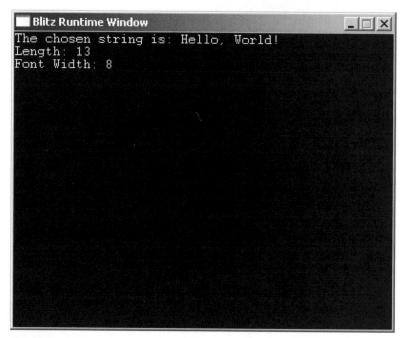

Figure 3.32
Len and FontWidth().

What Is SeedRnd?

You might wonder why I always use the command SeedRnd Millisecs() before using the Rand function. The fact is no computer is random. Because it was created to do certain tasks correctly each time, it cannot truly create random numbers. Because of this fact, using Rand by itself in a program would cause the same number to be generated over and over. The program uses SeedRnd to change the starting point of the random generator each time, so it does not generate the same numbers over and over. MilliSecs() is a good function to use to seed the generator because MilliSecs() is never the same twice.

The command

```
Dim blocks(BLOCKROWS, BLOCKCOLUMNS)
```

creates a multidimensional array called blocks. If you recall, a multidimensional array is just like a regular array but it has rows as well as columns. This fits in easily with the block setup.

Refer to Figure 3.33 to see the block rows and columns, complete with subscripts. You can see that the columns extend from the top to the bottom, and the rows extend from the left to the right.

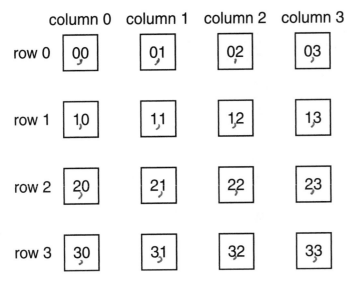

Figure 3.33
Rows and columns.

The next two variables created are ball and player. These two variables create the ball and player from the ball and paddle types.

Finally, you initialize the level by calling NewLevel(). This user-defined function creates all of the blocks and sets up the ball and paddle. The function is defined as:

```
Function NewLevel()
For rows=0 To BLOCKROWS - 1
        For cols=0 To BLOCKCOLUMNS - 1
                blocks(rows,cols) = 1
        Next
Next
ResetLevel()
End Function
```

The first for loop counts each of the rows and the second for loop counts each of the columns. Notice that I make the for loops count to the number of rows and columns minus 1. This subtraction offsets the fact that the starting number in an array is 0. Referring to Figure 3.34, you can see that this counter goes through each of the columns in the first row before moving to the next row and starting again. Whenever you see dual for loops to count through the blocks, all of the columns in the first row are counted before moving to the next row. Each of the blocks is set to one, which means they will be drawn (if they are destroyed, the blocks are set to zero).

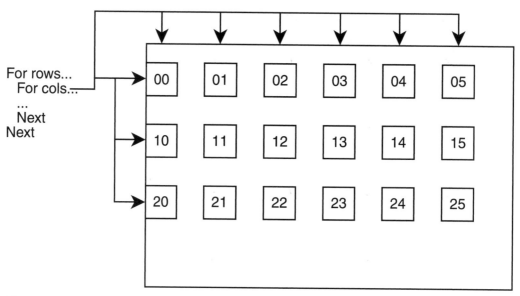

Figure 3.34
The for loops.

The next line calls the function ResetLevel(). ResetLevel() is defined as this:

```
Function ResetLevel()
ball\x = 320
ball\y = 150
ball\directiony = 12
ball\directionx = Rand(-5,5)
player\x = STARTX
player\y = STARTY
Delay 500

End Function
```

This function sets up the starting variables for the player and ball. The ball appears at the top-center of the screen and the player appears at the constant starting position. The ball is set to move toward the paddle at 12 pixels a frame and left or right randomly. The randomness of the ball's movement can sometimes cause a problem, however. There is always a chance that directionx will be equal to 0, and the ball will move straight up and down, without moving left or right at all. I left this problem in the program to illustrate a problem with random functions and to give you an exercise. Try to fix this problem so a directionx of 0 can never occur!

Well, that was initialization. Next up, the game loop:

```
While Not KeyDown(1)
     Cls

     DrawHUD()
     TestInput()
     DrawBlocks()
     DrawPaddle()
     CheckBall()

     Flip
Wend
```

As you can see, the loop does almost nothing other than calling other functions. If you look at Figure 3.35, you will see the function layout for this program—which functions call which other functions, and so on.

Note

You might wonder what the Flip command does. This command switches the background buffer with the foreground buffer. Don't worry what this means—it is explained in Chapter 5.

The first call the loop makes is to DrawHUD(). Referring to Figure 3.36, you can see that DrawHUD() simply shows the players what level they are on, what their score is, and how many blocks they have hit.

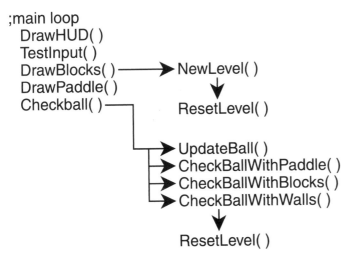

Figure 3.35
Textanoid!'s function outline.

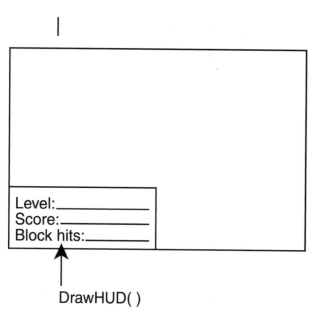

Figure 3.36
The DrawHud() function.

```
Function DrawHUD()
Text 0,440, "Level: " + level ;write the level
Text 0,450, "Score: " + score ;write the score
Text 0,460, "Block Hits: " + blockhits ;write the block hits
End Function
```

Not too bad, huh? The only thing you might want to notice are the coordinates. The x coordinate is 0, which means it is on the left side of the screen, and the y coordinate is 440, 450, and 460, which is pretty close to the bottom (the total height of this window is 480, as seen in the Graphics call at the beginning of the program).

The next call from the loop is to TestInput(). TestInput() determines if the player moves her paddle or quits the game.

```
Function TestInput()
If KeyDown(ESCKEY) ;hit Esc
        End ;quit the game
ElseIf KeyDown(LEFTKEY) ;hit left arrow
        player\x = player\x - 10 ;move paddle left
ElseIf KeyDown(RIGHTKEY) ;hit right arrow
        player\x = player\x + 10 ;move paddle right
EndIf
End Function
```

Just for review, the KeyDown(*scancode*) function determines if the selected key was pressed. This function tests the Esc key, the left arrow, and the right arrow. If the player pressed Esc, the game ends. The left and right arrows move the paddle around the board.

The next function is DrawBlocks(). This function loops through each block and draws it if it is equal to 1. If a block is set to 0 (a block is set to 0 when it is hit by the ball), it is not drawn.

```
Function DrawBlocks()

     x = BLOCKXORIGIN
     y = BLOCKYORIGIN
;This variable creates a new level if there are no blocks
     newlevel = 0


;For all the rows
     For rows = 0 To BLOCKROWS - 1
;reset rows position
          x = BLOCKXORIGIN
          For cols = 0 To BLOCKCOLUMNS - 1

               ;If the block exists, draw it onscreen
               If (blocks(rows,cols) = 1) Then
                    Text x,y, BLOCKSTRING$
                    newlevel = newlevel + 1
               EndIf
               ;Move over to the next block
               x = x + BLOCKXGAP

          Next
          ;Move to the next column
          y = y + BLOCKYGAP
     Next
     If newlevel = 0
          level = level + 1
          NewLevel()
     EndIf



End Function
```

BLOCKXORIGIN = 16
BLOCKYORIGIN = 8

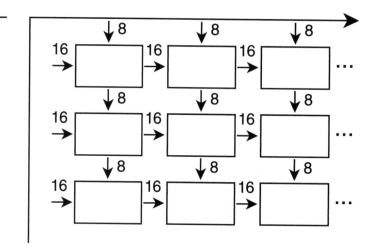

Figure 3.37
The X and Y origins.

This might be tough to understand, but I'm here to help! The function starts with setting x and y to BLOCKXORIGIN and BLOCKYORIGIN. Refer to Figure 3.37 to see how the origin variables define how far from the top-left corner the first block is.

The newlevel variable determines if there are any blocks left. Every time a block is found, newlevel is incremented. At the end of the function, if newlevel equals 0, a new level is created.

The function now creates two for loops to iterate through the rows and columns of blocks (just like in NewLevel()). The only line between the two for loops is

```
x = BLOCKXORIGIN
```

This line resets the x value to BLOCKXORIGIN after all of the columns in one row have been tested. This line is necessary; if it were not included, the program would believe that the second row started offscreen. This is shown in Figure 3.38.

The next few lines test each block:

```
If (blocks(rows,cols) = 1) Then;If the block exists
        Text x,y, BLOCKSTRING$
        newlevel = newlevel + 1
EndIf
```

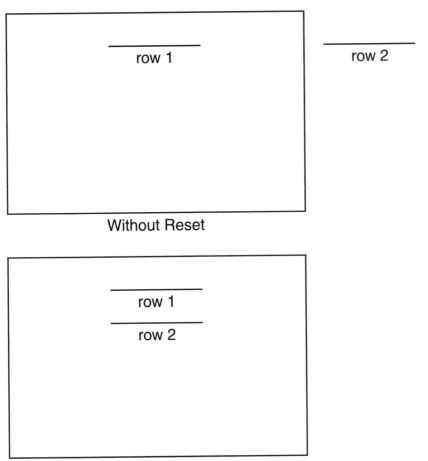

Without Reset

With Reset

Figure 3.38
`DrawBlocks()` with and without resetting the x value.

Figure 3.39 shows how each block is tested. If the current block is equal to 1, the block is drawn; if not, it is not drawn. At least one block must be drawn to continue the level; if no blocks are drawn, the `newlevel` variable never increases and stays at zero.

The final line before the column loop's `Next` command is

`x = x + BLOCKXGAP`

This line advances the x variable to the next block. The `BLOCKXGAP` constant contains the number of pixels between each block in a single row (otherwise known as every column).

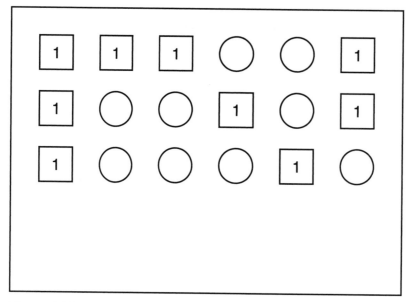

Figure 3.39
The block test.

After all the columns in the first row have been tested, the loop moves to the next row. This is achieved by adding a gap to the y variable:

```
y = y + BLOCKYGAP
```

Just like BLOCKXGAP, BLOCKYGAP is the number of pixels between each row. After all the boxes in one row are tested, the y value moves down a few pixels to begin drawing a new row.

The final lines of the function test the newlevel variable to determine if any blocks were hit. If none were (and newlevel equals 0), the level is increased and NewLevel() is called. This call begins the next level and redraws all the blocks.

Back to the game loop, the next function called is DrawPaddle(). DrawPaddle() is very simple.

```
Function DrawPaddle()

Text player\x,player\y,PADDLESTRING$

End Function
```

The only action this function performs is drawing the players at their x and y positions.

Finally, the game loop makes its final call—CheckBall().

```
Function CheckBall()

UpdateBall() ;Move and draw ball
CheckBallWithPaddle()
CheckBallWithBlocks()
CheckBallWithWalls()
End Function
```

This function is the biggest one in the program. First off, it updates the position of the ball.

```
Function UpdateBall()
ball\x = ball\x + ball\directionx ;Move the ball to the left or right
ball\y = ball\y + ball\directiony ;Move the ball up or down
Text ball\x, ball\y, BALLSTRING$   ;Draw the ball
End Function
```

This function begins by moving the ball based on its directionx and directiony variables. Then it draws the ball on the screen.

Next, the CheckBall() function calls CheckBallWithPaddle().

```
Function CheckBallWithPaddle()
If ball\x >= player\x And ball\x <= player\x + PADDLEWIDTH
        And ball\y + BALLHEIGHT>= player\y
        And ball\y + BALLHEIGHT <= player\y + PADDLEHEIGHT
ball\directiony = -ball\directiony + Rand(-3,3)
EndIf
End Function
```

This function is pretty simple. The If statement determines if the ball hit the paddle. You might have trouble understanding the If test, so I'll explain it to you.

See Figure 3.40 to understand how the test works. The line tests the ball and determines whether its x value falls between the left side of the paddle and the right side and whether its y value falls between the top and the bottom of the paddle.

If the ball has collided with the paddle, the directiony variable is flipped. This makes the direction move upward instead of downward. Also, if it hits the paddle, the speed of the ball increases by a value between –3 and 3 (if it increases by a negative value, the ball slows down).

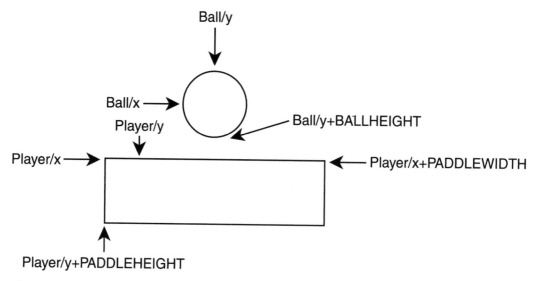

Figure 3.40
The ball-paddle collision.

Next, the CheckBall() function calls CheckBallWithBlocks(). This function tests the ball to determine if it has hit any blocks.

```
Function CheckBallWithBlocks()
;y is the first row
y = BLOCKYORIGIN

For rows=0 To BLOCKROWS - 1

    ;Reset x to first block of column
    x = BLOCKXORIGIN

    For every column of blocks
    For cols = 0 To BLOCKCOLUMNS - 1;

        ;If it exists
        If blocks(rows,cols)

            ;If the ball hit the block, delete the block
            If ball\x >= x And ball\x <=  x + BLOCKWIDTH
    And ball\y >= y And ball\y <= y + BLOCKHEIGHT

                blocks(rows,cols) = 0
                ;Delete block
```

```
                    ball\directiony = -ball\directiony + Rand(-2,2)
                      ;Reverse its direction and add randomizer

                    score = score + 75

                    blockhits = blockhits + 1

                    ;It can't hit more than one block, so leave function
                    Return
                EndIf
            EndIf

            ;move to next column
            x = x + BLOCKXGAP
    Next

    ;move to next row
    y = y + BLOCKYGAP
Next
End Function
```

This function might seem tough, but it is a lot like DrawBlocks(). The first thing the function does is set up the origins. Then it begins the row's loop and resets the x value, just as in DrawBlocks(). Now, in the column loop, the block is tested to see if it exists. If it does, the ball is tested with the block. If the ball does hit the block, the block is deleted (by setting it to 0) and the direction is reversed along with a random speed increase. Finally, the score is updated, the blockhits variable is increased, and the function returns (because the ball can't hit two blocks in one frame).

The last action the CheckBall() function performs is to check the ball with the walls.

```
Function CheckBallWithWalls()
;If ball hits the left wall, reverse its direction and add randomizer
If ball\x <= 0
        ball\directionx = -ball\directionx + Rand(-2,2)

;If ball hits top wall, reverse its direction and add randomizer
ElseIf ball\y <= 0
        ball\directiony = -ball\directiony + Rand(-2,2)
```

```
; If it hits right wall, reverse its direction and add randomizer
ElseIf ball\x >= 640 - BALLWIDTH
        ball\directionx = -ball\directionx + Rand(-2,2) ;

;If ball hits lower wall, dock points for missing ball
ElseIf ball\y >= 480
        score = score - 200

        ;Reset the level
        ResetLevel()
EndIf
End Function
```

If the ball hits the top, left, or right wall, it is reversed. If it hits the bottom wall (if the paddle fails to hit it), 200 points are subtracted from the score, and the level is reset.

Hey, take a look at Figure 3.41. It's the final version of Textanoid!

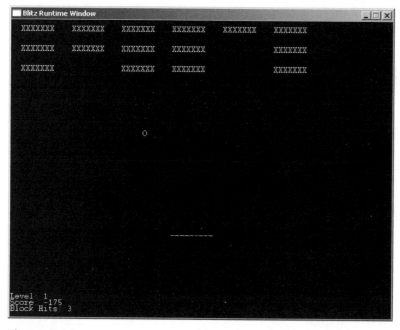

Figure 3.41
Textanoid!

Summary

Well, this has been one heck of a chapter. We learned about loops, functions, arrays, and types and created our first animated game! This chapter is probably one of the most important in the book. You learned the basics of any Blitz3D program, and you are now able to write any text-based program you can think of. I suggest you take a break now and try to digest and understand what you have read. You might want to reread the parts you don't understand and go through the listings again. Also, read and try to understand the full game from Chapter 1. It uses everything you have learned here with a small bit of graphics code added. Again, you can ask for help online at www.maneeshsethi.com or by e-mailing me at maneesh@maneeshsethi.com if you have any questions.

I have an exercise for you, if you feel like expanding on your learning. When you play the final game from this chapter, you might notice that every once in a while, the ball moves only straight up and down or slows to a complete stop. Try to fix this issue so the ball cannot slow down too much or stop moving left and right. (Hint: try randomizing `directionx` to make sure it does not move straight up and down.)

This chapter covered the following concepts:

- Loops

- Functions

- Arrays

- Types

- Creating Textanoid!

Okay, this chapter is now officially over. Get some rest and have some fun, or whatever. I'll be waiting for you whenever you feel like learning some more.

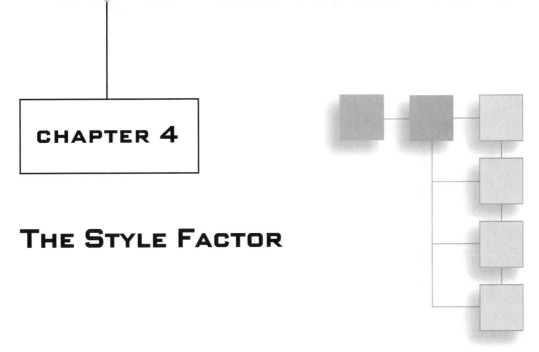

CHAPTER 4

THE STYLE FACTOR

I intend to make this chapter short and sweet, so that we can get on to the graphics stuff as soon as possible. A question you may be asking yourself right now is "What is style?" Well, my computer dictionary says that style is "Distinctive and stylish elegance."

In my eyes, style is not just how something looks. Style is how something *feels*. I have looked at one piece of code with contempt and another with understanding, simply because of the way it feels. But, of course, to achieve the feeling, you have to create the look.

Style in computer programming is creating code that is understandable and readable. It is code that you can see day after day and not detest. Style is one of the most overlooked and underappreciated parts of computer programming. This chapter quickly introduces you to the foundations of style and leads you to create your own.

Another thing to note is that a lot of times, ugly code is also poorly written. It is illogical and tough to understand, and that usually leads to unnecessary bad coding. Try to keep the code neat and your programs will be better.

Developing Style

Everyone has his or her own style of coding; it's an inevitable fact. No two people enjoy their code the same way. Basically, to create a style for yourself, you just

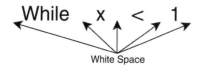

Figure 4.1
White space.

have to discover what is right for you and stick with it. Lesson one in the style primer: *Be Consistent*.

Let's start out with the most basic form of style: white space. Examples of white space are tabs, spaces, and new lines. Under most circumstances, you can add as much white space as you like to the beginning and end of most lines. White space can also be included between test commands (such as < and >) and what is being tested, as in Figure 4.1.

White Space and Indentation

The easiest way to see the use of white space is with examples. The first code snippet I will show you is a block of code using white space. This is what your code should look like. You can ignore what the program actually does and just see how it looks.

```
For x = 0 To 10
      If x > 5
            Print "x is greater than 50; it's equal to " + x + "."


        If x > 7
                Print "Wow, x is really high, it's " + x + " ."
            EndIf


      Else
            Print "Too bad, x is less than or equal to 50."
      EndIf
Next
```

Not a bad looking format, eh? It's pretty easy to figure out which If statement goes with which EndIf statement, right? Well, the next example is the same code with absolutely no white space. Try understanding it now!

```
For x = 0 To 10
If x > 5
Print "x is greater than 50; it's equal to " + x + "."
```

```
If x > 7
Print "Wow, x is really high, it's " + x + " ."
EndIf
Else
Print "Too bad, x is less or equal to 50."
EndIf
Next
```

This code is much harder to understand. If you wanted to actually comprehend its meaning, you would have to look closely and try to follow through the If commands. Now, imagine this code block was 10 or 15 times the length of the one I just showed you (programs can commonly grow that large in big games). It would be terribly difficult and a waste of time trying to understand all that code!

One thing you should know: adding white space does not affect the output of the program at all. There will be neither extra spaces nor new lines anywhere in the output of your program. See Figures 4.2 and 4.3 to see the outputs of both programs: white space and no white space.

Comments

I talked a little about comments previously, but I am going to explain them in depth now. Comments, as you know, are simply statements you write within your program to explain what you are doing. In a program, comments look like this:

```
Print "This is a statement." ;this is a comment
```

Make sure you notice the semicolon before the comment. The semicolon is required for every comment; in fact, it is how a comment is identified to the compiler. Comments are used to explain how a part of a program works: it may define what a single statement does, or it may tell what a whole block of statements does. I use almost one comment every other line in my programs; it helps because I often forget what I was trying to do after I finish a program. When I come back a few days or weeks later, the comments are still there to help guide me through my code.

Comments aren't only used to offer help for a single statement. I usually create a block of comments at the beginning of my programs to explain what the program

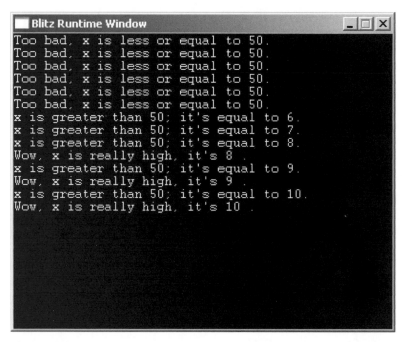

Figure 4.2
Output of programs with white space.

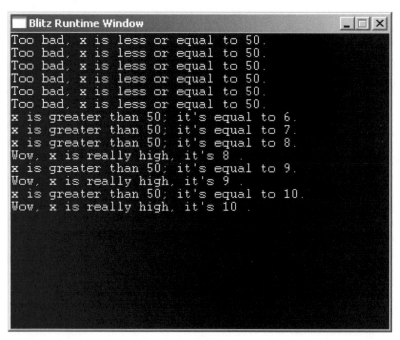

Figure 4.3
Output of programs without white space.

does. I often use a large box to draw my eyes toward it like this (the full listing for this program is named demo04-01.bb on the CD):

```
;;;;;;;;;;;;;;;;;;;;;;;;;;;;;;;;;;;;;;;;;;;;;;;;;;;;;
; HelloWorld.bb;;;;;;;;;;;;;;;;;;;;;;;;;;;;;;;;;;;;;;;
; By Maneesh Sethi;; ;;;;;;;;;;;;;;;;;;;;;;;;;;;;;;;;;
; This program prints "Hello World to the screen.;;;;;
; There are no input variables required;;;;;;;;;;;;;;;
;;;;;;;;;;;;;;;;;;;;;;;;;;;;;;;;;;;;;;;;;;;;;;;;;;;;;
```

As you can see, this box of comments is the intro to a HelloWorld program. I put a box like this at the top of most programs. It tells the reader four things: what the file name is, who the author is, what the purpose of the program is, and any extra info the user needs to use it.

There are some extra rows of information that you can add to the box. Maybe you want to tell the reader what version of the program this is, and you might want to reference others who helped you with it. Perhaps you have some special restrictions on the program ("this program does not run on Windows XP"), or something of that nature.

The next part of the program is the actual code. With comments, it might look something like this:

Note

This program is way more complex than it needs to be. There isn't much sense in using functions and variables in a simple Hello World program. The only reason I used functions and variables in this program is to demonstrate the use of comments.

```
;VARIABLES
;The hello string to be printed on the screen
hellostr$ = "Hello World!";END VARIABLES

;MAIN PROGRAM
;Pass "hellostr$" to PrintString function
PrintString(hellostr$)

;Wait for five seconds before closing
Delay 5000
;END MAIN PROGRAM
```

```
;FUNCTIONS
;;;;;;;;;;;;;;;;;;;;;;;;;;;;;;;;;;;;;;;
;Function PrintString(strng$);;;;;;;;;;;
;This function prints the variable strng$
;Parameters: strng$ - the string to be printed
;;;;;;;;;;;;;;;;;;;;;;;;;;;;;;;;;;;;;;;
Function PrintString(strng$)
;Print str$ on screen
Print strng$
End Function
;END FUNCTIONS
```

And there you have it! A fully commented version of Hello World, as in Figure 4.4.
Let's take a look at some of these comments.

Pre-Program Comments

Before the actual main program, I create a few commented sections that I call the
pre-program comments. This usually includes local variables, global variables,
constants, array dimensions, and anything else that you declare before the
program starts. For each section, I write a line of code that explains what is

Figure 4.4
Hello World!

following. For example, in demo04-01.bb, I created a section for variables. At the end of the declarations, I add a line of code that tells the reader that it is the end of the section (END VARIABLES in the Hello World example).

I also comment each variable individually to explain what it does specifically. Adding these simple lines of code makes it much easier to find out what a variable is named and what its value is simply by searching the top of a program.

Main Program Comments

I add some simple comments to the beginning of and inside the actual main program. At the beginning, I add a comment detailing the starting point of the actual program. I also add comments after statements, just as in the rest of the program.

Main program comments also tell where the main game loop begins and ends. I add those comments at the top and bottom of the While...Wend loop. Comments are usually included near function calls, such as the call to PrintScreen(strng$) in demo04-01.bb. The comments detail which function it calls and what the function does.

Function Comments

The function comments are written at the beginning of each and every function. I usually begin the function definitions after the end of the main program; consequently, I comment the ;FUNCTION header directly after ;END OF MAIN PROGRAM.

Refresher: The Difference between a Declaration and a Definition

I use the terms definition and declaration a lot in this chapter, and now is as good a time as any to go over the difference again. A declaration simply refers to or states a function or variable, and a definition actually defines it. For example, the declaration of PrintString is PrintString(strng$). The actual definition, however, is

```
Function PrintString(str$)
Print str$ ;Print str$ on screen
End Function
```

In summary, when I refer to the declaration of a function, I am talking about the call to it in code or the title of the function. When I refer to the definition of a function, I am talking about the actual code inside the function.

Before I define any functions, I always create a box that explains the function. On demo04-01.bb the `PrintString(strng$)` function is commented like this:

```
;;;;;;;;;;;;;;;;;;;;;;;;;;;;;;;;;;;;;;;;;;
;Function PrintString(strng$);;;;;;;;;;;;;
;This function prints the variable strng$
;Parameters: strng$ - the string to be printed
;;;;;;;;;;;;;;;;;;;;;;;;;;;;;;;;;;;;;;;;;;
```

As you can see, this block states the name of the function, its purpose, and its parameters. Make sure you add a block like this to the beginning of every function—it makes understanding them a heck of a lot easier.

Function and Variable Names

Naming your variables correctly can help solve a lot of problems in programs. Every once in a while you might come across the problem of not knowing what a variable does. You will have to backtrack and follow your program from the beginning. A way to solve this problem, however, is to name your variables a very easy-to-understand name. This can help reduce, if not eliminate, later forgetfulness.

Names

When declaring and defining variables, make sure you come up with a name that easily describes what the variable does. For example, when writing the Hello World program, I could have easily named the variable anything. I could have chosen names like

```
i$

row$

howareyou$

_123$

hellostr$
```

but there is a reason I didn't. For most of them, they don't make sense. For example, what does `howareyou` have to do with a string? (Unless, of course, I am asking how the user is feeling.) You may be wondering, though, why I didn't pick `hellostr$`. In this program, it would have been fine; however, in most programs, the contents of a variable change. Because they usually do change, creating a variable that tells exactly what is inside the variable rather than what kind of data it contains can create the exact same problem it is supposed to fix. If you changed the program so that `hellostr$` was equivalent to "`Today is my birthday,`" the `hellostr$` no longer makes sense in the context, and you might have to change all of the variable names in the program.

Naming Format

The format of your variable names is largely up to you. There are no rules set in stone as to how to name your functions and variables. The only thing that is required is that your format stays consistent throughout the program.

Here are some different ways to format the same variable.

```
hellostr$

Hello_Str$

helloStr$

HelloStr$

Hellostr$
```

As you can see, these variables are all the same. However, each name is slightly changed.

The first variable is my choice for regular variables. I keep it simple: both words are in lowercase. Some people use two words separated by an underscore (an underscore is a key achieved by pressing Shift+Dash). Others use the two words in different capitalization patterns.

Functions can also be named in similar ways. For example:

```
PrintString

printstring

Print_String
```

```
printString
```

```
Printstring
```

I usually choose the first method for functions: two joined words that are both capitalized. Once again, feel free to pick whichever you like, but make sure you stick with it.

Some other naming formats you might like to vary are constants, global variables, and array names.

I usually keep all the letters in a constant uppercase, like this:

```
Const CONSTANT = 1
```

My global variables are usually the same as regular variables, like this:

```
globalvar = 10
```

A lot of people prefer to add a g_ to the beginning of global variables. I choose not to, but feel free to try it.

For arrays, I keep it simple. I use one word if possible, and I keep it lowercase.

```
Dim array(numofelements)
```

Summary

Well, I hope you enjoyed this chapter. I tried to give the best explanation of style that I could, and hopefully I did a good job. I wrote this chapter because I believe style and clarity are important to every program and also because it is tough to find any style primers out there.

Once again, nothing in the chapter must be followed *exactly*. Style is an individual thing; what may appeal to one person may not appeal to the next. Try out all of the given styles and see which one fits you. The only thing I request of you is that you make your program simple and easy to understand. There is no need to use complex commands if you can get away with using a simpler block of code, even if it is a bit longer.

Try to get your programs to read like an essay—keep it organized and straightforward. Make sure you have your pre-program section listed, and try to comment any line of code that requires it. Make sure your style is consistent; if one function has an underscore between two words, make sure the next one does, too. Other than that, keep experimenting, and eventually you will develop your own style.

This chapter covered the following concepts:

- Developing style

- Comments

- Function and variable names

Hey, we just finished Part I. Take a break if you feel like it, or jump straight into Part II. We are finally getting into graphics; I guarantee it'll be more fun than you've ever had.

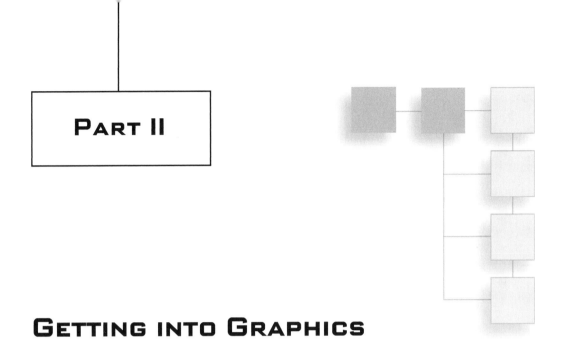

Part II

Getting into Graphics

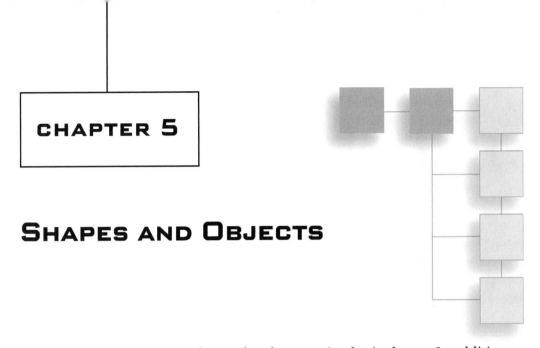

CHAPTER 5

SHAPES AND OBJECTS

This chapter explores everything related to creating basic shapes. In addition to learning how to create shapes, you'll discover how to dress them up by adding colors, patterns, and textures. The compiler you're using, Blitz3D, allows you to create several basic 3D shapes including spheres, cubes, cylinders, and cones. Of course, creating a shape is only the first step in the equation. After your shape is created, you'll learn how to position it, resize it, and change its shape.

Although the use of basic shapes is necessary in almost every 3D game, you may want to create something a little more sophisticated. There are dozens of programs on the market that allow you to create 3D objects. Later in the book, you'll explore some of the options you have when it comes to creating 3D objects, but for now, let's get to creating basic shapes.

Understanding the 3D World

Before we begin, it's important that you understand the concept of a 3D world. Start by looking at your monitor. Your monitor screen is actually two-dimensional; you can't reach in and grab an object on your computer's screen. So 3D games aren't really 3D, they just pretend to be 3D by using a variety of lighting and positioning techniques. Take a look at Figure 5.1. Just like the monitor on your computer, the pages of this book are in two dimensions, but we can create the illusion of three dimensions by cleverly using lighting and positioning. Both

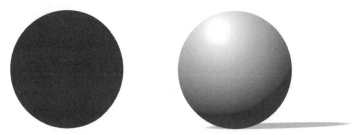

Figure 5.1
These two circles started off the same but now look distinctly different. The circle on the left looks two-dimensional but the one on the right looks three-dimensional because of the lighting applied to it.

objects are simple circles, but the one on the right looks three-dimensional because of the lighting applied to it.

A 2D world is made of up two axes: an x axis, which represents the horizontal part of your game, and a y axis, which represents the vertical part of your game. Think of the x and y axes as two rulers going across your monitor—one (the x axis) goes left and right, and the other (the y axis) goes up and down (see Figure 5.2).

Objects that you create in a two-dimensional game are positioned along the x and y axes. Their positions on the screen are called coordinates. Take a look at

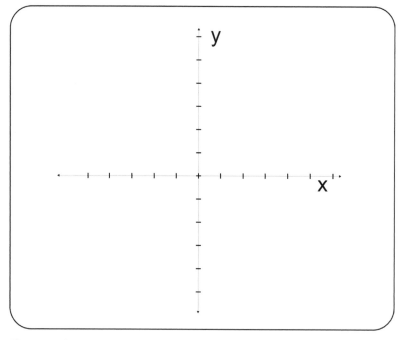

Figure 5.2
The x axis runs left to right across your screen and the y axis goes up and down.

Figure 5.3, which has an object in the top-right corner. The coordinates for this object would be (2,3). The first number represents the object's position on the x axis—in this case, two units to the right. The second number, 3, represents the object's position on the y axis—in this case, three units up.

On the x axis, positive numbers represent objects that are to the right of the center point, and objects to the left are represented by negative numbers. On the y axis, positive numbers represent objects that are above the center point, and negative numbers are those objects below the center point. Take a look at Figure 5.4, which shows several objects in different positions with their coordinates in brackets.

To create the illusion of near or far in a 3D world, the size of the object will change. Take a look at Figure 5.5, which has two objects: one that seems close and one that seems far away. We can tell that they are near or far because one is bigger than the other. In a 3D world, there is one more axis, the z axis, which represents objects that are near or far on the screen. On the z axis you can control how near or far an object is.

The position of an object in a 3D program is represented by three coordinates: an x axis, a y axis, and a z axis number. Positive numbers on the z axis represent how

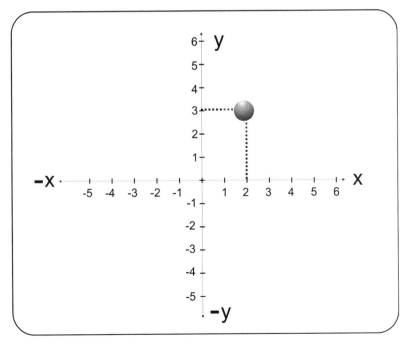

Figure 5.3
This object has the coordinate (2,3) because it is two units to the right of the center point and 3 units up.

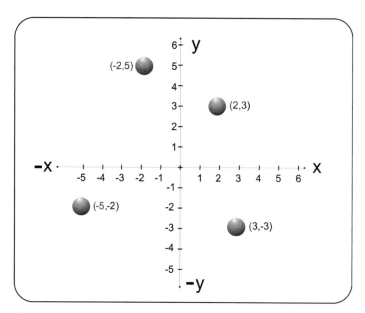

Figure 5.4
Each object is positioned at different coordinates.

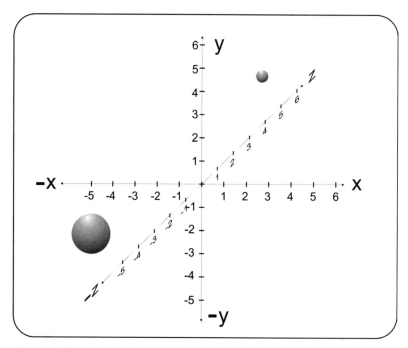

Figure 5.5
The z axis controls how near or far an object is.

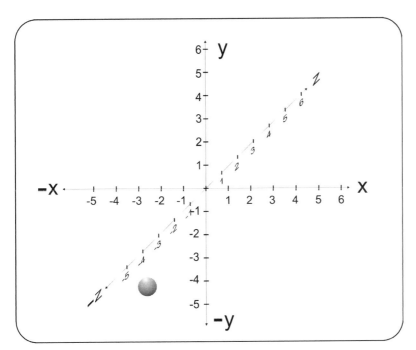

Figure 5.6
This object is positioned at location (−3, −4, −4).

far away the object is. For example, if the z axis number is 2, the object will be relatively close to the center point while a z axis value of 100 would mean that it is far away. A negative number will mean that the object will be on the close side of the center point, while a positive number represents a position on the far side of the center point. An example of coordinates of an object in a 3D world would be (−3,−,4,−4), which means the object would be at position −3 on the x axis, −4 on the y axis, and −4 on the z axis, as seen in Figure 5.6.

Note

Near or Far?

Keep in mind that terms like near, far, up, down, and left and right are all relative terms in Blitz3D because your "eyes" are the camera. Although the camera starts at position 0, 0, 0, it can be moved to any position in the 3D universe.

Creating Basic Shapes

When creating a basic shape, you need to tell Blitz3D two things: what type of shape you would like to create and where you would like to position it.

Creating a Cone

Let's start by entering the code for creating a cone and then going through each line to see what we have accomplished.

```
; demo05-01.bb - Creating a Basic Cone
; - - - - - - - - - - - - - - - - - -

Graphics3D 640,480
SetBuffer BackBuffer()

Const ESC_KEY = 1
; Create camera
camera = CreateCamera()
; Create a light
light = CreateLight()

; This is the code for creating the cone
cone = CreateCone()
PositionEntity cone,0,0,5


; This following code makes our program run
While Not KeyDown(ESC_KEY)
        RenderWorld
        Flip
Wend
End
```

You can find this code on the CD; it is titled demo05-01.bb. Open it up into Blitz3D and press the Run button to see the masterpiece you have created. With any luck, what you see on your screen should look exactly like what you see in Figure 5.7. After you are done admiring your beautiful work, press the Esc key to close the window and return to our programming session.

Now let's take a closer look at the code itself to see what we've done. In the previous chapter, we touched briefly on some of the code that was necessary to start our program, see our screen, and make things run, so here we will only concentrate on the specific code we used to create our cone:

```
; This is the code for creating the cone
cone = CreateCone()
PositionEntity
cone,0,0,5
```

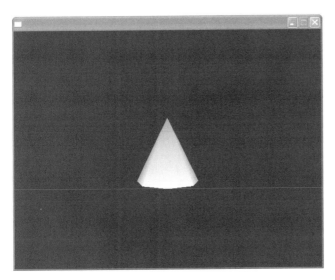

Figure 5.7
The demo05-01.bb program.

The first part of the code is `cone=`. This is what we are calling our cone. If you were to create a game with several cones, you'd want to create a separate name for each cone—for example, `cone1=`, `bigcone=`, `smallcone=`, and `smallshape=`. The point I'm trying to get across is that this first part of the code is simply a name you are giving your shape. You can call it anything; it doesn't even have to have the word "cone" in the name. You'll see this in practice in our next exercise.

The next part of the code is the `CreateCone()` command. This command tells Blitz3D to create a cone and give it the name you specified.

The next line of the code indicates where you would like to put your cone on the screen. As you learned earlier, your 3D world is broken up into x, y, and z values.

Using the `PositionEntity` command, you tell Blitz3D where to position a specific object in the 3D world. In the command we used, `PositionEntity cone,0,0,5`, we told Blitz3D to position the object called `cone` to the values on the screen where x=0, y=0, and z=5.

Now that you've created a cone, save your "game" so that you can always return back to this point. Click File > Save As to open a dialog box (see Figure 5.8) where you can select a directory in which to save your program. Call the program "cone" and then press the Save button.

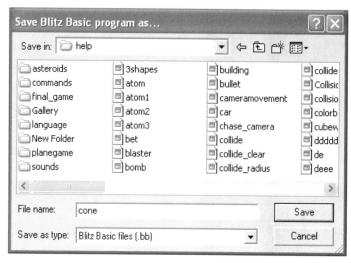

Figure 5.8
Make sure to save your files often.

Creating Multiple Cones

Now that you've created one cone, I'm going to show you how you can create others and position them in different locations on your screen. I'll also demonstrate that you can give your cones any names you'd like. Start off by deleting the cone you created earlier by erasing this code in your program:

```
; This is the code for creating the cone
cone=CreateCone()
PositionEntity cone,0,0,5
```

Now replace that code with the following, and run it once you are finished.

```
;Create and position four cones
coneleft = CreateCone()
PositionEntity coneleft,-3,2,5
apple = CreateCone()
PositionEntity apple,3,1,5
cone = CreateCone()
PositionEntity cone,-3,-2,5
coneyisland = CreateCone()
PositionEntity coneyisland,0,0,5
```

You should end up with the same display of cones as seen in Figure 5.9.

Notice that some of the cones have names that have nothing to do with cones at all. Remember that they are just names, and you can call them whatever you'd

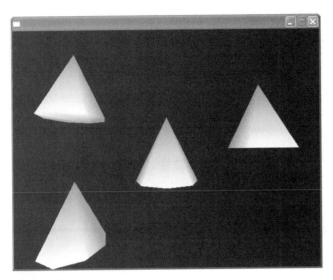

Figure 5.9
The demo05-02.bb program.

like, as long as it makes sense to you and others with whom you might be sharing the program code.

However, these strange names were only used for demonstration purposes. As we talked about in Chapter 4, it is better to only call the cones names that make sense, like cone1, cone2, cone3, etc.

Note

Identifiers

The names that you give to your objects are called identifiers.

You have noticed that some of the cones you created in the last step (see Figure 5.9) appear to be skewed. It's not that the shapes of the cones are altered, it's just that you've moved them around in your 3D world while your source of light and your camera have remained in the same spot. I'll cover cameras and lighting a little later on in the book.

Creating Cubes, Cylinders, and Spheres

There are several other shapes that you can create using Blitz3D, all of which are created in the exact same manner as you created the cone earlier. The only difference is that the create command you use will be different for each shape.

- `CreateSphere()`—This will create a sphere.

- `CreateCube()`—This will create a cube.

- `CreateCylinder()`—This will create a cylinder.

Don't forget that, when using any of these commands, you'll need to specify a name for the shape you are creating as well as a location. Here is an example of how you would create a cube within a program.

```
; This is the code for creating a cube
cube=CreateCube()
PositionEntity cube,0,0,5
```

Note

Now You Try

Take a look at Figure 5.10. Try to replicate what you see here on your own. Once you are done, compare your code to the actual code used to create it.

```
; demo05-03.bb - Creating a bunch of shapes
; - - - - - - - - - - - - - - - -
Graphics3D 640,480
SetBuffer BackBuffer()

Const ESC_KEY = 1
; Create camera
camera = CreateCamera()
; Create a light
light = CreateLight()
```

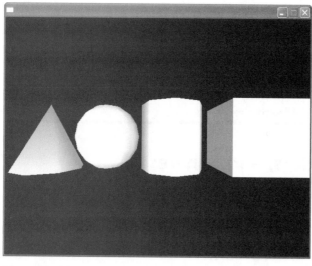

Figure 5.10
The demo05-03.bb program.

```
;Create and position four different shapes
cone=CreateCone()
PositionEntity cone,-3.5,0,5
cube=CreateCube()
PositionEntity cube,3,0,5
sphere=CreateSphere()
PositionEntity sphere,-1.6,0,5
cylinder=CreateCylinder()
PositionEntity cylinder,0.5,0,5


; This following code makes our program run
While Not KeyDown(ESC_KEY)
       RenderWorld
       Flip
Wend
End
```

We have managed to create four different 3D shapes! Check out Figure 5.10 to see what we made!

Segments

When you create spheres, cones, and cylinders, you can specify the number of segments that each is made of. A segment controls the number of polygons that are used to make up your shapes. This will control how "smooth" the shape will appear onscreen.

You may have noticed that the command you used for creating your shape was also followed by a series of parentheses. Typically, those parentheses can contain a definition of the number of segments, and they can define a parent. Don't worry about parents right now, but I will discuss segments. You can specify the number of segments in the brackets. For example, in this instance, the cone would be made of 25 segments:

```
cone=CreateCone(25)
```

Take a look at Figure 5.11, which compares a sphere with 8 segments versus a sphere with 32 segments.

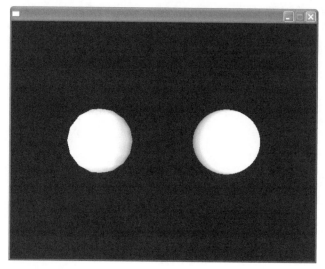

Figure 5.11
The sphere with 32 segments on the right appears much smoother.

N o t e

Default Segments

If you don't specify the number of segments, the number of segments will be 8 by default.

Resizing and Reshaping Objects

In most cases, the size of the shape that you have created will need to be adjusted to fit the purpose you had in mind. You can resize or even reshape an object by using the ScaleEntity command. The difference between resizing and reshaping an object is just a matter of what numbers you enter for the x, y, and z values.

Resizing or Scaling

To resize a shape, you use the ScaleEntity command and use the same number for the x, y, and z values. For this exercise, we are going to use the "cone" file that you saved earlier, so go ahead and open it. If, for some reason, you didn't save the file or you skipped the earlier section on creating a cone, you can find the file on the accompanying CD.

Let's say we want to double the size of the cone we created. To do this we'd add the ScaleEntity command as follows:

Figure 5.12
The sphere on the right has been enlarged by twice its size using the ScaleEntity command with the values 2,2,2.

```
; This is the code for creating the cone
cone = CreateCone()
PositionEntity cone,0,0,5
ScaleEntity cone, 2,2,2
```

Notice that the only line we added to double the size of our cone was the Scale-Entity cone, 2,2,2 command. ScaleEntity tells Blitz3D that there is an object whose size we want to change, cone tells Blitz3D the name of the object we'd like to resize, and the 2,2,2 informs Blitz3D that we want the size to double on the x, y, and z axes.

What if we wanted to reduce the size of the cone instead of increasing it? In that case, we would enter an integer for the x, y, and z values. For example, if you wanted to scale the cone in half (see Figure 5.12), you would use the following code:

```
cone = CreateCone()
PositionEntity cone,0,0,5
ScaleEntity cone, 0.5,0.5,0.5
```

Here's a quick reference for some size changes:

- 1/10 the size = 0.1

- 1/4 the size = 0.25

- 1/2 the size = 0.5

- Double the size = 2

- Triple the size = 3

- Ten times the size = 10

Note

ScaleEntity for All!

The `ScaleEntity` command can be used on more than just basic shapes that you create. Other objects that you create or import can be scaled using this command.

Reshaping

Reshaping an object works in much the same ways as scaling or resizing in that it uses the `ScaleEntity` command. The difference this time is that if you want to stretch or squish an object, the number that you enter for the x, y, and z values will be different. Let's go back and open the saved version of the "cone" file we created earlier to illustrate how we reshape our object. With this code, we will stretch the cone along the y axis.

```
cone = CreateCone()
PositionEntity cone,0,0,5
ScaleEntity cone, 1,2,1
```

We entered the numbers 1,2,1 which mean we are going to scale the x axis by multiplying it by 1 (which will result in no change, because any number multiplied by 1 remains the same), multiplying the y axis by 2, which will double the size of the shape along the y axis, and multiplying the z axis by 1. The result is that we end up with a cone that has been stretched along the y axis, as seen in Figure 5.13.

Note

Now You Try

Take a look at Figure 5.13, which is an image of a cylinder that has been stretched along one axis and reduced along another. Try to re-create this effect and then compare it to the actual code below.

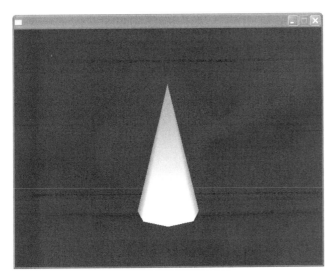

Figure 5.13
We stretched this cone by using ScaleEntity cone, 1,2,1.

```
; demo05-04.bb - Resizing a cone
; ------------------
Graphics3D 640,480
SetBuffer BackBuffer()

Const ESC_KEY = 1
; Create camera
camera = CreateCamera()
; Create a light
light = CreateLight()

;Create the cone
cone=CreateCone()
PositionEntity cone,0,0,5
ScaleEntity cone, 3,0.5,1


; This following code makes our program run
While Not KeyDown(ESC_KEY)
     RenderWorld
     Flip
Wend
End
```

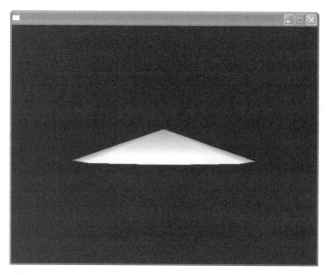

Figure 5.14
The demo05-04.bb program.

Figure 5.14 shows what this program looks like when run.

Flipping an Object

The process of flipping an object works the exact same way as resizing or scaling, with the exception that you use negative numbers as your x, y, or z values. In fact, you can resize, reshape, and flip your objects all at the same time. Just decide along which axis you'd like to reshape and resize your object, and then change the value to a negative number to flip the object. Here's an example of the code you would use to flip your cone along the z axis (see Figure 5.15).

```
cone = CreateCone()
PositionEntity cone,0,0,5
ScaleEntity cone, 1,1,-1
```

Coloring

So far, you've created simple shapes that have been white but appear slightly shaded because of the light source. You'll now learn how to apply a color to your shapes. Once again, start by opening the file "cone" that we created earlier. The EntityColor command allows you to apply color to an object. Here we will give our cone a color:

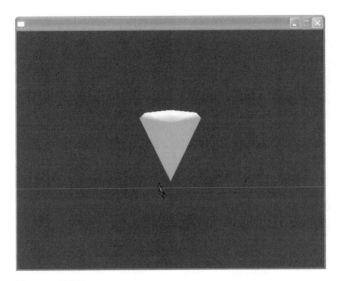

Figure 5.15
We flipped this cone on the z axis by using the command ScaleEntity cone, 1,1,-1.

```
; This is the code for creating and coloring the cone
cone=CreateCone()
PositionEntity cone,0,0,5
EntityColor cone, 125,201,190
```

After you enter the code EntityColor, you enter the name of the entity you want to color—in this case, it is called cone. You'll then notice three numbers—in this case, 125,201,190—which represent the red, green, and blue values. In this case, the 125 would be the red value, 201 would be the green value, and 190 would be the blue value. The colors on your computer monitor are created by mixing different values of red, green, and blue. By entering the three values for red, green, and blue (commonly referred to as RGB), you are telling what mix of colors you want to use to color your shape.

Now the million-dollar question: How do you know what combination of red, green, and blue make up a specific color? In others words, if you entered 12, 123, 204, what color would you get? Or if you wanted to color an object purple, what numbers would you enter? Well, almost every major graphics program provides a method for you to enter an RGB value to see the resulting color or select a color and get the RGB values.

Corel PHOTO-PAINT, which is included on the accompanying CD, provides an excellent way to get RGB values. After you launch PHOTO-PAINT, follow these instructions to get your RGB values:

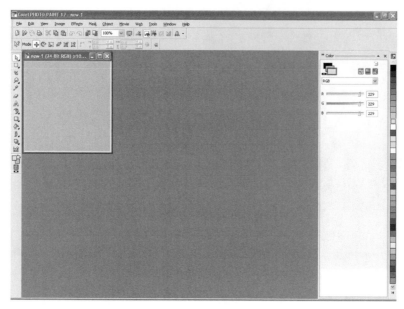

Figure 5.16
Pressing Ctrl+F2.

1. After opening a new document, press Ctrl+F2 on the keyboard. The Color docker (see Figure 5.16) will open on the right side of the screen, and by default, it will be set to RGB mode. You now have several options. You can enter specific values for R, G, and B and see the result of the values in a preview box. You can also click and drag the sliders to manipulate the RGB values.

2. If you prefer to select a color and then see what the RGB value is, you can click on the Show Color Palettes button, which will show you a square of color palettes. You can scroll through the colors and click on the swatch that you like, and the RGB values will be displayed as seen in Figure 5.17.

Wireframe

Every 3D object in your game is made up of triangles and polygons. If you want to see the triangle makeup of any object, you can go into wireframe mode (see Figure 5.18). This is best illustrated by creating a sphere and converting it to

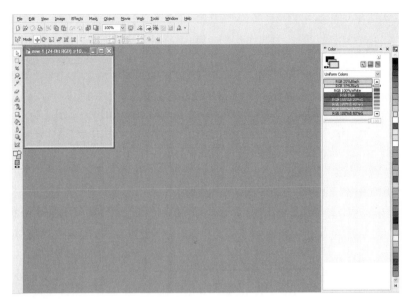

Figure 5.17
You can select colors from a palette.

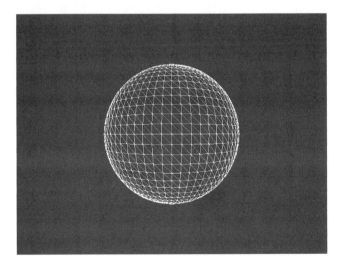

Figure 5.18
You can see the polygon makeup of your objects by using the `WireFrame` command.

wireframe. The command you use for wireframe is simply `WireFrame`. Here is the code for creating a sphere and then converting it to wireframe:

```
; This is the code for creating a sphere and making it wireframe
```

```
sphere=CreateSphere()
WireFrame sphere
```

Transparency

If you're a fan of the television series *Star Trek* (and if you're reading this book, you probably are), you're probably familiar with the term "cloaking." When a Klingon ship wanted to make itself invisible, it would cloak itself so that it couldn't be detected. We can "cloak" objects that we have created in Blitz3D by using the `Alpha` command. The `Alpha` command allows you to set a level of transparency for an object. Typically, you would set a number for the Alpha between 0 and 1. For example, if you entered an Alpha level of 0.5, the object would be 50% see-through. If you entered a value of 0, the object would be invisible, and if you entered a value of 1, the object would be seen in its entirety. Figure 5.19 shows an example of different alpha values applied to a sphere. Here is the code for creating a cube and then making it 50% transparent:

```
sphere = CreateSphere()
EntityAlpha sphere, 0.5
```

Textures and Texture Mapping

This is where things really get interesting. Texture mapping is the key to amazing graphics in 3D games. A very common analogy used for texture mapping is the

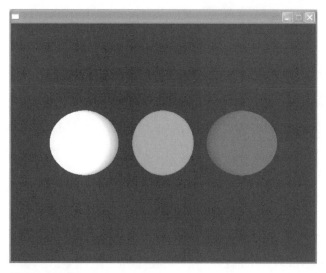

Figure 5.19
The sphere on the far left has an `EntityAlpha` of 1, the one in the middle has a value of 0.5, and the one on the right has a value of 0.2.

wrapping of birthday presents. When you wrap the sheet around the gift, the paper takes on the form of the gift. That's pretty much how texture mapping works. You take a flat image, a pattern, or text (the wrapping paper) and wrap it around a shape or an object you have created or imported.

Applying Image Textures

To get a "realistic" look for your objects, the best approach is to wrap an image around your shapes. To do this, you must create a texture and then tell Blitz3D what object you would like to wrap that texture around. In the following example, we will create a sphere and then wrap an image around it.

Note

Texture Location

It is very important to note that the file that contains your texture must be saved in the same location as your program file or you must specify the folder where it is located. After you have entered the following code, save it to a location and then copy the texture file to the same location as the program file.

```
; demo05-05.bb - Putting a texture on a sphere
; ------------------
Graphics3D 640,480
SetBuffer BackBuffer()

Const ESC_KEY = 1
; Create camera
camera = CreateCamera()
; Create a light
light = CreateLight()

; Create our sphere
sphere=CreateSphere(32)
PositionEntity sphere,0,0,5
ScaleEntity sphere, 2,2,2

; Create the texture
tex=LoadTexture( "texture.bmp" )
EntityTexture sphere, tex
```

Figure 5.20
The demo05-05.bb program.

```
; This following code makes our program run
While Not KeyDown(ESC_KEY)
     RenderWorld
     Flip
Wend
End
```

Run the program and you should see the same textured sphere shown in Figure 5.20.

Let's take a closer look at the code that loaded and applied the texture:

```
; Creating the texture
tex = LoadTexture( "texture.bmp" )
EntityTexture sphere, tex
```

The first part tex= is just a name. You can name your texture anything, but in this case, we called it tex. LoadTexture is the actual command that tells Blitz3D to load a specific texture. Within the brackets, you tell Blitz3D which file to load. In this case, the file is called texture.bmp.

Note that the file that you choose to load must be in the same folder that your program is saved in. In this example, texture.bmp would have to be in the same folder that your saved program is in, unless you specify another folder.

The next line, EntityTexture followed by sphere, tex, tells Blitz3D to put the texture, in this case called tex, onto the shape called sphere.

Scaling Textures

After you've applied your texture, you may find that it is either too big or too small for the object you are wrapping it around. You can use the ScaleTexture command to increase or decrease the scale of the texture.

Here is the line we would add to our code to scale the texture:

```
; Creating the texture
tex=LoadTexture( "texture.bmp" )
ScaleTexture tex, 2,2
EntityTexture sphere,tex
```

After the ScaleTexture command, you tell Blitz3D which texture you want to scale—in this case it is the one called tex. You then specify how much you would like to scale the object. Because the image you used as your texture was two-dimensional, you only have to enter a number for the amount you want to scale the x and y axes. Any numbers you enter above 1 will increase the size of the texture, and any integer between 0 and 1 will decrease the size of the texture. For example, if you entered 0.5,0.5 for the scale, the texture would be reduced by half.

Object Order

When you have more than one object on the screen, there is a chance that they can overlap each other and you won't be able to see one or the other. Sometimes you'll actually want an object to be hidden by others, and you can create this effect by controlling the order of an object. Let's create a program that contains two spheres that overlap and then change their order using the EntityOrder command. This will be demo05-06.bb on the CD.

First, try on your own to create two overlapping spheres, each with different colors (see Figure 5.21), and then compare it to the following code:

```
; demo05-06.bb - Creating two spheres without setting order
; ------------------
Graphics3D 640,480
SetBuffer BackBuffer()

Const ESC_KEY = 1
; Create camera
camera = CreateCamera()
; Create a light
light = CreateLight()
```

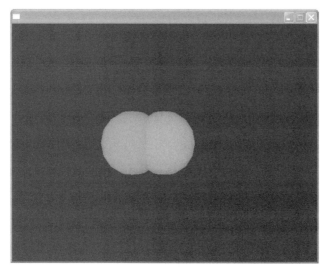

Figure 5.21
When two objects overlap, they'll blend into one another unless you adjust their order.

```
; Create our spheres
sphere1 = CreateSphere(32)
sphere2 = CreateSphere(32)
PositionEntity sphere1,-1,0,5
EntityColor sphere1, 102,23,231

sphere2=CreateSphere()
PositionEntity sphere2,0,0,5
EntityColor sphere2, 21,78,199


; This following code makes our program run
While Not KeyDown(ESC_KEY)
     RenderWorld
     Flip
Wend
End
```

Now when you run the program, you'll see that the two shapes blend together at the point where they overlap. Rather than having the objects blend together, you can have one overlap the other by changing the order in which they are drawn using the EntityOrder command. With the EntityOrder command you can enter a number either below or above 0 to change the order of an object. For example, let's say we had an object called sphere. If we entered the code EntityOrder sphere, -1, the sphere will be drawn behind other objects; if the code was EntityOrder sphere, 1, the sphere would be drawn in front of the other objects. Let's try this in our code. Change this code (just add the last line):

```
sphere1 = CreateSphere()
PositionEntity sphere1,-1,0,5
EntityColor sphere1, 102,23,231
```

to this:

```
sphere1 = CreateSphere()
PositionEntity sphere1,-1,0,5
EntityColor sphere1, 102,23,231
EntityOrder sphere1, -1
```

This is on the CD, at demo05-07.bb. Now run the program and see how it looks. Then go back and change the –1 to a 1 and run the program again to see how it affects how the spheres seem to overlap. Figure 5.22 shows how, now, the images overlap correctly!

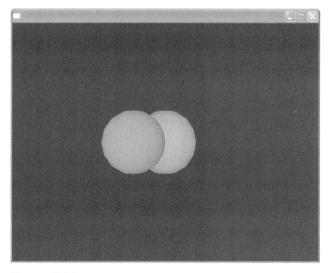

Figure 5.22
The demo05-07.bb program.

Summary

We've finally finished with the basics of BASIC programming and moved on to some of the graphical elements. With the skills you've just started learning, you will soon be able to make your own fully three-dimensional games!

This chapter might have seemed a little simple. While we have just started learning to make simple shapes, these are the building blocks of much more complex objects. Using these shapes, we will be able to make much more complex things in the upcoming chapters.

This chapter covered the following concepts:

- An overview of the 3D world

- Creating basic shapes

- Coloring

- Textures

- Object order

In the next chapter, we will learn how to move and control the objects we just created. Sweet!

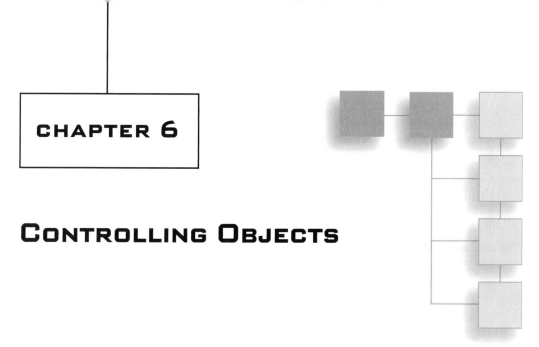

CHAPTER 6

CONTROLLING OBJECTS

What's the difference between watching a video and playing a video game? In a video game you have a certain amount of control over your players, the environment, and certain objects, but while watching a video you just watch the events unfold. This chapter is all about control—controlling the objects you create by moving them around the screen. You have a variety of choices when it comes to moving your objects. You can decide along which axis you want them moved, by what increments, and what controls will be used to navigate your objects. This chapter will also explore rotating objects and creating pivots.

Moving Objects

Now that you know how to create objects, we're going to have some fun and start moving them around the screen. We'll start off by taking a simple object (a sphere with the brick texture map applied to it) and create controls so that by using our keyboard we can move it around the screen. First, open the file called moving a demo06-01.bb from the CD, or enter the following code. Save the file to a new folder and copy the file called brick.jpg to that folder.

```
;demo06-01.bb - Moving a sphere
; ------------------
Graphics3D 640,480
SetBuffer BackBuffer()
```

```
;Key constants
Const A_KEY = 30
Const Z_KEY = 44
Const LEFT_KEY = 203
Const RIGHT_KEY = 205
Const UP_KEY = 200
Const DOWN_KEY = 208
Const ESC_KEY = 1

; Create camera
camera=CreateCamera()
; Create a light
light=CreateLight()

;Create sphere
sphere=CreateSphere(16)
PositionEntity sphere,0,0,5

;Load the texture
tex=LoadTexture( "brick.jpg" )
ScaleTexture tex, .5,.5
EntityTexture sphere,tex

; This following code moves our sphere:
While Not KeyDown(ESC_KEY)

    If KeyDown(A_KEY) TranslateEntity sphere,0,-.3,0
    If KeyDown(Z_KEY) TranslateEntity sphere,0,.3,0
    If KeyDown(LEFT_KEY) TranslateEntity sphere, -0.3,0,0
    If KeyDown(RIGHT_KEY) TranslateEntity sphere, 0.3,0,0
    If KeyDown(UP_KEY) TranslateEntity sphere,0,0,0.3
    If KeyDown(DOWN_KEY) TranslateEntity sphere,0,0,-0.3

    RenderWorld
    Flip
Wend
End
```

Run the program now, and what you see on the screen should look similar to Figure 6.1. You can control the sphere with the A and Z keys and the arrow keys.

Figure 6.1
The demo06-01.bb program.

Now take a closer look at the part of the program that actually controls the movement:

```
; This following code moves our sphere:
While Not KeyDown(ESC_KEY)

    If KeyDown(A_KEY) TranslateEntity sphere,0,-.3,0
    If KeyDown(Z_KEY) TranslateEntity sphere,0,.3,0
    If KeyDown(LEFT_KEY) TranslateEntity sphere, -0.3,0,0
    If KeyDown(RIGHT_KEY) TranslateEntity sphere, 0.3,0,0
    If KeyDown(UP_KEY) TranslateEntity sphere,0,0,0.3
    If KeyDown(DOWN_KEY) TranslateEntity sphere,0,0,-0.3

    RenderWorld
    Flip
Wend
```

Let's examine this section of code piece by piece to see what is going on.

`While Not KeyDown(ESC_KEY)`—This basically means: as long as the Esc key is not pressed down, continue the program.

`If KeyDown(A_KEY) TranslateEntity sphere,0,-.3,0`—This line is saying that when the letter A is pressed on the keyboard, move the object down the y axis by 0.3 units. The command that tells Blitz3D to actually move the object is `TranslateEntity`. The rest of the lines basically say the same thing, but using different keys and designating different movements along the x, y, and z axes.

Rotating Objects

Rotating your objects is similar to moving them in that you need to define which keys you want to use to rotate your objects and on which axis you'd like to rotate them. The axis for the rotation will determine how your objects will spin. Rotation can occur along the x axis, the y axis, or the z axis (see Figures 6.2, 6.3, and 6.4).

Using the same program as above, let's add the following code above the RenderWorld line to add rotation controls:

```
; Change rotation values depending on the key pressed
If KeyDown(N_KEY)= True Then pitch#=pitch#-1
If KeyDown(M_KEY)=True Then pitch#=pitch#+1
```

Pitch

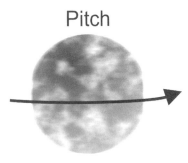

Figure 6.2
Rotation along the x axis.

Yaw

Figure 6.3
Rotation along the y axis.

Roll

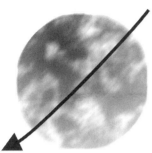

Figure 6.4
Rotation along the z axis.

```
If KeyDown(COMMA)=True Then yaw#=yaw#-1
If KeyDown(PERIOD)=True Then yaw#=yaw#+1
If KeyDown(X_KEY)=True Then roll#=roll#-1
If KeyDown(C_KEY)=True Then roll#=roll#+1

;Rotate
RotateEntity sphere,pitch#,yaw#,roll#
```

Now, run the program and you'll see that, by pressing the keys M, N, comma, period, X, and C, you can rotate your object along the different axes. Here's a breakdown of the code that we just entered:

`If KeyDown (N_KEY)= True` means that when the letter "n" is pressed on the keyboard, then do the following. `Pitch#=pitch#+1` basically says that the pitch of the object should change positively (in other words, rotate clockwise) on the x axis by one unit. The rest of this section of code is the same but changes the values positively and negatively for pitch, yaw, and roll.

The next section tells Blitz3D what to rotate:

`RotateEntity sphere,pitch#,yaw#,roll#`

Here we are telling Blitz3D to rotate the object called `sphere` by the amount we defined in the previous section of code.

Rotating Objects on Their Own

In the previous section, you learned how you could rotate an object via keyboard commands. What if you wanted to just have an object rotate on its own? To do this, you just have to slightly modify the code you used in the last section. Here is the code for a program that contains a single cube that rotates on its own:

```
;demo06-03.bb - Rotating a cube on its own
; -----------------
Graphics3D 640,480
SetBuffer BackBuffer()

;Key constants
Const ESC_KEY = 1

; Create camera
camera=CreateCamera()
; Create a light
light=CreateLight()

;Create cube
cube = CreateCube()
PositionEntity cube,0,0,5

; This following code rotates our cube:
While Not KeyDown(ESC_KEY)

    pitch# = pitch# - 1
    ;Rotate
    RotateEntity cube,pitch#,yaw#,roll#

    RenderWorld
    Flip
Wend
End
```

Basically, the program we just created is a simple cube with one element of code that makes it rotate:

```
While Not KeyDown(ESC_KEY)

    pitch# = pitch# - 3
    ;Rotate
    RotateEntity cube,pitch#,yaw#,roll#
```

The `While Not KeyDown(ESC_KEY)`, as usual, says that as long as the Esc key isn't pressed, do the following. The code `pitch#=pitch#−1` controls the speed, direction, and angle of rotation for your cube. The value of the pitch will always change because we entered this code within the game loop. This way, it will continue to rotate on its own. Because we didn't define a starting speed, the pitch will start at 0. After the first loop of the game, the pitch will be −1, after the second loop, it will be −2, and so on. To slow down the rotation, you would enter an integer between 0 and 1, and to speed it up, enter a number greater than 1. For example, if you used pitch#=pitch#=+0.2, the rotation would be extremely slow, while using pitch#=pitch#=+5 would create an extremely fast rotation. If the number you enter is negative, the rotation will be toward you, and a positive number means the rotation will be away from you.

N o t e

Don't Forget the + and −

You have to enter a + or − sign before the speed of rotation number or the code won't work. For example, pitch#=pitch#1 wouldn't work because there is no plus or minus sign in front of the 1. It would have to be either pitch#=pitch#−1 or pitch#=pitch#+1 because we are decreasing or increasing it by one unit.

In this example, we rotated the cube along the x axis. If we wanted to rotate the cube on the y or z axis, we would have entered yaw#=yaw#−1 or roll#=roll#−1 instead of the pitch#=pitch#−1.

N o t e

Rotate Around Multiple Axes

You are not restricted to rotating around one axis at a time. You can have your objects rotate around the x, y, and z axes individually or with any combination of the three. For example, if I wanted the cube in the last section to rotate around all three axes, I would have entered the following code in the run section:

```
While Not KeyDown( 1 )
pitch#=pitch#-1
yaw#=yaw#=+1
roll#=roll#-1
RotateEntity cube,pitch#,yaw#,roll#
```

N o t e

Now You Try

Experiment with different rotation speeds, angles, and directions until you're comfortable with it. It's always a good idea to apply a texture to your object before you start rotating it so that you can really see the effects of the rotation.

Orbiting (a.k.a. Pivoting)

What's the difference between rotating and pivoting? Let's look to the galaxies for our answer. Think of how the earth orbits around the sun. While the earth is rotating, it is also orbiting (in the case of Blitz3D we'll call this pivoting) around the sun. The sun is set as the pivot point, and the earth orbits around it. Let's re-create this scene and combine both rotating and orbiting using Blitz3D. To make our scene look a little more realistic, we'll add a texture map to both the sun and the earth. On the CD you'll find the two textures that were used: sunskin.jpg and earthskin.jpg.

The key to this program is the item called the *pivot*. Think of the pivot item as an invisible anchor that sets the point of rotation. Have you ever seen someone do the discus or hammer throw at the Olympics? The athlete stays in one spot and spins as the hammer or discus "orbits" around him until he lets go. If we were to compare this to Blitz3D code, the athlete, who acts as the center of the rotation, would be the "pivot." Take a look at Figure 6.5, which provides an illustrated example of a pivot.

Before we get to the code of this little program, I should warn you: You might get a little confused. There are a lot of concepts in this program, and I combine a few different elements, so if you are a little confused, don't worry; I'll break it down nicely afterward and give you plenty of help.

Here's the code we use to create the program:

```
;demo06-04.bb - Demonstrating orbiting
; ------------------
Graphics3D 640,480
SetBuffer BackBuffer()
```

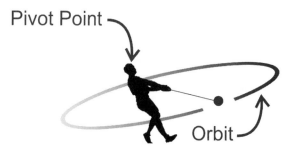

Figure 6.5
The athlete is the pivot and the ball twirling around him is the orbit.

```
;Key constants
Const ESC_KEY = 1

; Create camera
camera=CreateCamera()
PositionEntity camera,0,0,-10

; Create a light
light=CreateLight()
RotateEntity light,90,0,0

;Create the Sun
sun = CreateSphere(16)
ScaleEntity sun, 2,2,2
PositionEntity sun, 2,3,1

;Give a texture to the sun
tex=LoadTexture( "sunskin.jpg" )
EntityTexture sun,tex

; Create a pivot.
pivot = CreatePivot()
PositionEntity pivot,2,3,1

; Create the planet earth. Make the pivot the parent of the earth.
earth = CreateSphere(16,pivot)
tex1 = LoadTexture( "earthskin.jpg" )
EntityTexture earth, tex1

; Position planet so that it is offset from the sun
PositionEntity earth,5,0,0

; This following code runs the simulation
While Not KeyDown(ESC_KEY)

    ; Turn pivot, making planet orbit around the pivot point.
    TurnEntity pivot,0,1,0
    ; Rotate the earth.
    pitch#=pitch#+1
    RotateEntity earth,pitch#,yaw#,roll#
RenderWorld

    Flip
```

```
Wend
End
```

Now take a close look, and I'll explain the important parts of the above code:

```
;Create the Sun
sun = CreateSphere(16)
ScaleEntity sun, 2,2,2
PositionEntity sun, 2,3,1

;Give a texture to the sun
tex=LoadTexture( "sunskin.jpg" )
EntityTexture sun,tex
```

There's nothing in this code that you haven't seen already. We simply created the sun by making a sphere and then applied the texture sunskin.jpg to it. The line you should take note of is the position of the sun at 2,3,1. We offset the sun on purpose, to illustrate that the pivot we create later in the program will have to be located in the same spot to make it look as if the sun is the center of the orbit.

```
; Create a pivot.
pivot = CreatePivot()
PositionEntity pivot,2,3,1
```

With this code, we name our pivot—in this case we were very original and called it pivot. This is followed by the actual command to create the pivot: CreatePivot(). In the next line we position the pivot. We put it in the exact same location (2,3,1) that we put the sun so that it will appear as if the planet we create is orbiting the sun. The truth is that the planet will actually be orbiting the pivot point. If you deleted the sun, the planet we created would still orbit the same location.

```
; Create the planet earth. Make the pivot the parent of the earth.
earth = CreateSphere(16,pivot)
tex1 = LoadTexture( "earthskin.jpg" )
EntityTexture earth, tex1
```

The creation of the earth is fairly straightforward, but you are seeing a piece of code that you have not seen before. In the first line, notice the word pivot after the 16:

```
earth = CreateSphere(16,pivot)
```

By doing this we are making the pivot the *parent* of the earth. A parent is a piece of code that will tie the two objects together. Anything that we do to the parent—

in this case, the pivot—will also affect the child, which in this case is the earth. Parents are awesome—you may not think so in real life, but in Blitz3D, they can save you a lot of time and effort. I'll talk a little more about parents later in the book and you'll see how they can benefit you.

```
; Position planet so that it is offset from the sun
PositionEntity earth,5,0,0
```

Here we are just placing the earth on the screen, a little ways from the sun. Next we enter the code that actually makes the program run:

```
While Not KeyDown(ESC_KEY)
; Turn pivot, making planet orbit around the pivot point.
TurnEntity pivot,0,1,0
; Rotate the earth.
pitch#=pitch#+1
RotateEntity earth,pitch#,yaw#,roll#
RenderWorld
Flip
Wend
End
```

We've discussed `While Not KeyDown(ESC_KEY)` already in this book. Again, it says that as long as the Esc key is not pressed, do the following. `TurnEntity pivot 0,1,0` tells the program to continually orbit the pivot (this also includes the earth because we made the pivot the parent of the earth) around the y axis. If you wanted the orbit to go around the x axis, you would've entered 1,0,0, and if you wanted it to orbit around the z axis, you would have used 0,0,1. You could have also changed the direction of the pivot by making the pivot value a negative number.

The earth doesn't just orbit around the sun; it also rotates as it is orbiting. To set the rotation, we used the same code you learned in the last section, but we just took out the `If` statement. Without the `If` statement, the earth spins continually.

Now You Try

Create a replica of an atom with protons orbiting around the nucleus, as seen in Figure 6.6. Give the protons a different color. Once you've tried this, compare it to the actual code used. Keep in mind that we used the texture sunskin.jpg for the nucleus and orbit.jpg for the orbits. You can use those or create your own.

```
;demo06-05.bb - Modeling a nucleus
; -------------------
```

```
Graphics3D 640,480
SetBuffer BackBuffer()

;Key constants
Const ESC_KEY = 1

; Create camera
camera=CreateCamera()
PositionEntity camera,0,0,-10

; Create a light
light=CreateLight()
RotateEntity light,90,0,0

;Create the Sun
nucleus = CreateSphere(16)
PositionEntity nucleus, 0,0,1

;Give a texture to the sun
tex=LoadTexture( "sunskin.jpg" )
EntityTexture nucleus,tex

; Create a pivot for each orbit
pivot1=CreatePivot()
PositionEntity pivot1,0,0,1
pivot2=CreatePivot()
PositionEntity pivot2, 0,0,1
pivot3=CreatePivot()
PositionEntity pivot3, 0,0,1

; Create each orbit.
orbit=CreateSphere(16,pivot1)
tex1=LoadTexture( "orbit.jpg" )
EntityTexture orbit, tex1
ScaleEntity orbit, 0.3,0.3,0.3
PositionEntity orbit,4,0,0

orbit2=CreateSphere(16,pivot2)
tex2=LoadTexture("orbit.jpg")
EntityTexture orbit2, tex1
ScaleEntity orbit2, 0.3,0.3,0.3
PositionEntity orbit2, 0,0,4
```

```
orbit3=CreateSphere(16, pivot3)
tex2=LoadTexture("orbit.jpg")
EntityTexture orbit3, tex1
ScaleEntity orbit3, 0.3,0.3,0.3
PositionEntity orbit3, 4,0,0


; This following code runs the simulation
While Not KeyDown(ESC_KEY)

    ; Turn pivots, making atom orbit around the nucleus.
    TurnEntity pivot1, 0,3,0
    TurnEntity pivot2, 3,0,0
    TurnEntity pivot3, 0,0,3
    ; Spinning the nucleus.
    pitch#=pitch#+3 yaw#=yaw#+3 roll#=roll#+3
    RotateEntity nucleus,pitch#,yaw#,roll#
    RenderWorld

    Flip
Wend
End
```

Run the program now, and what you see on your screen should look similar to Figure 6.6.

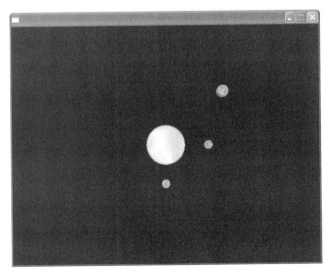

Figure 6.6
The demo06-05.bb program.

Summary

With what you've learned in this chapter, you can now create objects that actually move on the screen. You noticed that we created objects that even move on their own (such as the pivoting orbits). Allowing objects to move on their own is the basic idea of artificial intelligence, but we will go over that more later.

This chapter covered the following concepts:

- Moving objects

- Rotating objects

- Pivoting objects

In the next chapter, we will learn more about using lights and cameras to showcase what is occurring in our 3D world.

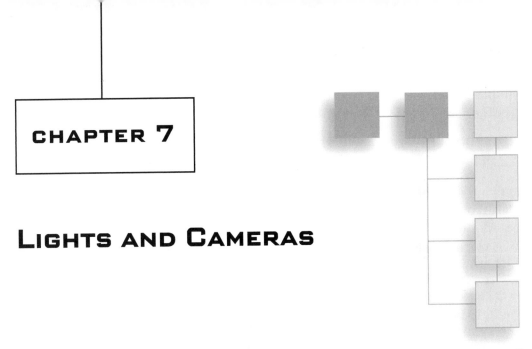

CHAPTER 7

LIGHTS AND CAMERAS

As you've seen from the previous chapters, two of the essential components of your Blitz3D programs are lights and cameras. In fact, in every program we've created so far, we've created at least one light and one camera by entering the following code:

```
camera=CreateCamera()
light=CreateLight()
```

Blitz 3D allows you to do so much with both lights and cameras. You can change the type of lights, as well as their strength and position; you can tie the camera to objects, add multiple cameras, and rotate and move the camera, among other things. In this chapter, you'll be using some of the techniques you learned in the previous chapters on creating and moving objects, so just be sure you have a good grasp on those chapters before you move on.

Working with Cameras

The camera acts as the eyes for the player of the game. Where you place the camera or cameras will directly determine the action that the player sees. Blitz3D makes it easy to manipulate the location, angle, and zoom level of our cameras. Most of the camera settings we will apply in this chapter will be performed on a simple cylinder. Before continuing, either open the program called demo07-01.bb or enter the following code:

```
; Lighting and Cameras
; ----------------------------------
Graphics3D 640,480
SetBuffer BackBuffer()
; Create camera
camera=CreateCamera()
; Creating a light
light=CreateLight()
; This is the code for creating the cylinder
cylinder=CreateCylinder()
PositionEntity cylinder,0,0,5
EntityColor cylinder, 0,26,125
; The following code makes our program run
While Not KeyDown(1)
RenderWorld
Flip
Wend
End
```

When you run this program, you should see a cylinder (see Figure 7.1).

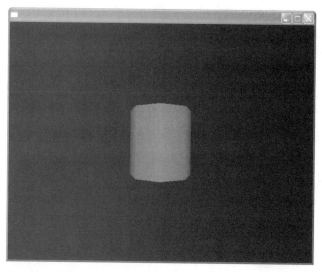

Figure 7.1
The demo07-01.bb program.

Creating and Positioning a Camera

You've actually created a camera several times already by using the `Create-Camera()` command. Just like with creating shapes, you need to give your camera a name. Typically when coding a camera you should give the camera a generic name like `camera` or `camera1` to make things easier. For example, if we wanted to create and name a camera called `camera1`, we would enter the following code:

```
camera1=CreateCamera()
```

The next step is to position your camera. Cameras can be positioned like most other objects using the `PositionEntity` command. You simply need to specify where on the screen you would like the camera to be.

For this example, remove the existing code under `;Create Camera` in the demo07-01.bb program and replace it with this:

```
; Create camera
camera1=CreateCamera()
PositionEntity camera1, 1,-3,-1
```

Now when you run the program, it may seem as though the cylinder has moved, but it hasn't (see Figure 7.2). What has actually happened is that you've moved the location of your camera, and the cylinder is actually in the same spot it always was.

Figure 7.2
The cylinder hasn't really moved, just the location of the camera.

Rotating a Camera

Just like other objects, you can rotate a camera to change the angle of your view. By using the RotateEntity command, you can specify the axis on which you want the rotation to occur. To test this out, we're going to place a camera on top of our shape and rotate it so that it is facing downward. Replace the code under ;Create camera with the following:

```
; Create camera
camera1 = CreateCamera()
PositionEntity camera1,0,5,5
RotateEntity camera1,90,0,0
```

After you run the program, you'll notice that you now have a view of the cylinder, as if you were on the ceiling looking down (see Figure 7.3).

Let's take a closer look at the code to see how we created this.

PositionEntity camera1, 0,5,5 moved the camera along the y and z axes so that the camera was directly over the cylinder (remember the cylinder is at position 0,0,5). If you ran the program at this point, you wouldn't see anything because the camera is pointing straight ahead instead of downward at the cylinder. To correct this, we rotate the camera by entering this code:

```
RotateEntity camera1,90,0,0
```

The 90,0,0 rotated the camera 90 degrees along the x axis.

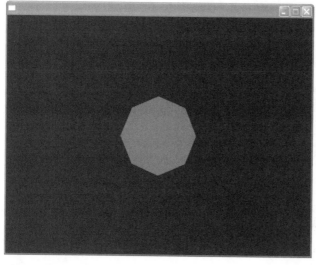

Figure 7.3
A view of the cylinder from the top.

Using Two Cameras

Normally when you watch television you sit back, relax, and let the show entertain you. While you're sitting there relaxing, there's a lot of hard work going on, especially in the TV director's control room. Whether it's a sporting event, a sitcom, the local news, or a soap opera, there are typically three or more cameras that are continuously being switched by the director.

In the following example, we will create two cameras around our cylinder and then switch to each one, using the HideEntity and ShowEntity commands. While the program is running, we'll switch each camera as if we were big-time television directors!

We'll make this demo07-02.bb. The first thing we'll do is create two cameras:

```
; Create camera
camera1=CreateCamera()
PositionEntity camera1,0,5,5
RotateEntity camera1,90,0,0
camera2=CreateCamera()
PositionEntity camera2,0,0,0
```

If we ran the program right now, the view would be from camera2 because it was the last camera created, as seen in Figure 7.4.

Figure 7.4
The view would be from camera2 because it's the last one created.

Now we have to create the code to control the program while it is running.

```
; The following code makes our program run
While Not KeyDown( 1 )
RenderWorld
If KeyHit(2) HideEntity camera2
If KeyHit(3) ShowEntity camera2
Flip
Wend
End
```

The following two lines of code are the ones that control the camera:

```
If KeyHit(ONE_KEY) HideEntity camera2
If KeyHit(TWO_KEY) ShowEntity camera2
```

The first line, If KeyHit(ONE_KEY) HideEntity camera2, says that if you press the number 1 on the keyboard, then the camera will be hidden. When the camera is hidden with the HideEntity command, the view will default to the other camera, camera1. To show camera2 again, we use the ShowEntity command by pressing the number 2 on the keyboard, as seen in Figure 7.5.

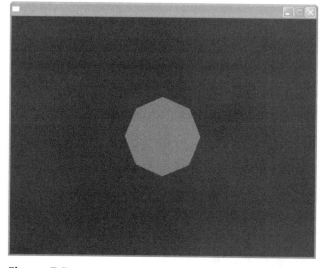

Figure 7.5
The demo07-02.bb program. When you press the numbers 1 and 2, the second camera is activated or deactivated.

Switching Cameras Virtually

While switching cameras is one way of changing the viewpoint, another easier way to change the viewpoint is to simply move or reposition a camera when an event occurs. In the following example, we'll change the position of the camera when certain keys are hit. Enter the following code to create a simple cylinder:

```
; Lighting and Cameras
; ----------------------------------
Graphics3D 640,480
SetBuffer BackBuffer()
;Create camera
camera=CreateCamera()
; Creating a light
light=CreateLight()
; This is the code for creating the cylinder
cylinder=CreateCylinder()
PositionEntity cylinder,0,0,5
; This following code makes our program run
While Not KeyDown( 1 )
RenderWorld
Flip
Wend
End
```

If you run the program now, you should just see a cylinder as in Figure 7.6.

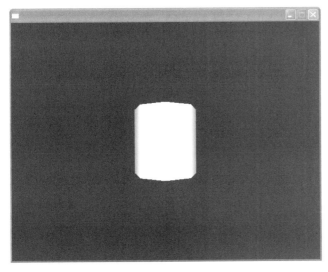

Figure 7.6
The code you created should produce this cylinder.

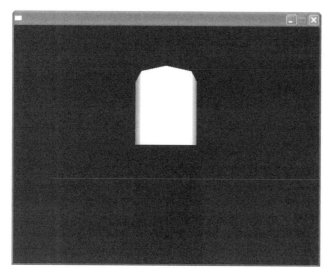

Figure 7.7
View 1 of demo07-03.bb.

The following code will move the camera when certain keys are pressed:

```
While Not KeyDown(ESC_KEY)

    If KeyHit(ONE_KEY) Then PositionEntity camera, 0,-1,0
    If KeyHit(TWO_KEY) Then PositionEntity camera, 0,1,0
    If KeyDown(THREE_KEY) Then PositionEntity camera, 1,0,0
    If KeyDown(FOUR_KEY) Then PositionEntity camera, 0,0,0

    RenderWorld
    Flip
Wend
```

When you run the program, pressing the keys 1 through 4 will change the viewpoint (see Figures 7.7–7.10).

Splitting Views

Another option you have when working with cameras is to use a split screen. When you have more than one camera, you can split the screen in two so that you can see the view from both cameras at once. To split the screen, you use the

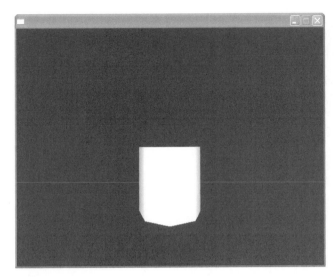

Figure 7.8
View 2 of demo07-03.bb.

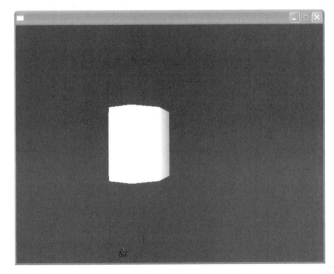

Figure 7.9
View 3 of demo07-03.bb.

CameraViewport command. Start by entering the following code or by opening demo07-04.bb to create a program with two cameras:

```
; Lighting and Cameras
; ------------------------------------
Graphics3D 640,480
SetBuffer BackBuffer()
```

Figure 7.10
View 4 of demo07-03.bb.

```
; Create camera
camera1=CreateCamera()
PositionEntity camera1,0,5,5
RotateEntity camera1,90,0,0
camera2=CreateCamera()
PositionEntity camera2,0,0,0
; Creating a light
light=CreateLight()
; This is the code for creating the cylinder
cylinder=CreateCylinder()
PositionEntity cylinder,0,0,5
; This following code makes our program run
While Not KeyDown( 1 )
RenderWorld
Flip
Wend
End
```

Now we'll create the split screens using the `CameraViewport` command by entering the following code in bold:

```
; This is the code for creating the cylinder
cylinder=CreateCylinder()
PositionEntity cylinder,0,0,5
; Using CameraViewport
```

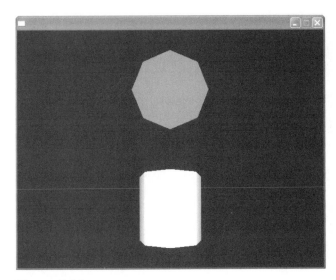

Figure 7.11
The view is now split.

```
CameraViewport camera1,0,0,GraphicsWidth(),GraphicsHeight()/2
CameraViewport camera2,0,GraphicsHeight()/2,
GraphicsWidth(),GraphicsHeight()/2
```

Now when you run the program, you'll see the screen split in two. The top section is a view of the cylinder from the top, and the bottom section is a face-on view, as seen in Figure 7.11.

Okay, this code is made up of a bunch of different numbers and text, so let's break it down step by step.

`CameraViewport camera1`—This creates the split screen portion for `camera1`.

`,0,0`—This tells you the x and y coordinates (starting from the top-left corner of the screen) for this section of the split screen.

`GraphicsWidth()`—This tells you how wide this section of the split screen should be in relation to the entire screen. Let's say you wanted the width of this split to be half the size of the screen. You would enter `GraphicsWidth()/2` in this section of code. The "divided by 2" code (`/2`) tells Blitz3D to divide the width of the screen in two.

`GraphicsHeight()/2`—This indicates what the height of the split screen should be. In this case the `/2` divides the screen in two horizontally so we have one split screen at the top of the screen and one at the bottom.

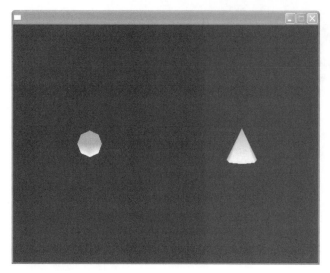

Figure 7.12
The demo07-05.bb program.

Note

Now You Try

In the last example, the screen was split horizontally through the middle. Try on your own to create a split vertically down the middle of the screen with a cone. Once you are done, compare your code with the actual code used to create Figure 7.12, demo07-05.bb.

```
;demo07-05.bb - Split views with cones
; ------------------
Graphics3D 640,480
SetBuffer BackBuffer()

Const ESC_KEY = 1

; Create camera
camera1=CreateCamera()
PositionEntity camera1,0,5,5
RotateEntity camera1,90,0,0
camera2=CreateCamera()
PositionEntity camera2,0,0,0


; Create a light
light=CreateLight()
```

```
; This is the code for creating the cone
cone=CreateCone()
PositionEntity cone,0,0,5
EntityColor cone, 0, 26, 125

; Using CameraViewport
CameraViewport camera1,0,0,GraphicsWidth()/2,GraphicsHeight()
CameraViewport camera2,GraphicsWidth()/2,0,GraphicsWidth()/2,
GraphicsHeight()

; This following code deals with cameras and cylinders
While Not KeyDown(ESC_KEY)

    RenderWorld
    Flip
Wend
End
```

Zooming

Rather than having to move a camera to get closer or farther away from an object, you can take advantage of Blitz3D's camera zooming capabilities. In this exercise, we'll create a sphere that seems far off in the distance and then give the player the ability to zoom in and out using the CameraZoom command.

Start by creating a program that contains only a simple sphere, as designated by the following code. Alternatively, if you want to save a little time typing, open the program called demo07-06.bb.

```
;demo07-06.bb - Camera zooming
; -----------------
Graphics3D 640,480
SetBuffer BackBuffer()

Const ESC_KEY = 1
Const UP_KEY = 200
Const DOWN_KEY = 208

; Create camera
camera=CreateCamera()
zoom# = 1
```

```
; Create a light
light=CreateLight()

; This is the code for creating the sphere
sphere=CreateSphere()
PositionEntity sphere,0,0,9
ScaleEntity sphere, .2, .2, .2
EntityColor sphere, 0, 26, 125

; This following code deals with cameras and cylinders
While Not KeyDown(ESC_KEY)

    If KeyDown(UP_KEY) Then zoom# = zoom# + 1
    If KeyDown(DOWN_KEY) Then zoom# = zoom# - 1

    If zoom# < 1 Then zoom# = 1
    CameraZoom camera, zoom#


    RenderWorld
    Flip
Wend
End
```

The program should look like Figure 7.13 when it is run.

Figure 7.13
The demo07-06.bb program, initial zoom.

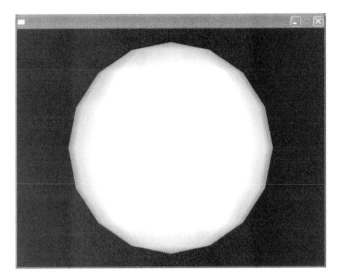

Figure 7.14
The demo07-06.bb program with the zoom level at 30: the sphere looks much, much closer.

Now that we have a camera and a simple sphere far off in the distance, we can add some parameters that will allow us to zoom. The first thing that we do is set the starting zoom values. The zoom value, or zoom level, is represented in the code by zoom#. You can set the zoom value to any number you want. The number 1 represents no zoom at all, any number greater than 1 will zoom you in, and any number less than 1 will zoom you out. For our program, we'll set the default zoom level at 30 to test the zoom.

The next step is to apply the CameraZoom command to our camera:

```
; Applying the zoom
CameraZoom camera,zoom#
```

Go ahead and run the program now. You'll see that the sphere that was previously so far away is now in your face (see Figure 7.14) because we zoomed in so strongly.

Let's take a look at the main loop.

```
; This following code deals with cameras and cylinders
While Not KeyDown(ESC_KEY)

    If KeyDown(UP_KEY) Then zoom# = zoom# + 1
    If KeyDown(DOWN_KEY) Then zoom# = zoom# - 1
```

```
    If zoom# < 1 Then zoom# = 1
    CameraZoom camera, zoom#


    RenderWorld
    Flip
Wend
```

What this code says is that if the down arrow is pressed, then the zoom level (zoom#) decreases by 1, and the opposite if the up arrow is pressed. We make sure the zoom never goes too low by saying that if the zoom is less than 1, it becomes 1 again. Then, using the CameraZoom function, the new zoom is attached each frame to the camera!

Camera Movement

Like just about any other object, the camera that you create can be moved around and rotated to either follow the action or survey your surroundings. In this example, we will work with a file we created earlier in the book called demo06-05.bb—a file that has some protons and electrons floating around a spinning nucleus. We will create a camera that can be moved around and rotated so that you can navigate through the atom. First we'll add controls that will allow us to turn and move the camera. Add this code before the RenderWorld line near the end of the program:

```
;Moving the Camera
If KeyDown(RIGHT_KEY) TurnEntity camera,0,1,0
If KeyDown(LEFT_KEY) TurnEntity camera,0,-1,0
If KeyDown(UP_KEY) MoveEntity camera,0,0,1
If KeyDown(DOWN_KEY) MoveEntity camera,0,0,-1
```

Basically what we've done is set the camera to turn by an increment when the arrow keys are pressed. The MoveEntity command moves the physical location of the camera, while the TurnEntity command turns it by an increment on the axis specified. You can enter different numbers and different increments to see how the camera will react. You can also specify other keys to have the camera move and turn on a different axis.

By using the arrow keys, you can change the viewpoint by moving the camera (see Figures 7.15 and 7.16).

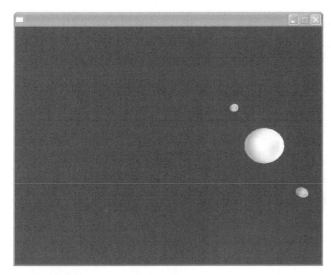

Figure 7.15
Camera view 1 of demo07-07.bb.

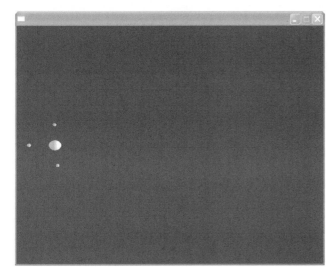

Figure 7.16
Camera view 2.

Following an Object

Having a camera follow an object automatically is a common technique used by 3D video games. Whether it's a race car, plane, or character, being able to automatically follow an object as it moves is the key to game play in certain programs. The goal of this chapter is to give you the groundwork for creating, moving, and switching cameras. There are several methods for having a camera follow an object, all of which are quite involved and are beyond the scope of this chapter. We'll attack this challenge a little later on in the book.

Light

If you don't create light in your Blitz3D programs, you'll be left in darkness! Every Blitz program that you create requires at least one light. You can change the type, position, and effect of your lights by altering the codes.

Types of Lights

Unlike your local Home Depot, which has thousands of different varieties of lights, Blitz3D offers you only three different light types. Take a look at the code used to create a light:

```
light = CreateLight()
```

The first part of the code, `light=`, is just the name that you give to your light. The next part of the code, `CreateLight`, actually creates the light, and, finally, the brackets, `()`, tell Blitz3D what type of light to create. You can specify one of three different types of lights:

■ **Directional Light** created by the code `light = CreateLight()` or `light = CreateLight(1)`. Everything that faces the light will be equally lit (see Figure 7.17).

■ **Point Light** created by the code `light = CreateLight(2)`. This type of light starts strong at a specific point and fades out the farther away you get from the light (see Figure 7.18).

■ **Spot Light** created by the code `light = CreateLight(3)`. Think of spot light as holding a flashlight on an object (see Figure 7.19).

Note

Now You Try

Create a program with a cone or sphere. Try each variety of light to see how the light affects the object.

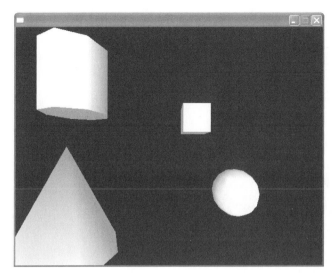

Figure 7.17
Directional lighting.

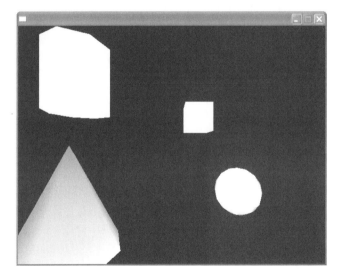

Figure 7.18
Point lighting.

Light Range

You can control how "strong" a light is by adjusting its range. The stronger the range is, the farther it will reach. In the next example, we'll create a sphere that is far off in the distance and is lit by a spotlight. We'll then change the light range to

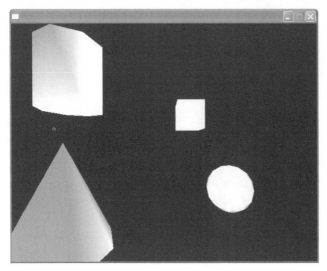

Figure 7.19
Spot lighting.

see how it affects our image. The code used to adjust the range is `LightRange` followed by the name of the light and the amount of range. Open the file called demo07-08.bb or enter this code:

```
;demo07-08.bb - Lights and Cameras
; -------------------
Graphics3D 640,480
SetBuffer BackBuffer()

Const ESC_KEY = 1

; Create camera
camera=CreateCamera()

; Create a light
light=CreateLight(3)
LightRange light, 50


; This is the code for creating the sphere
sphere=CreateSphere()
PositionEntity sphere,0,0,9
ScaleEntity sphere, .5, .5, .5
```

```
EntityColor sphere, 0, 26, 125

; This following code deals with cameras and cylinders
While Not KeyDown(ESC_KEY)

    RenderWorld
    Flip
Wend
End
```

When you run the program, you should see a sphere, as in Figure 7.20.

Now we are going to adjust the range of the light to make it stronger by adding this code in the Creating a light section. We'll increase the range to 50.

```
; Creating a light
light=CreateLight()
LightRange light, 50
```

You'll now see that the object appears brighter (see Figure 7.21) because we've increased its intensity using this code.

Figure 7.20
This is what the object looks like without the LightRange command.

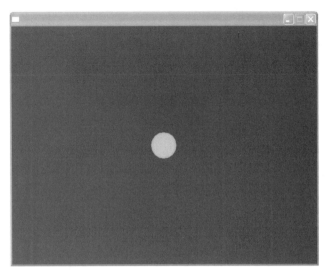

Figure 7.21
Adding `LightRange` to demo07-08.bb.

N o t e

Now You Try

Experiment with this code, adjusting the intensity (currently set at 50) to see the results you get by changing the range of a light.

Summary

We've gone over some important concepts in this chapter. Without a camera, no one would able to see your games, and without lights—well, the game would be awfully boring if there were no light!

This chapter covered the following concepts

- Working with cameras

- Splitting views

- Zooming

- Types of light

- Light range

In the next chapter, we are going to discuss how to actually create the graphics used in our games! Get ready!

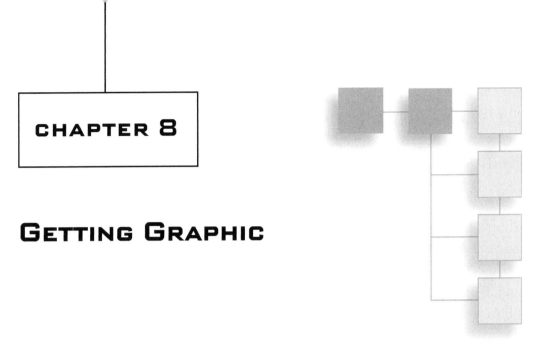

CHAPTER 8

GETTING GRAPHIC

It's time to take a break from programming for a minute. I know what you're thinking: We've only been programming for a few chapters and already we are taking a break? Well, because graphics play such an important part in the world of 3D gaming, I thought it might be wise to spend some time showing you how to create graphics that you'll include in your games. You will need these graphics as you get deeper into the book. Besides, as you'll soon see, creating graphics can be a lot of fun.

There are two categories of graphics that I will cover in this chapter. This first is *heightmaps*. A heightmap defines the landscape of your terrain. In other words, it informs the program where any bumps, mountains, and valleys should occur. The next category of images that you'll create is *textures*. Textures can include the cover to any type of surface including terrains, the sky, walls, and other objects. From grass to mud to ice to brick, you'll create several different types of terrains in this chapter.

All of the graphics that you create in this chapter will be made using either Corel PHOTO-PAINT or CorelDRAW. Both of these programs are found on the accompanying CD and are arguably the most powerful graphics applications on the market. As with most of the technology you are learning in this book, the specific tools you use aren't all that important—it's the process of creating and the thinking behind it that is most important. For that reason, to create the same effects we will accomplish here, you can use almost any graphics applications, including Adobe Photoshop and Illustrator, PaintShop Pro, CorelPainter, and many others.

Heightmaps

A heightmap is an image that defines the landscape of your game. Keep in mind that your game doesn't necessarily need a heightmap, but they are perfect for driving, racing, and role-playing games.

Heightmap images are made in Grayscale mode, which means that there is no color in them, but just 256 shades of gray. You can create mountains and valleys and plains in a heightmap through the use of different shades. Anything that is fully white represents the highest peak, whereas anything that is completely black represents the lowest point (see Figure 8.1).

Now on to the fun part. We are going to create some heightmaps in PHOTO-PAINT. There are hundreds of thousands of possible combinations we can use to create a heightmap, but here I will discuss three different methods. Once you have reviewed these methods, try creating some heightmaps on your own.

Creating Heightmaps with Textured Fills

Corel PHOTO-PAINT comes with a library of textures that are perfect for creating heightmaps. With a few clicks of the mouse button, you can create your

Figure 8.1
The image on the left is the heightmap that was used to create the image on the right. As you can see, the areas that were white represent the high points and the areas that were black represent the low areas.

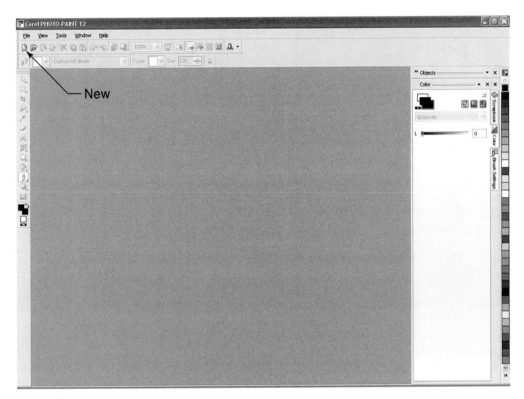

Figure 8.2
Start with a new file by clicking the New icon.

perfect heightmap. Start off by launching PHOTO-PAINT. A Welcome screen will appear.

1. Click the New icon (see Figure 8.2). If the Welcome screen doesn't appear, or if you are already in PHOTO-PAINT, just click File > New. A new document dialog box will now appear where you can set the parameters for your heightmap.

2. Take a look at Figure 8.3 and make sure that your settings are the same. You want the Color mode to be 8-bit Grayscale, the width and height to be 256 pixels, and the resolution to be 72 dpi. You'll probably have to change the units of measurement to pixels to be able to enter these numbers. Click OK once you have all the settings entered.

3. Press the Ctrl key and the Backspace key at the same time. This will open the Fill dialog box.

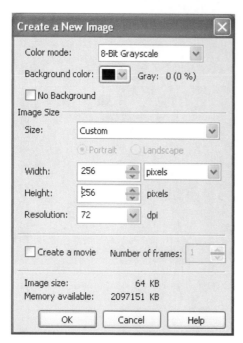

Figure 8.3
Enter your image settings for color, size, and resolution.

4. At the bottom of the dialog box you will see a row of buttons with little pictures on them. Click the button on the far right called Texture Fill.

5. Now click the Edit button. This will open a dialog box where you can choose a texture for your heightmap (see Figure 8.4).

6. Scroll through the different textures and click on a texture name to see a preview of it. The textures are grouped into seven different categories. You can change categories by clicking on the Texture Library drop-down arrow. There are dozens of different textures to choose from with literally millions of combinations. That's right, I said millions! Every time you click on the Preview button in this dialog box, the pattern will be changed slightly so you can choose from an infinite number of different combinations (see Figure 8.5).

7. Once you find a pattern that you like, you can click the OK button to return to the last dialog box. You'll have to click OK again to be returned to PHOTO-PAINT where you will now see your heightmap. As you make your decision on a heightmap, keep in mind again that the darker an area is, the flatter it will be, while the lighter an area is, the more it will be raised.

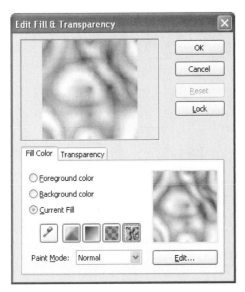

Figure 8.4
Choose a texture for your heightmap.

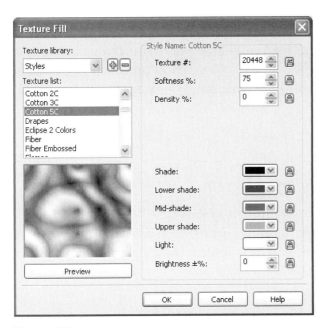

Figure 8.5
You can create millions of different combinations by clicking the Preview button.

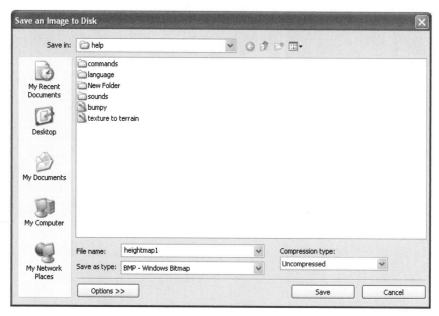

Figure 8.6
Save the heightmap as a .bmp file.

8. Now that your heightmap is created, it is a good idea to save it. Generally speaking, you should save it as a .bmp file. In PHOTO-PAINT, click File > Save As to open a dialog box (see Figure 8.6) where you can save your file. Click the Save As Type drop-down arrow and scroll until you can select Windows BMP—Windows Bitmap. Now give your file a name—call this heightmap1.bmp—and then click the Save button. That's it. You've created your first heightmap.

Creating Heightmaps with a Brush

Another way that you can create a heightmap in PHOTO-PAINT, or just about any other graphics application, is to simply paint one. Just remember as you paint that the darker the shade of gray, the flatter the surface will be and vice versa. Start by launching PHOTO-PAINT.

1. Click the New icon. If the Welcome screen doesn't appear, or if you are already in PHOTO-PAINT, just click File > New. A new document dialog box will now appear where you can set the parameters for your heightmap.

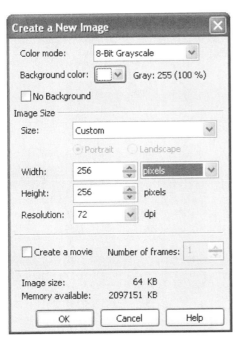

Figure 8.7
Enter your image settings for the color, size, and resolution.

2. Take a look at Figure 8.7 and make sure that your settings are the same. You want the Color mode to be 8-bit Grayscale, the width and height to be 256 pixels, and the resolution to be 72 dpi. You'll probably have to change the units of measurement to pixels to be able to enter these numbers. Click OK once you have all the settings entered.

3. Click on the Paint tool button in the toolbox, as shown in Figure 8.8.

4. Click on the Shape drop-down menu from the Property bar. You'll now see a list of different brush sizes and shapes, as shown in Figure 8.9. You can choose from any of these brushes.

5. Click on any color in the Colors palette. Keep in mind that your color won't actually be a color; it will be a shade of gray because we are working in Grayscale mode. The darker the color you choose, the flatter the heightmap will be and vice versa.

6. Click and drag across the page to draw, as shown in Figure 8.10. You can select different colors to change the amount of shading in order to create different heights.

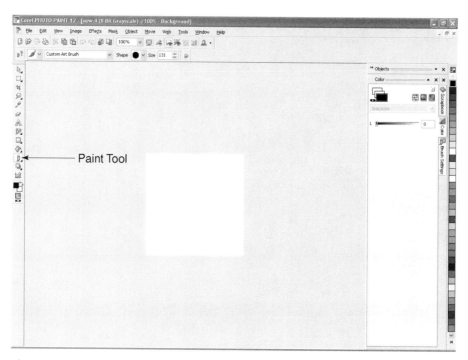

Figure 8.8
Select the Paint tool button in the toolbox.

7. Now that your heightmap is created, it is a good idea to save it. Generally speaking, you should save it as a .bmp file. In PHOTO-PAINT, click File > Save As to open a dialog box where you can save your file. Click the Save As Type drop-down arrow and scroll until you can select BMP— Windows Bitmap. Now give your file a name—call this heightmap2.bmp— and then click the Save button.

Creating Heightmaps with Effects

There are hundreds of different ways to create a heightmap using effects in PHOTO-PAINT. What's the key to creating a cool heightmap with effects? Experiment. After you've followed these instructions, experiment on your own with different combinations of effects. First launch PHOTO-PAINT and then follow these steps:

1. Click the New icon. If the Welcome screen doesn't appear, or if you are already in PHOTO-PAINT, just click File > New. A new document dialog box will now appear where you can set the parameters for your heightmap.

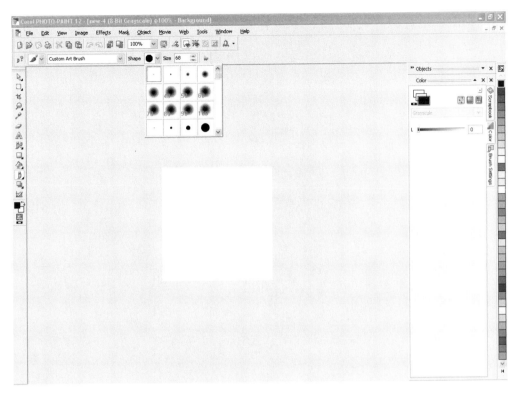

Figure 8.9
Choose from any of the brushes displayed.

2. Take a look at Figure 8.11 and make sure that your settings are the same. You want the Color mode to be 8-bit Grayscale, the width and height to be 256 pixels, and the resolution to be 72 dpi; the background color is white. You'll probably have to change the units of measurement to pixels to be able to enter these numbers. Click OK once you have all the settings entered.

3. Click Effects > Art Strokes > Palette Knife. A dialog box (see Figure 8.12), will appear where you can enter different settings for this effect. Simply accept the defaults and click the OK button. You'll be left with a gray and white image. Now we will smooth things out and make them a little more even.

4. Click Effects > Texture > Relief Sculpture. This will open a dialog box (see Figure 8.13) where you can adjust the settings. Enter the following settings and then click OK. Detail: 51, Depth: 23, Smoothness: 37. You will now be left with a useable heightmap.

5. Now that your heightmap is created, it is a good idea to save it. Generally speaking, you should save it as a .bmp file. In PHOTO-PAINT click File >

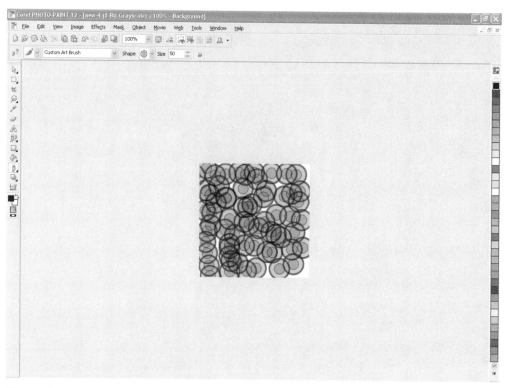

Figure 8.10
Drag across the page to apply the brush.

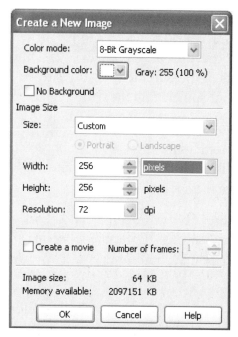

Figure 8.11
Enter your image settings for color, size, and resolution.

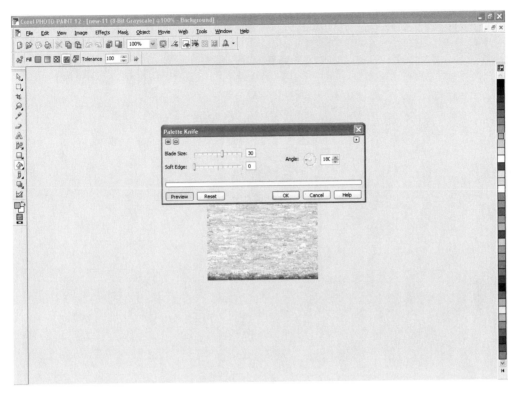

Figure 8.12
Accept the default settings by clicking OK.

Save As to open a dialog box where you can save your file. Click the Save As Type drop-down arrow and scroll until you can select BMP—Windows Bitmap. Now give your file a name—call this heightmap3.bmp—and then click the Save button.

Creating Textures

Textures can make the difference between a good game and a fantastic game. As mentioned earlier, we'll be using a feature called texture mapping to wrap around our objects. Whether it's a wall, a sky, the ground, or floating objects, most get their "feel" from the textures we create. The good news is that creating your own textures is a breeze, whether you're creating them in PHOTO-PAINT or other graphics applications. In this section, we'll create a variety of different textures for walls, terrains, skies, and other objects. The techniques discussed here are not the only options for creating textures, but they will give you a good foundation

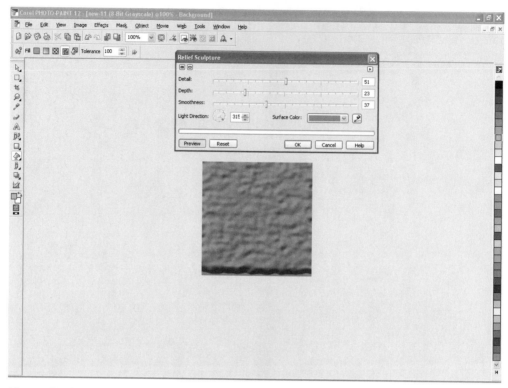

Figure 8.13
Enter the settings in the dialog box to adjust the Relief Sculpture effects.

for creating textures in PHOTO-PAINT. Once you get more familiar with PHOTO-PAINT, experiment with different effects, brushes, and techniques to create your own textures. Start by launching PHOTO-PAINT and clicking New in the Welcome screen. From there, follow any of these steps to create a texture.

Walls

How can you create a wall? Let me count the ways. The truth is that PHOTO-PAINT provides several dozen options for creating a wall. Below you'll find two samples, but again, I encourage you to experiment on your own to create all types of walls.

Brick Walls

There is actually an effect in PHOTO-PAINT that will allow you to instantly create a brick wall.

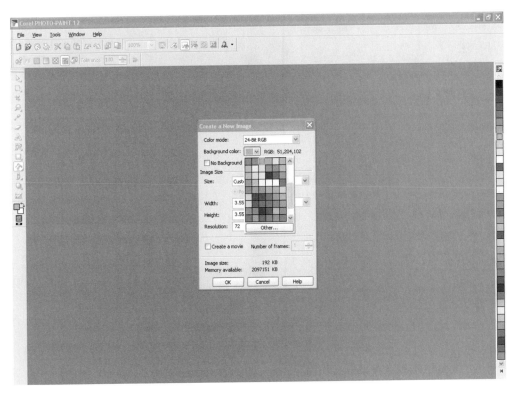

Figure 8.14
Choose any color for your brick wall.

1. Set the Color mode to 24-bit RGB and click the Background color drop-down arrow and select a color for your brick wall (see Figure 8.14).

2. For the rest of the settings, take a look at Figure 8.15 and make sure that your settings are the same. You want the width and height to be 256 pixels and the resolution to be 72 dpi. You'll probably have to change the units of measurement to pixels to be able to enter these numbers. Click OK once you have all the settings entered.

3. Click Effects > Texture > Brick Wall. This will open a dialog box (see Figure 8.16), and at the same time you'll be able to preview the effect. You can click and drag the Roughness slider and adjust other settings like the width and height of the brick and grout. Once you've got the brick wall the way you like it, click OK.

4. Now that your brick wall is created, it is a good idea to save it. Generally speaking, you should save it as a .jpg file. In PHOTO-PAINT, click File > Save

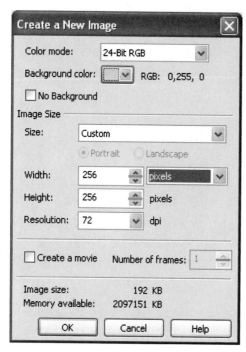

Figure 8.15
Enter your image settings for color, size, and resolution.

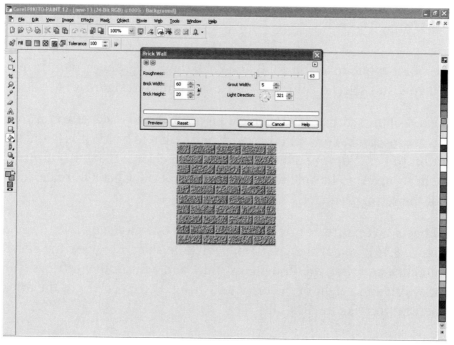

Figure 8.16
Drag any of the sliders to adjust the settings.

As to open a dialog box where you can save your file. Click the Save As Type drop-down arrow and scroll until you can select JPG—JPEG Bitmaps. Now give your file a name—call this wall1.jpg—and then click the Save button.

Plaster Wall

You can create the look of a plaster wall by using the same technique used for the brick wall but just applying a different effect.

1. Click the Background color drop-down arrow and select a color for your plaster wall. For the rest of the settings, take a look at Figure 8.17 and make sure that your settings are the same. You want the Color mode to be 24-bit RGB, the width and height to be 256 pixels, and the resolution to be 72 dpi. You'll probably have to change the units of measurement to pixels to be able to enter these numbers. Click OK once you have all the settings entered.

2. Click Effects > Texture > Plaster Wall. This will open a dialog box (see Figure 8.18), and at the same time you'll be able to preview the effect. You

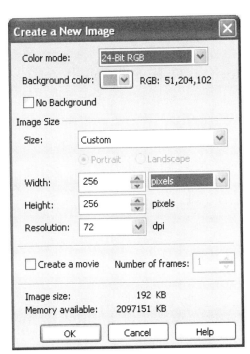

Figure 8.17
Enter your image settings for color, size, and resolution.

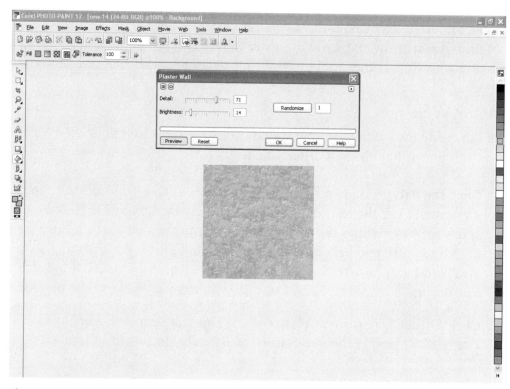

Figure 8.18
Adjust the sliders to change the effect.

can click and drag the sliders to adjust the wall. Once you've got the plaster wall the way you'd like it, click OK.

3. Now that your plaster wall is created, it is a good idea to save it. Generally speaking, you should save it as a .jpg file. In PHOTO-PAINT, click File > Save As to open a dialog box where you can save your file. Click the Save As Type drop-down arrow and scroll until you can select JPG—JPEG Bitmaps. Now give your file a name—call this wall1.jpg—and then click the Save button.

Note

Why Not Photos?

Rather than having to create textures, terrains, and skies from scratch, you can always use your own photos when texture mapping. Imagine that you wanted to create a realistic looking building in your game. Why not take a photo of a building and wrap it around a stretched cube? A great resource for finding photos of different objects is the Image search on Google. Just keep in mind that most images are copyrighted, so if you plan on distributing your game, make sure you have permission to use the images.

Terrains and Skies

A terrain is typically the ground that your players will walk, run, race, or drive on. Again, there are a variety of different ways you can create awesome looking terrains in seconds in PHOTO-PAINT.

Creating Terrains with Texture Fills

The best way to create a realistic looking terrain is to use the Texture fill option in PHOTO-PAINT. There is a complete library of different terrains you can select from and modify.

1. Take a look at Figure 8.19 and make sure that your settings are the same. You want the Color mode to be 24-bit RGB, the width and height to be 256 pixels, and the resolution to be 72 dpi. You'll probably have to change the units of measurement to pixels to be able to enter these numbers. Click OK once you have all the settings entered.

2. Press the Ctrl key and the Backspace key at the same time. This will open the Fill dialog box (see Figure 8.20).

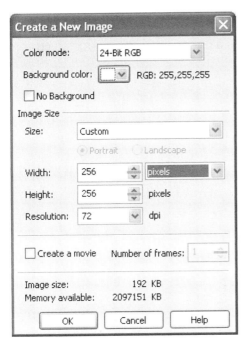

Figure 8.19
Enter your image settings for color, size, and resolution.

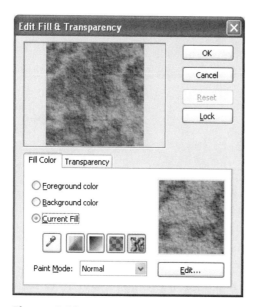

Figure 8.20
Click the Edit button to choose a texture for your heightmap.

3. At the bottom of the dialog box you will see a row of buttons with little pictures on them. Click the button on the far right called Texture Fill.

4. Now click the Edit button. This will open a dialog box where you can choose a texture for your heightmap.

5. Scroll through the different textures and click on a texture name to see a preview of it. The textures are grouped into seven different categories. You can change categories by clicking on the Texture Library drop-down arrow. There are dozens of different textures to choose from (see Figure 8.21) with millions of combinations. You can also adjust the colors in the texture by clicking on the drop-down arrow beside the color boxes. Just make sure you click the Preview button to see your changes. Following are some of the best textures you can use for terrains.

Under the Styles Texture library, there are a variety of textures that begin with the word Rock that are perfect to use:

- Rock-Cloudy-Cracked 2C
- Rock-Cloudy-Eroded, 2C
- Rock-Fractal-Cracked 2C
- Rock-Fractal-Eroded, 2C

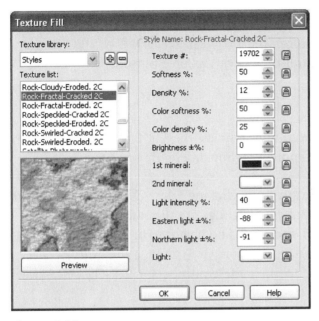

Figure 8.21
There are dozens of patterns to choose from.

- Rock-Speckled-Cracked 2C
- Rock-Speckled-Eroded, 2C

Under the Samples 7 Texture library, there are a variety of textures that are great for terrains, including:

- Drylands
- Polar Surface

For creating sky textures, there are a couple fills that are perfect. You'll have to change the colors to blue, but the results will be great. These two options can be found in the Sample 6 Texture library:

- Cotton Candy
- Exhaust Fume

6. Once you find a pattern that you like, you can click the OK button to return to the last dialog box. You'll have to click OK again to be returned to PHOTO-PAINT where you will now see your heightmap. As you make your decision on a heightmap, keep in mind again that the darker an area is, the flatter it will be, while the lighter an area is, the more it will be raised

7. Now that your texture is created, it is a good idea to save it. Generally speaking, you should save it as a .jpg file. In PHOTO-PAINT, click File >

Save As to open a dialog box where you can save your file. Click the Save As Type drop-down arrow and scroll until you can select JPG—JPEG Bitmap. Now give your file a name, and then click the Save button.

Wood

There are several bitmap fills that beautifully emulate the real-life wood from which you can create textures. These are applied slightly differently from texture fills.

1. Start by clicking the New button or by clicking File > New. Take a look at Figure 8.22 and make sure that your settings are the same. You want the Color mode to be 24-bit RGB, the width and height to be 256 pixels, and the resolution to be 72 dpi. You'll probably have to change the units of measurement to pixels to be able to enter these numbers. Click OK once you have all the settings entered.

2. Press the Ctrl key and the Backspace key at the same time. This will open the Fill dialog box.

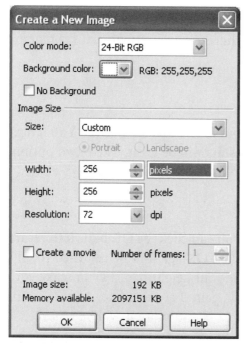

Figure 8.22
Enter your image settings for color, size, and resolution.

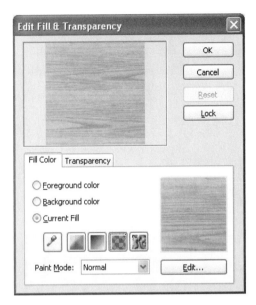

Figure 8.23
By clicking the Edit button, you can change the fill.

3. At the bottom of the dialog box, you will see a row of buttons with little pictures on them. Click the second to last button on the far right called Bitmap Fill.

4. Now click the Edit button. This will open a dialog box (see Figure 8.23) where you can choose a texture for your heightmap.

5. Click the down arrow to see a list of bitmap fills, and scroll to the bottom. At the bottom, you'll find several textures that resemble wood. Click on the one you would like to apply and then click OK. (See Figure 8.24.)

6. Click OK in the original dialog box, and your new texture will be created.

7. Now that your texture is created, it is a good idea to save it. Generally speaking, you should save it as a .jpg file. In PHOTO-PAINT click File > Save As to open a dialog box where you can save your file. Click the Save As Type drop-down arrow and scroll until you can select JPG—JPEG Bitmap. Now give your file a name, and then click the Save button.

Creating Terrains with Effects

Another option for creating terrains is to use the built-in effects of PHOTO-PAINT. The following two textures are great to use for terrains, walls, or other objects.

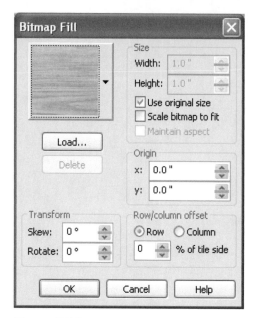

Figure 8.24
Choose a fill that looks like wood.

Cobblestone

The Cobblestone effect in PHOTO-PAINT is the perfect way to emulate a desert floor. Here's how you do it.

1. Click the Background color drop-down arrow and select a color for your wall. For the rest of the settings, take a look at Figure 8.25 and make sure that your settings are the same. You want the Color mode to be 24-bit RGB, the Background color should be a light brown, the width and height need to be 256 pixels, and the resolution should be 72 dpi. You'll probably have to change the units of measurement to pixels to be able to enter these numbers. Click OK once you have all the settings entered.

2. Click Effects > Texture > Cobblestone. This will open a dialog box, and at the same time you'll be able to preview the effect. You can click and drag the sliders to adjust the cobblestone settings (see Figure 8.26). The larger you slide the Size option, the more realistic the desert floor will look. Once you've got the effect the way you like it, click OK.

3. Now that your desert floor is created, it is a good idea to save it. Generally speaking, you should save it as a .jpg file. In PHOTO-PAINT, click File >

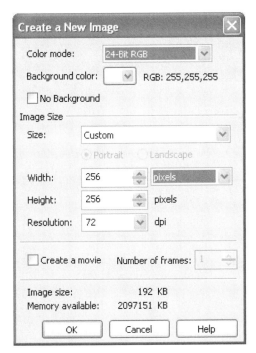

Figure 8.25
Enter your image settings for color, size, and resolution.

Save As to open a dialog box where you can save your file. Click the Save As Type drop-down arrow and scroll until you can select JPG—JPEG Bitmaps. Now give your file a name, and then click the Save button.

Mosaic Tile

From the bottom of pools to bathroom backsplashes to church floors, mosaic tiles are everywhere. You can nicely emulate a real mosaic tile to apply to walls, floors, or ceilings. Open up a new file and follow these steps:

1. Click the Background color drop-down arrow and select a color for your wall. For the rest of the settings, look at Figure 8.27 and make sure that your settings are the same. You want the Color mode to be 24-bit RGB, the Background color should be a light brown, the width and height need to be 256 pixels, and the resolution should be 72 dpi. You'll probably have to change the units of measurement to pixels to be able to enter these numbers. Click OK once you have all the settings entered.

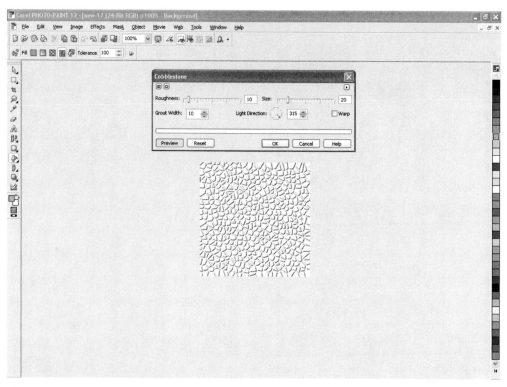

Figure 8.26
Drag any of the sliders to adjust the effect.

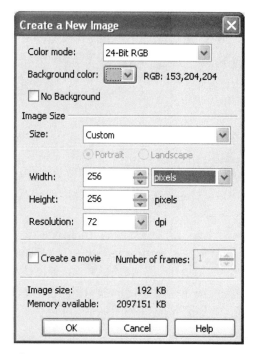

Figure 8.27
Enter your image settings for color, size, and resolution.

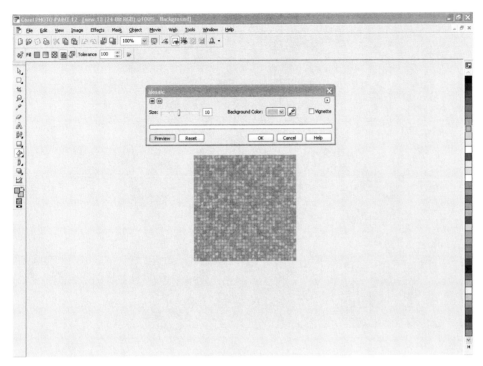

Figure 8.28
Drag the slider to change the size of the tiles.

2. Click Effects > Creative > Mosaic. This will open a dialog box (see Figure 8.28) and at the same time you'll be able to preview the effect. You can click and drag the slider to adjust the size of the tiles. Once you've got the effect the way you like it, click OK.

3. Now that your mosaic tile is created, it is a good idea to save it. Generally speaking, you should save it as a .jpg file. In PHOTO-PAINT, click File > Save As to open a dialog box where you can save your file. Click the Save As Type drop-down arrow and scroll until you can select JPG—JPEG Bitmaps. Now give your file a name, and then click the Save button.

Note

Now You Try

In this chapter you've created a variety of different textures. Take what you learned in the last chapter and apply some of the textures you created in this chapter to some basic shapes, as shown in Figure 8.29.

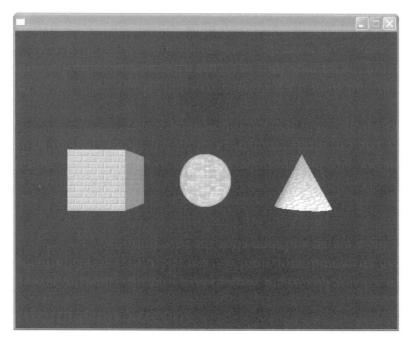

Figure 8.29
Create these shapes and apply a texture to them as shown here.

Information Screens

Most games have at least one or two information screens that provide the user with, well, information. This information usually includes directions on how to use the game or what is going on at that moment. Typical examples of information screens are Welcome screens, Pause screens, and Exit screens. In this section, we'll create a Welcome screen and Pause screen using CorelDRAW. I won't turn you into a graphic designer, but I will show you some cool design tricks. Once you get the hang of things, I suggest you experiment on your own creating different game screens.

Welcome Screen

The Welcome screen that we'll create includes the name of our game and instructions on how to control the game. We will actually use this Welcome screen in the final game that we create in this book. After the Welcome screen is created, we will export it to a format that can be understood by Blitz3D.

1. Launch CorelDRAW and click New in the Welcome screen that appears. The first thing that we need to do is change the units of measurement to

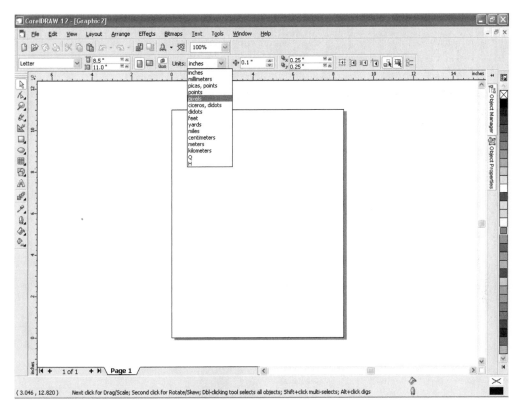

Figure 8.30
Change the units to pixels.

pixels. In the Units drop-down menu in the Property bar, select Pixels, as in Figure 8.30.

2. Select the Rectangle tool from the toolbox on the left side of the screen and click and drag a rectangle onto the page. It doesn't matter how big you make the rectangle since we are going to adjust this momentarily.

3. In the Property bar, change the dimensions of your rectangle to 1024 by 768, as in Figure 8.31. This will ensure that our Welcome screen will take up the entire screen when we later import it into our game.

4. With the rectangle still selected, click on the color Yellow in the Colors palette on the right side of the screen. The rectangle should now be yellow. Press Shift+F2 to zoom in to the rectangle.

5. Select the Text tool (the letter A button) from the toolbox on the left side of the screen and click anywhere inside the rectangle. A cursor should begin

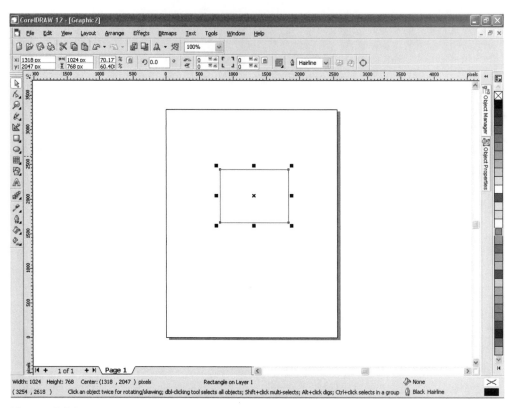

Figure 8.31
Adjust the size of the rectangle to be 1024 by 768.

flashing inside the rectangle. Click the Font Size drop-down menu from the Property bar and select 48, as in Figure 8.32.

Note

Font

In addition to changing the font size, you can also change the font face by clicking on the Font drop-down menu in the Property bar and selecting a different font.

6. Type the words "3D Gallery" and then select the Pick tool (the white arrow at the top of the toolbox on the left side of the screen). A series of black boxes called *handles* will appear around the text.

7. Position the mouse pointer over the x in the middle of the text and click and drag it until it is positioned as in Figure 8.33.

8. Click on the Interactive Fill tool (the bottom tool in the toolbox). Position the mouse pointer at the top of the G in "Gallery" and click and drag

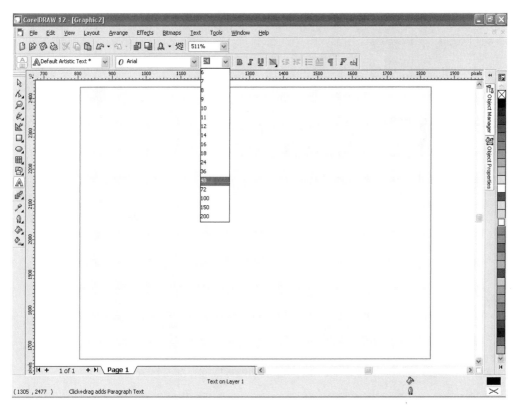

Figure 8.32
Select size 48 from the drop-down menu.

downward until you reach the bottom of the G. Two little colored boxes should appear—one at the top and one at the bottom of the G, as shown in Figure 8.34.

9. In the Property bar you should notice two Fill drop-downs: one that is black and another that is white. Click on the Fill drop-down list on the left and select a dark blue from the menu that appears. Click on the Fill drop-down list on the right and select a light-blue color, as shown in Figure 8.35.

10. Now we will make the text seem three-dimensional by using the Perspective effect. Click Effects > Add Perspective from the Menu bar. A red grid will appear around your text. Position your mouse pointer over the black handle in the top-right corner of the grid and click and drag it upward slightly. Now position the mouse pointer over the black handle in the bottom-right corner of the grid and click and drag downward slightly. You should be left with an image similar to the one you see in Figure 8.36.

Figure 8.33
Position the words "3D Gallery" in the top third of the rectangle, as shown here.

Figure 8.34
Click and drag from the top of the G to the bottom using the Interactive Fill tool.

Figure 8.35
Select the two colors for your text from the Fill drop-down menus.

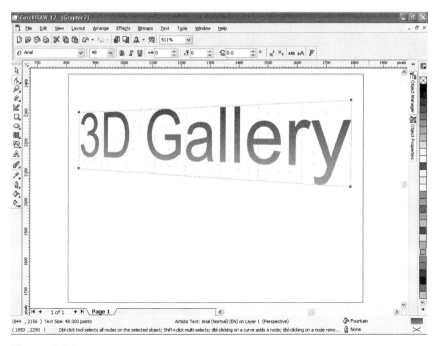

Figure 8.36
Make the text appear as if it is jumping off the page by using the Perspective feature.

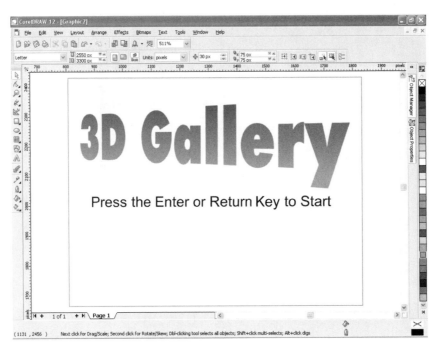

Figure 8.37
Position the text you created as shown here.

11. Click the Text tool again—click once in the rectangle, change the font size to 12, and choose your favorite font. Type "Press the Enter or Return Key to Start" and then position the text as shown in Figure 8.37. Notice too that I've changed the font of the words "3D Gallery" to something thicker, and the text stands out much better than before.

12. Select the Rectangle tool and click and drag a rectangle on the page, similar in size and position to the one shown in Figure 8.38. Click on your favorite color in the Color palette to give your rectangle some color. Right-click on the x in the top of the Color palette to remove the outline from the rectangle.

13. Select the Shape tool (the second tool from the top in the Tools palette). Four black handles will appear around the rectangle. Position your mouse pointer over any of these black handles and click and drag inward to round the corners of the rectangle, as shown in Figure 8.39.

14. Select the Text tool again and click within the rectangle you just created. Change the font size to 7. Type the following: "Up Arrow – Move Forward." Press the Enter key, and then type "Down Arrow – Move Backward." Continue adding the following new lines of text: "Left Arrow – Turn Left,"

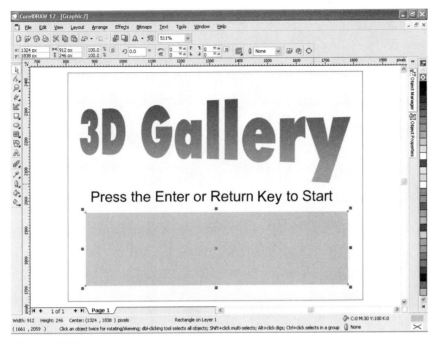

Figure 8.38
Create a rectangle similar to the one shown here.

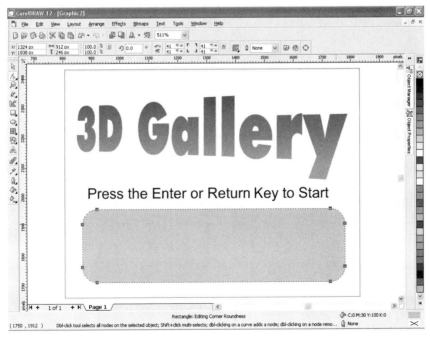

Figure 8.39
Round the corners of the rectangle using the Shape tool.

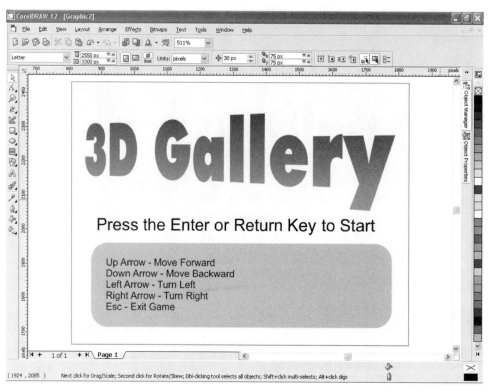

Figure 8.40
Position the text you created on the left side of the rectangle.

"Right Arrow – Turn Right," and "Esc – Exit Game." Select the Pick tool and move the text to the left side of the rectangle, as shown in Figure 8.40.

15. Repeat Step 14 to create another block of text that includes the following: "Space Bar – Fire," "P – Pause Game," "Mouse Button – Continue," "R – Reload Bullets," "V – Hover." Position this new block of text as shown in Figure 8.41

16. Now it's time to export our image to a format that Blitz3D can understand. In this case, we will convert our drawing into a .bmp image, but we could just as easily save it as a .jpeg or .gif. Click File > Export to open the Export dialog box. Click the Save As Type drop-down arrow and scroll until you can select BMP—Windows Bitmap. Now give your file the name "welcome," and then click the Export button.

17. In the Convert to Bitmap dialog box that appears, enter 1024 in the width box and 768 in the height box. Make sure the resolution is 96 dpi and the

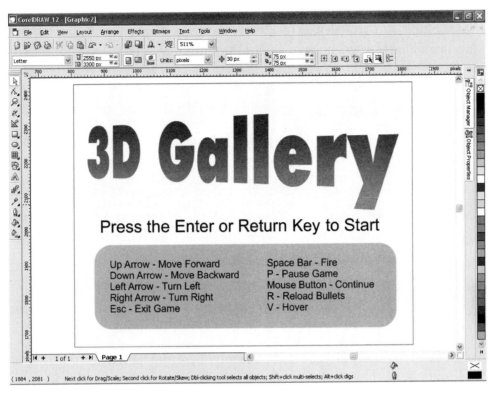

Figure 8.41
Position the remaining text as shown here.

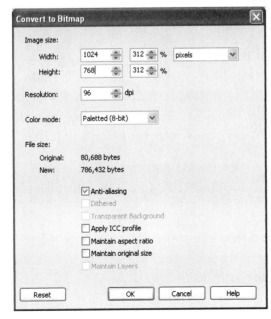

Figure 8.42
Ensure that these settings are entered.

Color mode is set to Paletted (8-bit), as shown in Figure 8.42. Click OK and another dialog box will appear. Click OK in this dialog box, and your file will be exported.

Pause Screen

When the player pauses the game, typically a Pause screen appears letting him know how he can restart the game. We will create a Pause screen that incorporates some design elements from the final game that we'll be creating in this book.

1. Launch CorelDRAW and click New in the Welcome screen that appears. The first thing that we need to do is change the units of measurement to pixels. In the Units drop-down menu in the Property bar, select Pixels.

2. Select the Rectangle tool from the toolbox on the left side of the screen and click and drag a rectangle onto the page. It doesn't matter how big you make the rectangle since we are going to adjust this momentarily.

3. In the Property bar, change the dimension of your rectangle to 1024 by 768. This will ensure that our Pause screen will take up the entire screen when we later import it into our game.

4. With the rectangle still selected, click on the color blue in the Colors palette on the right side of the screen. The rectangle should now be blue. Press Shift+F2 to zoom in to the rectangle.

5. Select the Text tool (the letter A button) from the toolbox on the left side of the screen and click anywhere inside the rectangle. A cursor should begin flashing inside the rectangle. Click the Font Size drop-down menu from the Property bar and select 24. You can also choose any font face you'd like.

6. Click on the color dark blue in the Color palette and right-click on the color white. This will give the text you are about to type a dark blue fill and a white outline.

7. Type the words "Game Paused" and then select the Pick tool (the white arrow at the top of the Tools palette on the left side of the screen). A series of black boxes called *handles* will appear around the words.

8. Position the mouse pointer over the x in the middle of the text and click and drag it until it is positioned as in Figure 8.43.

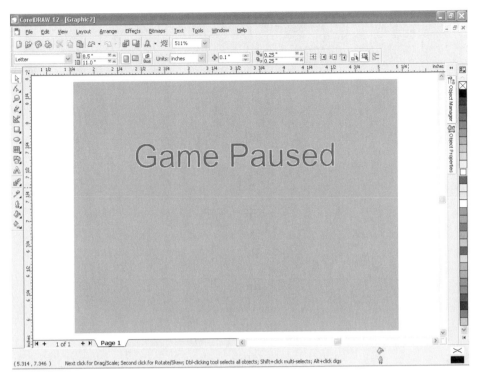

Figure 8.43
Position the text "Game Paused" about one third of the way down.

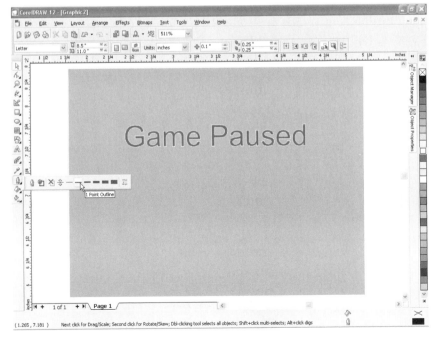

Figure 8.44
Change the outline thickness to 1 point, as shown here.

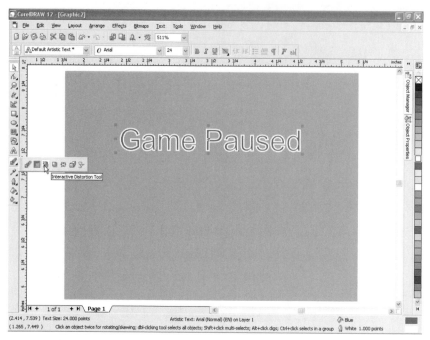

Figure 8.45
Select the Interactive Distortion tool, as shown here.

9. Click on the Outline tool flyout and select the 1-point outline as shown in Figure 8.44. This will thicken the outline.

10. Click and hold the button *under* the Text tool (letter A) in the toolbox. This will open a flyout of different tools. Select the Interactive Distortion tool, the third button in, as shown in Figure 8.45.

11. Click the Twister option from the Property bar. Position the mouse pointer over the middle of "P" in "Paused" and ever so slightly click and drag upward to twist the words, as shown in Figure 8.46.

12. Click the Text tool, then click once in the rectangle, change the font size to 12, and choose your favorite font. Type "Press the Mouse Button to," press Enter, and then type "Resume Play." Press Ctrl+E to center the text, and then select the Pick tool and position the text as shown in Figure 8.47.

13. Click and hold the button *under* the Text tool (letter A) in the toolbox. This will open a flyout of different tools. Select the Interactive Drop Shadow tool, the fourth button in.

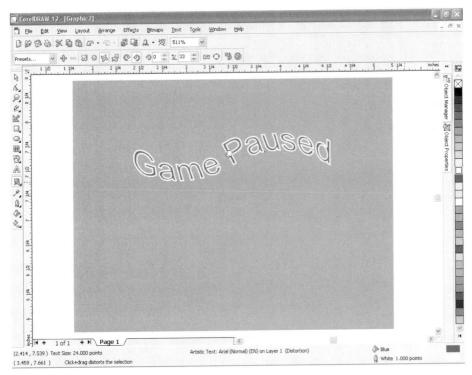

Figure 8.46
Twist the text using the Twister option.

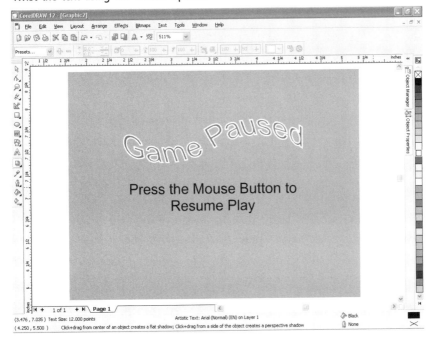

Figure 8.47
Position the text you created as shown here.

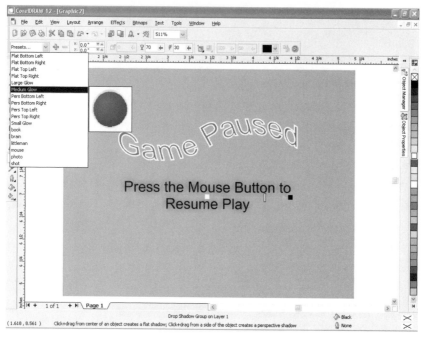

Figure 8.48
Select Medium Glow from the Presets drop-down menu.

14. From the Presets drop-down menu, choose Medium Glow, as shown in Figure 8.48. The text will now have a black glow.

15. We will now change the color of the glow. In the Property bar is a Drop Shadow Color box. Click on the drop-down button and choose the color white. The glow color will now change to white as shown in Figure 8.49.

16. Click File > Import to open the Import dialog box so that we can import an image of a 3D duck into our image. Navigate to the CD folder and click on the file called duck.cdr. Click the Import button. The dialog box will close and the mouse pointer will change into two lines connected at a right angle. Click once on the page to import the duck and it will appear. Using the Pick tool, position the duck in the bottom-left corner of the rectangle, as shown in Figure 8.50.

17. With the duck still selected, press Ctrl+D to make an exact duplicate of the duck. Position the mouse pointer over any of the corner handles of the duplicate duck and click and drag inward slightly to reduce its size. Position the duplicate duck in the bottom-right corner as shown in Figure 8.51.

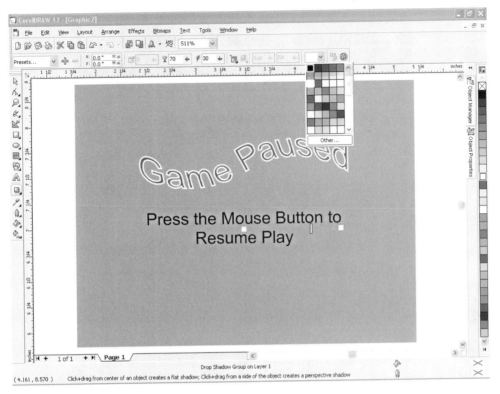

Figure 8.49
Change the glow color to white.

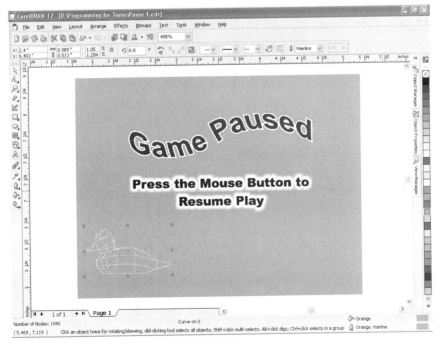

Figure 8.50
Position the duck you just imported in the bottom-left corner.

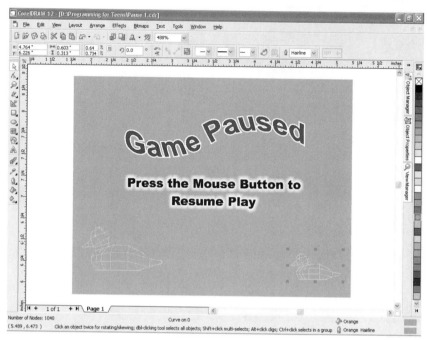

Figure 8.51
Position the duplicate duck in the bottom-right corner and slightly reduce its size.

18. Click and hold the button *under* the Text tool (letter A) in the toolbar. This will open a flyout of different tools. Select the Interactive Blend tool, the first button in, as shown in Figure 8.52.

19. Click on the small duck on the right and drag until the mouse pointer is over the larger duck on the left. When you release the mouse button, 20 copies of the ducks will appear between the first and the last as shown in Figure 8.53.

20. In the Property bar, change the number of transition steps from 20 to 4 (see Figure 8.54). There will now be four ducks between the first and the last. Also click the Counterclockwise Blend button to change the color of the ducks within the blend.

21. Click and hold the button right above the Text tool in the toolbox. A flyout of different tools will appear. Click the Star Shapes option.

22. From the Property bar, click the Perfect Shapes button and select the five-sided star as shown in Figure 8.55. Click and drag a star onto the rectangle and then click on the color red in the color palette to fill the star.

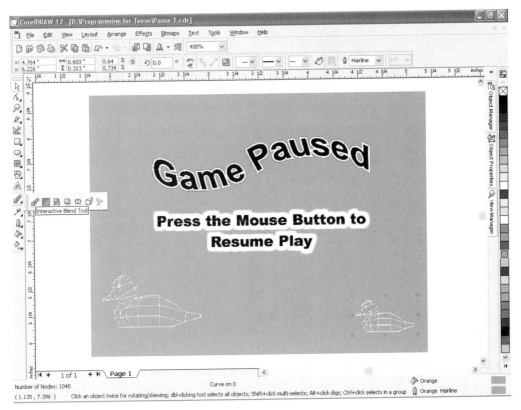

Figure 8.52
Select the Interactive Blend tool.

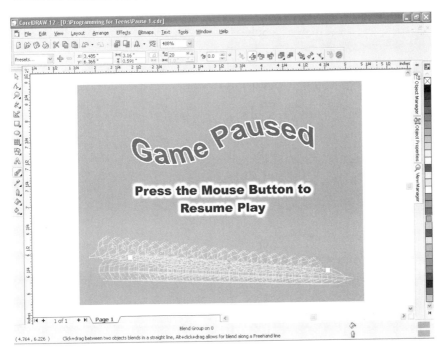

Figure 8.53
Using the Interactive Blend tool, blend the two ducks.

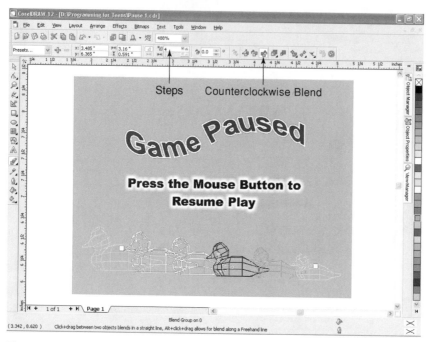

Figure 8.54
Change the number of blend steps to 4 and then click the Counterclockwise Blend button.

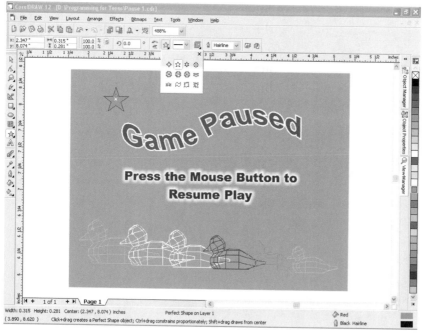

Figure 8.55
Create a star similar to the one shown here.

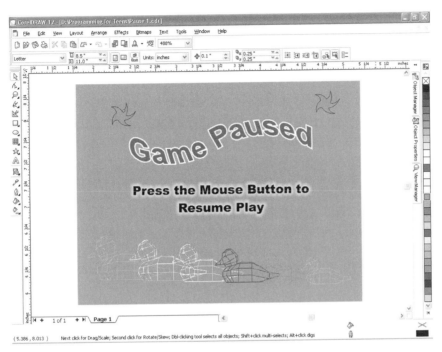

Figure 8.56
Twist the stars and then position them as shown here.

23. Using the technique you used in Step 11, apply a slight twister to the star. Duplicate the star by pressing Ctrl+D. Position the two stars as shown in Figure 8.56. You are now ready to export your file to a format that Blitz3D can understand. Follow Steps 16 and 17 from the Welcome screen section, this time saving the file as pause.bmp.

Summary

This chapter was definitely a tutorial—step by step, you learned how to use some graphic programs and create your own graphics.

This chapter covered the following concepts:

- Creating heightmaps
- Making walls
- Designing textures
- Building information screens

The next chapter will teach you how to create your game landscape. Chapter by chapter we are getting closer to building complete 3D games!

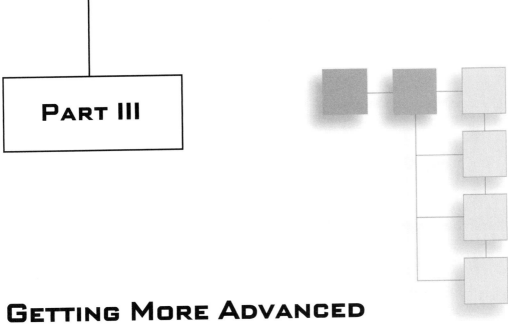

PART III

GETTING MORE ADVANCED

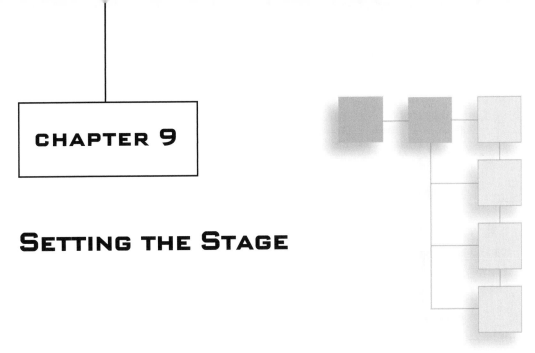

CHAPTER 9

SETTING THE STAGE

The environment of your game is the world in which the events of the game take place. The type of world that you create will depend heavily on the type of game that you are creating. An adventure game may include buildings that your character walks through, a race game may have a track, and a tank battle game may take place on a field. Regardless of the type of game you are creating, Blitz3D gives you all the tools necessary to create the "stage" on which your game takes place.

There are many different components that you can choose to create for your world, but several are fairly common throughout most games, including the ground, the sky, and buildings. Beyond that, the options are endless. Here we will explore creating those basic elements as well as some of the other options available to you. The techniques you use can vary from creating basic shapes to act as components in your world to using advanced techniques available in Blitz3D.

Creating a Terrain

One of the quickest ways to create a terrain (or the ground) for your games is to use the programming code called CreateTerrain. This code allows you to create and specify a size for the terrain (again, think of this as the ground) of your game. In this example, we'll add a terrain to an empty program. Take a basic program:

```
Graphics3D 640,480
SetBuffer BackBuffer()

Const ESC_KEY = 1

; Create camera
camera=CreateCamera()
; Creating a light
light=CreateLight()
; The following code makes the program run
While Not KeyDown(ESC_KEY)
RenderWorld
Flip
Wend
End
```

If you ran this program now, you would see only a blank, black screen. We are now going to add the code to create a terrain for this program. Add the following code under the "Creating a Light" section to create the terrain:

```
; Creating the terrain
ground=CreateTerrain (512)
```

If you ran this program right now, you'd see nothing because the camera isn't looking at the terrain (see Figure 9.1). We'll fix that in a moment, but for now

Figure 9.1
Oh, no! There's nothing on the screen. That's okay, the terrain is actually there—it's just out of the view of the camera.

let's take a closer look at the code we just entered. ground is just the name we are giving to the terrain, CreateTerrain is the code that creates the terrain, and the number in parentheses (512) is how far the terrain extends along the x and z axes.

Positioning a Terrain

To actually see the terrain, you have two options. Either you can reposition your camera or you can change the location of your terrain. The following sections will cover both methods.

Repositioning the Camera

We need to change the position of the camera. The terrain begins at position 1 on the y axis, and in this case, our terrain extends to the position 512,1,59. Since the default camera is at position 0,0,0, we need to bring it up to 0,1,0 so that we can see the terrain. Add the following lines to the camera code to position it so that we can see the terrain:

```
; Create camera
camera=CreateCamera()
PositionEntity camera,0,1,0
```

If you run the program right now, you'll see the beginning of the terrain we created. Not much of a terrain yet—just a gray box (see Figure 9.2).

Let's add some controls so that we can navigate around the terrain with our arrow keys.

```
; This following code deals with cameras and terrain
While Not KeyDown(ESC_KEY)

    If KeyDown(RIGHT_KEY) = True Then TurnEntity camera,0,-1,0
    If KeyDown(LEFT_KEY) = True Then TurnEntity camera,0,1,0
    If KeyDown(DOWN_KEY) = True Then MoveEntity camera,0,0,-0.05
    If KeyDown(UP_KEY) = True Then MoveEntity camera,0,0,0.05

    RenderWorld
    Flip
Wend
```

Figure 9.2
There's our terrain from demo09-01.bb. Beautiful, isn't it? You can move the terrain or the camera to get a better view.

Figure 9.3
By adding code that allows us to move the camera, we can get a better view of our terrain.

Now run this program and use the arrow keys to move the camera around so that you can navigate around your terrain (see Figure 9.3).

Repositioning the Terrain

Rather than changing the position of the camera in order to see the terrain, you can simply reposition the terrain. To do this, we make use of the PositionEntity command, as is done in demo09-02.bb (see Figure 9.4). All we have to do is add one line.

```
; Creating the terrain
ground=CreateTerrain (512)
PositionEntity ground, -500,-1,-500

; This following code deals with cameras and terrain
While Not KeyDown(ESC_KEY)

    If KeyDown(RIGHT_KEY)=True Then TurnEntity camera,0,-1,0
    If KeyDown(LEFT_KEY)=True Then TurnEntity camera,0,1,0
    If KeyDown(DOWN_KEY)=True Then MoveEntity camera,0,0,-0.05
    If KeyDown(UP_KEY)=True Then MoveEntity camera,0,0,0.05

    RenderWorld
    Flip
Wend
```

We've lowered the plane so that it is now below the camera and can be seen. Here we chose a position of 0,-1,0, but you can choose any starting position that you'd like. In fact, try the same program above but replace the position of the terrain with different numbers to get the hang of it.

Figure 9.4
The terrain above is positioned at -500,-1,-500 in demo09-02.bb.

Changing the Terrain Color

By default, the terrain you created was gray in color. You can change the color of a terrain just as you would any other object by using the `EntityColor` command.

```
; Create terrain
ground=CreateTerrain(512)
EntityColor ground, 125,36,32
```

Applying a Texture to a Terrain

More often than not, rather than coloring a terrain, you'll probably want to apply a texture to it. You can apply a texture to a terrain just as you would any other entity. Before you continue, open the file called demo09-03.bb and make sure that the file grass1.jpg is in the same folder as the program. Add the following code to apply a grass texture to our terrain.

```
; Create the terrain
ground=CreateTerrain(512)
texture=LoadTexture ( "grass1.jpg" )
EntityTexture ground, texture
```

Go ahead and run the program now and you'll see that your terrain now has the grass texture applied to it (see Figure 9.5).

Figure 9.5
A grassy texture has been applied to the terrain in demo09-03.bb.

Changing the Size of a Terrain

We'll use the ScaleEntity command to change the size of a terrain. In the example we've been using, we'll scale the terrain by 15 times on the y axis and 10 times on the x and z axes by adding the following code (in bold):

```
; Creating the terrain
ground=CreateTerrain(512)
PositionEntity ground, -500,0,-500
ScaleEntity ground, 10,15,10
```

Using the ScaleEntity command, you can increase or decrease the size of your playing field.

Creating a Plane

One of the easiest ways to make a "playing field" for your game is to create a plane. A *plane* is an endless surface that continues on and on into infinity. The biggest advantage of a plane is that it goes on forever, so there is no chance that your players will fall off the edge of the playing surface. This is a great alternative to creating a terrain.

Creating a plane is quite simple; it can be made as easily as any shape. Planes act much like shapes in that they can be colored or textured. In the following example, we'll add a plane to an empty program.

Start by entering the following code into Blitz3D. Once you have entered the code, save it with a new name.

```
Graphics3D 640,480
SetBuffer BackBuffer()
; Create camera
camera=CreateCamera()
PositionEntity camera,0,1,0; Creating a light
light=CreateLight()
; Creating a plane
myplane=CreatePlane()
; The following code makes our program run
While Not KeyDown( 1 )
RenderWorld
Flip
Wend
End
```

Figure 9.6
This plane was positioned at 0,-1,0.

The name of the plane we created in this example is "myplane," but we could have called it anything. The actual code that creates the plane is `CreatePlane()`.

Applying a Heightmap

You may have noticed something peculiar about the terrain you created in the last section—it was flat. If you want the terrain to have a more realistic look to it, you can load a heightmap. A heightmap defines the landscape of your terrain. In other words, it informs the program where any bumps, mountains, and valleys should occur. Heightmap images are made in Grayscale mode, which means that there is no color in them, just 256 shades of gray. Anything that is fully white in the heightmap represents the highest peak, while anything that is completely black represents the lowest point. The shades of gray in between will make up the valleys and mountains in your terrain. Look at Figure 9.7 to see how the heightmap would convert into actual terrain.

I discussed the creation of heightmaps earlier in this book in Chapter 8, "Getting Graphic." There, we created a heightmap, but we didn't actually apply it using any code. You can refer back to that chapter to learn how to actually create a heightmap.

Once you have a heightmap created, you can simply load it using the `Load-Terrain` command and then apply a texture to it. In the following example, we

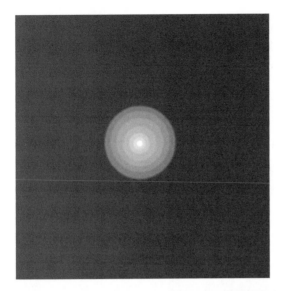

Figure 9.7
The heightmap on the top was used to create the terrain on the bottom.

will start by creating a program with nothing at all in it and then apply three different heightmaps so that you can get a good idea of how they would look in the games you create. Open up demo09-04.bb, or type in the following code. Make sure that the files spikey.jpg, valley.jpg, highmountain.jpg, and greenery.jpg are in the same folder. Notice in the code how we've positioned the camera 15 units above the ground so that we can get a good view of our landscape once it is created.

```
;demo09-04.bb - Beginning a terrain
; ------------------
Graphics3D 640,480
SetBuffer BackBuffer()

Const ESC_KEY = 1
Const LEFT_KEY = 203
Const RIGHT_KEY = 205
Const UP_KEY = 200
Const DOWN_KEY = 208

; Create camera
camera=CreateCamera()
PositionEntity camera,0,1,0

; Create a light
light=CreateLight(3)

; Loading the heightmap
terrain=LoadTerrain ( "highmountain.jpg" )
ScaleEntity terrain,5,100,5
PositionEntity terrain,-500,0,-500
tex=LoadTexture( "greenery.jpg" )
ScaleTexture tex, 50,50
EntityTexture terrain,tex


; Create the terrain
ground=CreateTerrain(512)


; This following code deals with cameras and terrain
While Not KeyDown(ESC_KEY)

    If KeyDown(RIGHT_KEY)=True Then TurnEntity camera,0,-1,0
    If KeyDown(LEFT_KEY)=True Then TurnEntity camera,0,1,0
    If KeyDown(DOWN_KEY)=True Then MoveEntity camera,0,0,-1
    If KeyDown(UP_KEY)=True Then MoveEntity camera,0,0,1

    RenderWorld
    Flip
Wend
End
```

Let's look closely at the code used to load the heightmap:

```
; Loading the heightmap
terrain=LoadTerrain ( "highmountain.jpg" )
ScaleEntity terrain,5,100,5
PositionEntity terrain,-500,0,-500
tex=LoadTexture( "greenery.jpg" )
ScaleTexture tex, 50,50
EntityTexture terrain,tex
```

Run the program now, and with any luck your screen should be similar to the one shown in Figure 9.8.

Let's take a look at each line individually to see what we have done.

`terrain = LoadTerrain("highmountain.jpg")`—This code creates a terrain called `terrain` by loading up the heightmap file called highmountain.jpg.

`ScaleEntity terrain,5,100,5`—This is a very important piece of code when working with heightmaps. The heightmap file that we created is saved as a very small file format to save processing time. When we apply it to our terrain, we need to stretch it out. In order to retain the shape of our mountains, we need to ensure that the y axis is stretched out much more than the x and z axes. In

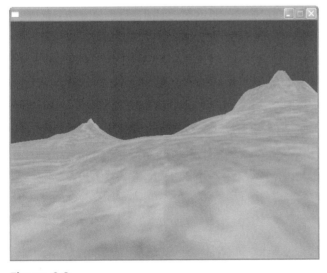

Figure 9.8
The heightmap highmountain.jpg has been loaded, and the texture greenery.jpg has been applied.

this case, we enlarged the y axis by 100 times and enlarged the x and z axes by 5 times. You can experiment with these numbers to see how it will affect your terrain.

PositionEntity terrain,-500,0,-500—With this code, we positioned the terrain at the 0 mark on the y axis and at -500 along the x and z axes.

tex=LoadTexture("greenery.jpg")—This code creates a texture that we called tex from the file greenery.jpg.

ScaleTexture tex, 50,50—Because we scaled our terrain, it's a good idea to stretch out our texture so that it retains the original look that we intended. Remember that a texture is a two-dimensional image that we apply to a three-dimensional object, so it has only x and y coordinates to adjust. In this case, we have scaled the x and y coordinates by 50 times.

EntityTexture terrain,tex—This command applies the texture we created, called tex, to the terrain.

Before we run the program, let's add the following code to the run section so that we can navigate through our terrain using the arrow keys:

```
; This following code deals with cameras and terrain
While Not KeyDown(ESC_KEY)

    If KeyDown(RIGHT_KEY)=True Then TurnEntity camera,0,-1,0
    If KeyDown(LEFT_KEY)=True Then TurnEntity camera,0,1,0
    If KeyDown(DOWN_KEY)=True Then MoveEntity camera,0,0,-1
    If KeyDown(UP_KEY)=True Then MoveEntity camera,0,0,1

    RenderWorld
    Flip
Wend
```

Go ahead and run the program now and use the arrow keys to navigate through the 3D world that you have created.

Note

Now You Try

In the code that you just created, replace the file highmountain.jpg with valley.jpg and then spikey.jpg to see how those heightmaps will look when applied to a game. Look at Figures 9.9 and 9.10 to see the results.

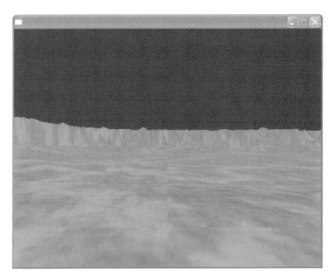

Figure 9.9
The valley.jpg heightmap.

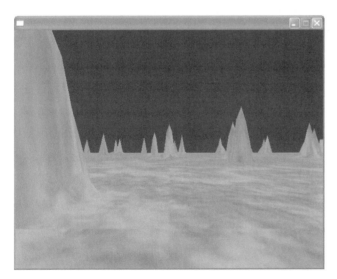

Figure 9.10
The spikey.jpg heightmap.

Shapes as Environments

Simple shapes will play an important part in the creation of your 3D worlds. You can use them in combination with your terrains or on their own to create entire environments or elements of your environment including the sky, ground, buildings, walls, and much more. Earlier in the book, you learned how to create simple shapes like spheres, cubes, and cylinders. Blitz3D gives you the ability to use any shape as the environment for your games. You can create a huge shape, such as a sphere or rectangle, and then have your game take place inside that sphere. You can then apply a texture to that shape and turn the texture inside out using the FlipMesh command so that you can see the texture when you are inside that shape. Does that sound confusing? The best way to clarify things is to take it piece by piece and learn by doing, as in the following sections.

Going Inside Shapes

What if you want to have a game inside of a room? You will have to go INSIDE of a shape to do so! The process of creating a shape to use as your 3D world isn't very difficult. You simply have to create a large version of the desired shape and then add a few commands to make things work. There are three new commands that we'll use in this section of code: FitMesh, FlipMesh, and EntityFX. I'll discuss each of these after we've entered the code.

Let's create a program that allows us to go inside shapes! Demo09-05.bb shows how it's done. Make sure that the file called wall.jpg is also placed in the same directory as demo09-05.bb.

```
;demo09-05.bb - Going inside a shape
; ------------------
Graphics3D 640,480
SetBuffer BackBuffer()

Const ESC_KEY = 1
Const LEFT_KEY = 203
Const RIGHT_KEY = 205
Const UP_KEY = 200
Const DOWN_KEY = 208

; Create camera
camera=CreateCamera()
PositionEntity camera,0,1,0

; Create a light
light=CreateLight()

;Create our Cube World
cubeworld=CreateCube()
```

```
FitMesh cubeworld,-250,0,-250,500,500,500
FlipMesh cubeworld
tex=LoadTexture( "wall.jpg" )
ScaleTexture tex, 0.5,0.5
EntityTexture cubeworld,tex
EntityFX cubeworld,1



; Create the terrain
ground=CreateTerrain(512)


; This following code deals with cameras and terrain
While Not KeyDown(ESC_KEY)

    If KeyDown(RIGHT_KEY)=True Then TurnEntity camera,0,-1,0
    If KeyDown(LEFT_KEY)=True Then TurnEntity camera,0,1,0
    If KeyDown(DOWN_KEY)=True Then TurnEntity camera,-1,0,0
    If KeyDown(UP_KEY)=True Then TurnEntity camera,1,0,0

    RenderWorld
    Flip
Wend
End
```

Take a closer look at the important part of this program.

```
;Creating our Cube World
cubeworld=CreateCube()
FitMesh cubeworld,-250,0,-250,500,500,500
FlipMesh cubeworld
tex=LoadTexture( "wall.jpg" )
ScaleTexture tex, 0.5,0.5
EntityTexture cubeworld,tex
EntityFX cubeworld,1
```

Run the program now and have a look around by pressing the arrow keys. You'll notice that you are now inside your cube world, which looks like a room made of hardwood walls, a ceiling, and a floor, as in Figure 9.11.

Now let's look at the code you just entered line by line to figure out exactly how we did what we did.

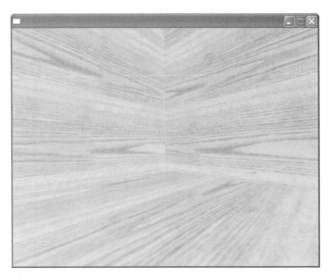

Figure 9.11
Navigate around your wooden room using the arrow keys.

cubeworld=CreateCube()—This code creates a standard cube at the default size. In this case, we called our cube cubeworld. You don't have to specify a size or location for the cube because you do so in the next command.

FitMesh cubeworld,-250,0,-250,500,500,500—The FitMesh command creates a mesh that will fit inside the cube that we created. After the FitMesh command, you need to specify the location of the mesh on the x, y, and z axes and the dimensions. The first three numbers specify the position of the mesh. In this case, it is at position −250 on the x axis, 0 on the y axis, and −250 on the z axis. The next three numbers specify the width, height, and depth of the mesh. In this case, we've made all three 500.

FlipMesh cubeworld—When we apply a texture to an object, that texture is wrapped around the outside of the object, not the inside. If you were to go inside an object that has a texture applied to it, it would appear dark. Think of the example of a box that is covered in gift wrapping. If you were inside the box, you would be in the dark because the wrapping paper is on the outside. Blitz3D has a function called FlipMesh that allows you to turn the wrapped object inside out so that the wrapping paper appears on the inside. That's exactly what we've done in this step. We've told Blitz3D that anything we wrap around the object cubeworld should be wrapped around the inside, not the outside.

tex=LoadTexture("wall.jpg")—This is the command we have used many times already to load a texture. In this case, we are using the image called wall.jpg as the texture that we are calling `tex`.

ScaleTexture tex, 0.5,0.5—We will reduce the scale of our texture by half by adding this command.

EntityTexture cubeworld,tex—This applies the texture to the cube. Remember, because we created a `FlipMesh`, the texture will be on the inside of the cube.

EntityFX cubeworld,1—It would be very dark inside our box if we didn't have a way of brightening the inside. To do this, we use the `EntityFX` command. The `EntityFX` command has several different effects. In this case, the number 1 indicates that the area should be filled with full brightness. Run the program without this code and you'll notice that the walls inside your cube are much darker.

Using Shapes with Terrains

What's better than chocolate mixing with peanut butter? How about terrains mixing with shapes? Maybe that's not quite as good, but combining a terrain with a shape is how many 3D games create their environments. Typically, the terrain will make up the ground, and the shapes will make up the sky and other objects within the game. In the following example, we'll create a sky using a shape and apply it to a standard. Start by opening the file called demo09-06.bb or entering the following code. Save the file with a new name into a new folder and make sure that the files called greenery.jpg and sky2.jpg are copied to that folder.

```
;demo09-06.bb - Shapes and Terrain
; -----------------
Graphics3D 640,480
SetBuffer BackBuffer()

Const ESC_KEY = 1
Const LEFT_KEY = 203
Const RIGHT_KEY = 205
Const UP_KEY = 200
Const DOWN_KEY = 208

; Create camera
camera=CreateCamera()
PositionEntity camera,0,1,0
```

```
; Create a light
light=CreateLight()

;Create our terrain
ground=CreateTerrain(512)
PositionEntity ground, -500,0,-500
ScaleEntity ground, 10,15,10
tex=LoadTexture( "greenery.jpg" )
EntityTexture ground, tex




; Create the terrain
ground=CreateTerrain(512)


; This following code deals with cameras and terrain
While Not KeyDown(ESC_KEY)

    If KeyDown(RIGHT_KEY)=True Then TurnEntity camera,0,-1,0
    If KeyDown(LEFT_KEY)=True Then TurnEntity camera,0,1,0
    If KeyDown(DOWN_KEY)=True Then MoveEntity camera,0,0,-0.5
    If KeyDown(UP_KEY)=True Then MoveEntity camera,0,0,0.5

    RenderWorld
    Flip
Wend
End
```

Run the program now and you should be able to see a green terrain and nothing (black) as the sky (see Figure 9.12). We are going to change all that by creating a sphere to act as the sky. We will make the sphere extremely large, apply a texture to it, and then use the FlipMesh function we learned earlier to put the texture on the inside of the sphere. Enter this code after the "Creating the terrain" section. (The file on the CD already has this code inserted. If you want to see the terrain without the blue sky, delete the following code from the file on the CD.)

```
;Creating the sky
sky = CreateSphere (40)
FlipMesh sky
ScaleEntity sky, 100,100,100
```

Figure 9.12
The program at this point has terrain and a black sky.

```
PositionEntity sky, 0,50,0
sky_tex = LoadTexture ( "sky2.jpg" )
EntityTexture sky,sky_tex
EntityFX sky,1
```

Run the program now to see the sky as in Figure 9.13.

Figure 9.13
We've now added a bright, beautiful sky to our terrain. This is the final demo09-06.bb program.

I have described in detail all of the previous code in earlier sections of this chapter. Here we are just adding it to the code of an existing terrain. If you run the program now, you'll see both the terrain and the sky. We've actually done something pretty cool here, and I want you to see how it works. We haven't really created a "sky"—we've just created a sphere that takes up most of the screen so that it looks like a sky. Want to see what I mean? Run the program and hold down the down arrow. You'll move backwards until you can see that your sky was simply a sphere. You wouldn't actually want this to happen in a real game, so there are measures that we can take to avoid having our "fake" sky from being discovered. First of all, in a real game we would make the sphere much bigger. Rather than having it scaled at 100 times (as we did with this line of code: ScaleEntity sky, 100,100,100), we would scale it much larger and we would create a "parent" so that as our player moved, the sphere that made up the sky would also move. You'll learn more about parents later in the book. You'll also notice that if you hold down the up arrow, you'll move toward the sky and eventually be able to go through it. In an actual game, setting up a "collision" would prevent this. You'll learn more about collisions in Chapter 11.

Summary

Now that you've finished this chapter, you know how to build a terrain! Now you can make some cool scenes for your 3D games!

This chapter covered the following concepts:

- Creating terrains

- Setting up environments

- Applying heightmaps

- Going inside shapes

We are going to learn how to do some 3D modeling in the next chapter!

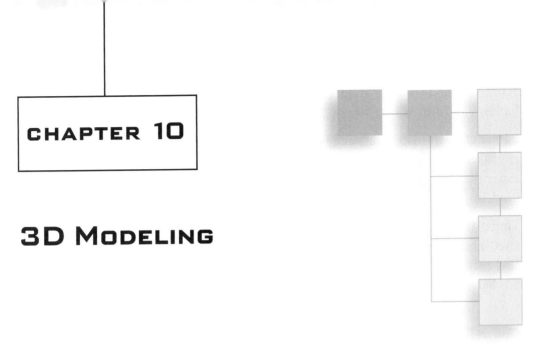

CHAPTER 10

3D MODELING

In Chapter 5, "Shapes and Objects," you learned how to create a few basic objects. Truth be told, to make your game a little more appealing, you'll probably want to create some out of the ordinary, wild, and interesting shapes. To do this, you'll need to use one of the 3D modeling software packages available on the market. In this book, you'll be using a program called Autodesk 3ds Max. This package is one of the gaming industry's standards for 3D modeling and has all the tools necessary for creating all types of 3D objects. Keep in mind that 3ds Max is not the only package available; dozens of other programs are used, including one called Maya that is also quite popular. I chose 3ds Max for several reasons. First of all, it allows you to export objects to a file format that can be opened in Blitz3D. In many other 3D programs, you can't save your file formats to something that Blitz3D will understand. However, there are many third-party programs (programs by other companies) that will convert the files for you. Another advantage of 3ds Max is that you can also try it out for free for 30 days. Finally, the skills you learn in 3ds Max can be transferred to other 3D modeling packages.

The purpose of this chapter is to give you an introduction to creating shapes in 3ds Max. As you'll see, there are thousands of different combinations of filters, effects, and objects that you can apply and create, and it would take several books to cover all the features. My goal is not to teach you everything about 3D modeling and 3ds Max but to give you a jump-start into learning the program and creating a few objects. If you are interested in pursuing

3D modeling further, I suggest you start by reading *Game Art for Teens* by Les Pardew, published by Course Technology.

Rather than showing you each tool and describing it, we will take a project-based approach. I'll show you how to create several objects, but then I encourage you to experiment on your own and go out and learn more about this and other 3D modeling packages.

To get the program for this book, you need to download the 30-day 3ds Max trial. You can get this from the Products tab at http://usa.autodesk.com. Just click where it says Products, then Free Product Trials, and then download the 3ds Max trial.

Creating a Bottle

This project will take you through the steps necessary to create a bottle and then export it to a format that Blitz3D will understand. The primary tool we will be using in this project is the Lathe tool. If you've ever taken woodworking, you know that a lathe is a machine that spins an object (usually a piece of wood or metal). By using a tool like a chisel on the object as it spins you can create interesting shapes or patterns. The Lathe modifier in 3ds Max allows you to create objects that look like they have been through a lathe.

Creating the Outline

To begin with, we'll create an outline of a bottle in two dimensions, which we will later convert to 3D.

1. Click on the window labeled Left. A yellow outline will appear around the window.

2. Click the Maximize Viewpoint toggle button (see Figure 10.1). This will expand the Left window so that it takes up the entire screen.

3. Click the Create button at the far-right side of the screen. It looks like a mouse pointer with a white star behind it.

4. Click the Shapes button. This will open a list of different object types from which you can select.

5. Click Line. The box will turn yellow to indicate that it is selected.

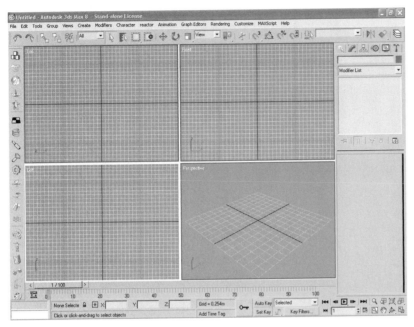

Figure 10.1
By clicking the Maximize Viewpoint toggle button, you can maximize the currently selected view.

6. Position the mouse pointer about ten grid squares up on the middle line and click once to start the line (see Figure 10.2).

7. Move the mouse pointer to the right on the grid square and click again.

8. Continue moving the mouse and clicking in the designated spots until you've created the outline of a bottle. If you hold down the Shift key when you draw lines, they will appear straight. When you click the point where you started, a dialog box will appear.

9. Click Yes in the Spline dialog box that appears (see Figure 10.3).

Lathing the Bottle

Now the fun part—we get to convert our two-dimensional bottle into a 3D object. We do this by using the Lathe modifier.

1. Click the Maximize viewport toggle button. This will return you to the main screen where you can see all views.

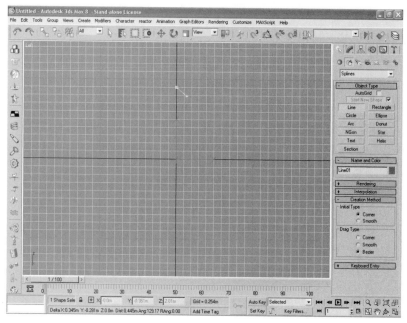

Figure 10.2
Click once about 10 squares up from the center to start the line.

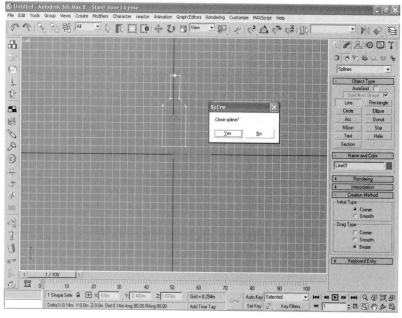

Figure 10.3
Click Yes in the dialog box that appears after you've finished creating the bottle shape.

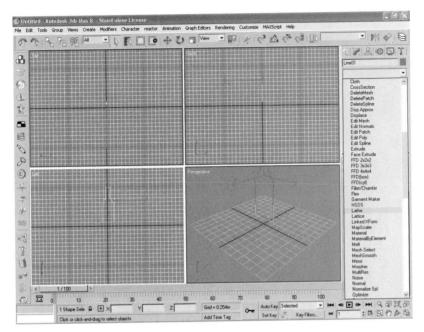

Figure 10.4
Choose Lathe from the Modifiers list.

2. Click the Modify button. The Modify button looks like a blue quarter oval.

3. Click the Modifiers list drop-down arrow to see a list of different modifiers (see Figure 10.4).

4. Scroll through the list and click Lathe (see Figure 10.5). Ta da! You've just created a 3D bottle!

Exporting the Bottle

Now we need to convert the bottle into a format that Blitz3D can understand. Before we do that, the bottle needs to be resized since it is currently huge.

1. Click the Select and Uniform Scale button. It looks like a square within a square. A series of yellow shaded triangles will appear around your bottle.

2. Position the mouse pointer over the middle of the yellow triangle in the Perspective window (see Figure 10.6).

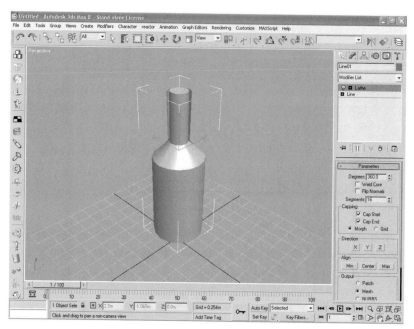

Figure 10.5
You should be left with an object that looks like a bottle as seen here.

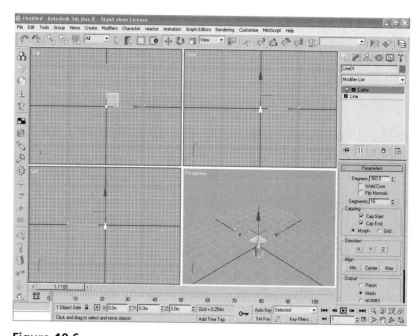

Figure 10.6
After you've selected the Select and Uniform Scale button, drag downward on the inner yellow triangle that appears.

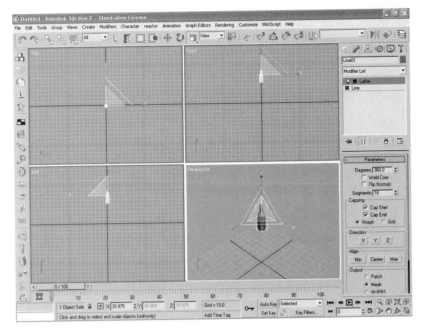

Figure 10.7
When you shrunk the bottle, it became off center.

3. Click and drag downward. As you drag, the bottle will shrink (see Figure 10.7). Doing this also moves the bottle off center, so we'll now move it back.

4. Click the Select and Move button from the toolbar. A yellow rectangle and several axes will appear around your object.

5. Position the mouse pointer over the middle of the yellow rectangle in the Perspective window.

6. Click and drag the bottle until it is in the middle of the grid (see Figure 10.8). Alternatively, you can just enter 0 in the X, Y, and Z fields at the bottom of the screen.

Note

Object Position

It's very important that you move your object to the middle of the grid before you export it. When you insert the object into your program, Blitz3D will remember its location from the point where it was exported. If the object was not in the center of the grid, you'll have a hard time positioning it within your game.

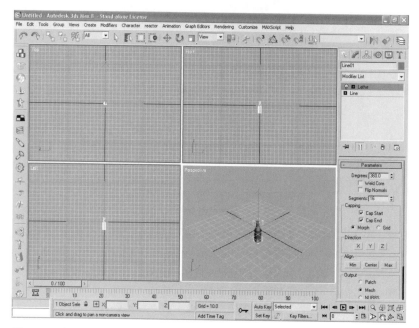

Figure 10.8
Position the bottle in the middle of the screen.

7. Click File > Export Selected. The Select File to Export dialog box will appear.

8. Click the Save As Type drop-down arrow and choose 3D Studio (*.3ds). This will save your file to the .3ds format, which can be read by Blitz3D.

9. Navigate to the folder where you would like to save the file, give it a name, and then click Save (see Figure 10.9). You've now successfully saved the file so that it can be used in Blitz3D.

Creating a Missile

In most good 3D video games, it's all about the weapons. How many you have, what kind, and how much damage they can do. In this section we are going to use 3ds Max to create a weapon that we can use over and over in our games: a missile. The missile itself is made from only a few basic shapes that we will manipulate and combine in order to get our final image. Although there are only a few shapes used in this image, working in the 3ds environment can be a little tricky,

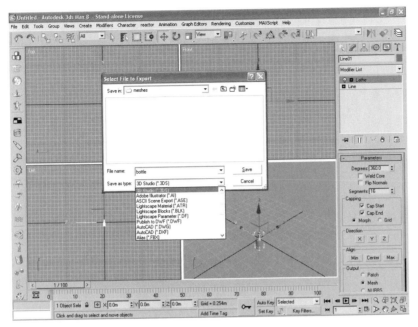

Figure 10.9
Save your file to the .3ds format that Blitz3D can easily understand.

especially if you are new to the program, so follow each instruction carefully and make sure not to skip any steps.

Creating the Missile Body

The main body of our missile is simply a long cylinder to which we will later add different parts. For most of this drawing we will use the Perspective viewport so we can actually see our final image as we draw.

1. Click anywhere in the Perspective viewport to select this window. A yellow border will appear around the window. Click on the Maximize viewport toggle button (or use the shortcut Alt+W) to maximize this viewport and hide the others, as seen in Figure 10.10.

2. Click Create > Standard Primitives > Cylinder. You can now set certain parameters for your cylinder.

3. Expand the Parameters panel by clicking on the + beside the word "parameters" if it is not already expanded.

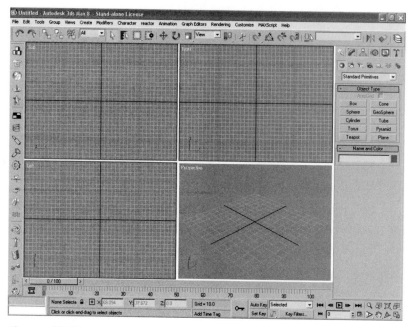

Figure 10.10
Maximize the Perspective window.

4. Enter 5 for both the Height Segments and Cap Segments, as shown in Figure 10.11. This is a very important step; if you don't do this, you'll have trouble later on.

5. Click and drag a circle across the screen. It doesn't matter what size it is; we'll adjust this later. When you release the mouse button, you'll be able to adjust the height of the cylinder. Drag upwards to extend the cylinder, and then release the mouse button. You should now have a cylinder similar to the one in Figure 10.12.

6. Now we are going to taper off the peak of the cylinder to make it look like a missile head. We'll do this by converting the cylinder into an editable poly and stretching out the peak of the cone. Click on the Modify panel if it's not already selected.

7. Right-click on the word "cylinder" and select Editable Poly from the menu that appears (see Figure 10.13).

8. Click on the Select and Move button in the toolbar. In the Selection panel, click on the Vertex button (three red dots). You should now see a series

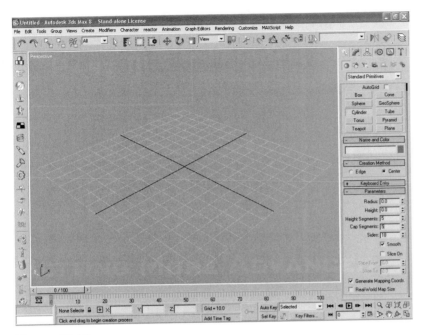

Figure 10.11
Make sure that you enter a 5 in the Cap Segments portion of the Parameters panel.

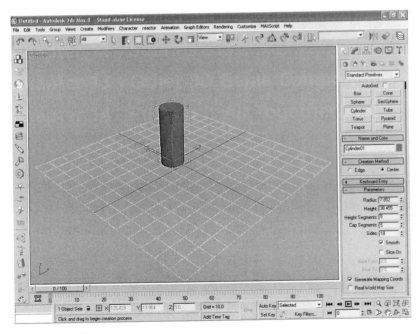

Figure 10.12
Try to create a cylinder similar in size to the one seen here.

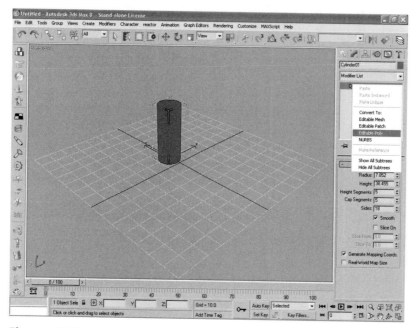

Figure 10.13
In the Modify panel, right-click on the word "cylinder" and select Editable Poly.

of dots appear all around the cylinder, as in Figure 10.14. We'll manipulate these dots in order to change the shape of the cylinder.

9. Click Vertex in the very middle of the cylinder. It should turn red, and three arrows should appear around it, as in Figure 10.15. You may have to zoom in to accomplish this. You can zoom in by selecting the Zoom tool (the magnifying glass at the bottom right of the screen) and clicking and dragging upwards. You can then pan to the top of the cylinder by using the Pan tool (the little white hand).

10. Expand the Soft Selection panel if it is not already expanded. In this panel, click the check box labeled Use Soft Selection. In the Falloff box, enter the number 20. The vertexes on top of the cylinder should be orange and yellow.

11. Position your mouse pointer over the blue z arrow and click and drag upwards until the cylinder has a cone peak, as in Figure 10.16.

12. Click on Editable Poly in the Modifier list. It will turn from yellow to gray, and the vertexes will no longer appear on the cylinder.

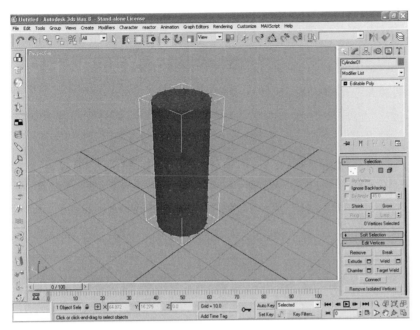

Figure 10.14
When you select the Vertex button, a series of dots will appear around the cylinder.

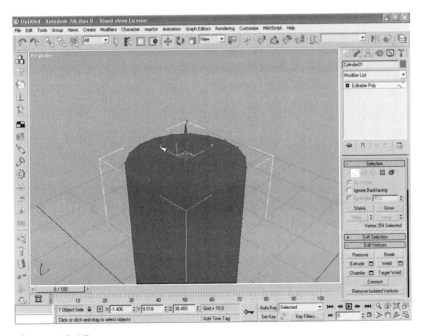

Figure 10.15
Select the center vertex and a series of arrows will appear around it.

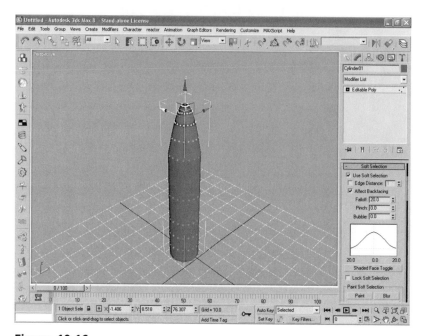

Figure 10.16
After you've created a 20-unit soft selection, click and drag upwards on the blue z arrow to create a
peak out of the top of the cylinder.

Creating the Wings

To create the wings that control the flight path of the missile, we will create and
modify a box. We'll then duplicate the manipulated cube several times and place
it in different locations around the missile.

1. Click Create > Standard Primitives > Box. The Parameter panel should
   appear on the right side of the screen. Make sure that the Length, Width,
   and Height boxes all have the number 1 in them.

2. Click and drag a rectangle across the screen. Try to make it about the size of
   the rectangle in Figure 10.17 in relation to the missile. When you release
   the mouse button, you'll be able to adjust the height of the box. Drag
   upwards to extend the box and then release the mouse button. You should
   now have a box similar to the one in Figure 10.17.

3. Right-click on the box to bring up a menu of different options. Click on the
   Convert To option and then select Convert to Poly (see Figure 10.18).

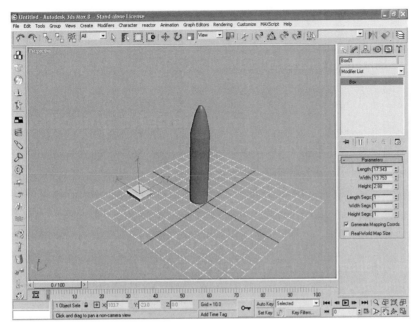

Figure 10.17
Create a box similar in size to the one seen here.

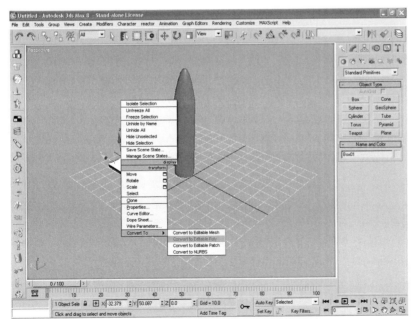

Figure 10.18
Convert the image to an Editable Poly by right-clicking on the box.

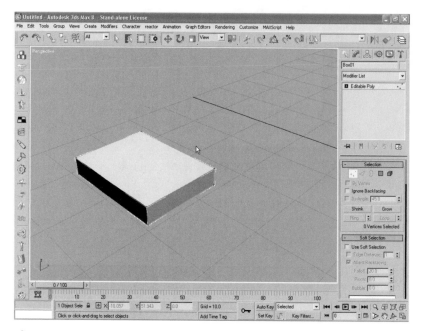

Figure 10.19
Drag the marquee around the corner of the box to select both the top and bottom corner nodes.

4. In the Selection panel, click on the Vertex button. You should now see a series of dots appear around the edges of the box. Position the mouse pointer to the outside of one of the corners of the box. Click and drag around the corner vertexes. As you drag, a marquee (see Figure 10.19) should appear surrounding both of the vertexes in the corner. When you release the mouse button, the corner vertexes should appear red. Green, blue, and red arrows should appear around the box.

5. Click and drag the green arrow upwards to bring in the corner of the box. Release the mouse button when the shape looks like the one in Figure 10.20.

6. Repeat Steps 4 and 5 for the vertexes on the other side. You should be left with the shape you see in Figure 10.21.

7. Click on Editable Poly in the Modifiers list. It will turn from yellow to gray, and the vertexes will no longer appear on the box.

8. Click on the Select and Rotate button. At the bottom of the screen, enter -90 in the Y box to rotate the wing (see Figure 10.22).

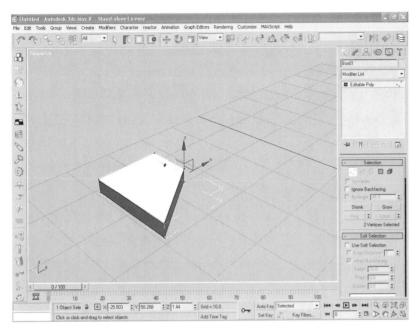

Figure 10.20
Drag the green arrow to bring in the two selected vertexes and create the shape you see here.

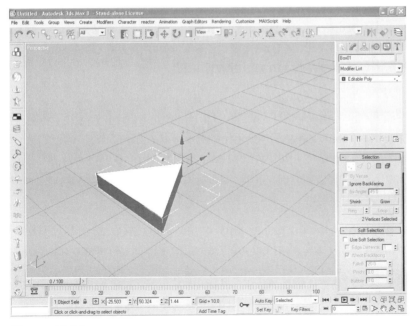

Figure 10.21
Using the same technique, bring in the other side.

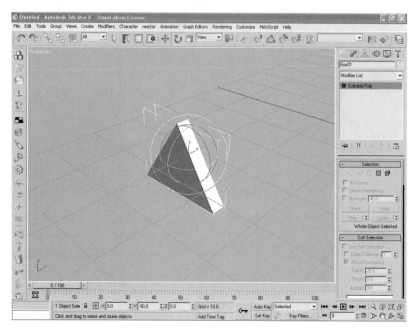

Figure 10.22
By entering -90 in the Y field, you can "stand up" your 3D triangle.

9. Click on the Select and Move button in the toolbox. Position the mouse pointer around the point where the three arrows meet. You'll know you're in the right place when a yellow transparent square appears. Click and drag the arrow until it is at the bottom of the cylinder.

10. You may need to resize the wing to make it fit in perspective with the rest of the missile. Click the Select and Uniform Scale button in the toolbar. Position the mouse pointer over the point where the three arrows meet. A yellow triangle will appear when you are in the right place. Click and drag up or down to increase or decrease the size of the wing as necessary. We've slightly enlarged our triangle, as seen in Figure 10.23.

11. Click Edit > Clone to make an exact copy of the wing. A dialog box will appear from which you should click the Copy option and then click OK.

12. We are now going to rotate this wing. Click the Select and Rotate button from the toolbox. A series of circular arrows will appear around the wing. At the bottom left of the screen, enter -90 in the X and Y boxes. This will flip the copy of the wing, as seen in Figure 10.24.

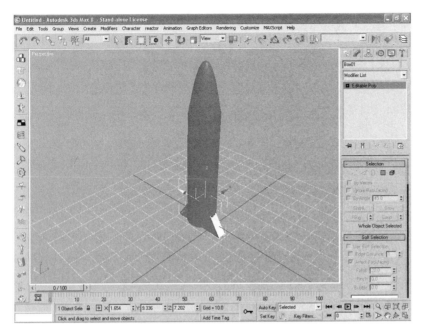

Figure 10.23
Using the Select and Uniform Scale button, resize and reposition the triangle so that it looks similar to the one shown here in relation to the cylinder.

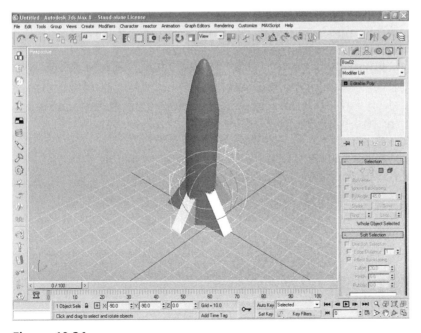

Figure 10.24
Flip the cloned triangle by entering -90 in the X and Y boxes at the bottom of the screen.

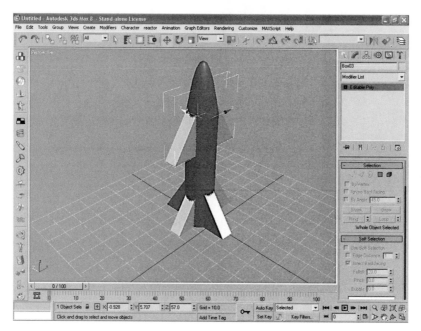

Figure 10.25
Move the cloned triangle about halfway up the cylinder.

13. Click Edit > Clone to make another exact copy of the wing. A dialog box will appear from which you should click the Copy option and then click OK.

14. Click the Select and Move button in the toolbar. Three colored arrows will appear around the wing. Position the mouse pointer over the blue z arrow, and click and drag upwards until the wing is halfway up the missile, as shown in Figure 10.25.

15. The middle wing is a little too big, so we are going to change its size. Click the Select and Uniform Scale button in the toolbar. Position the mouse pointer over the point where the three arrows meet. A yellow triangle will appear when you are in the right place. Click and drag down to decrease the size of the wing, as shown in Figure 10.26.

Exporting the Missile

We now need to convert the missile into a format that Blitz3D can understand. In this case, we'll export it to the .3ds format.

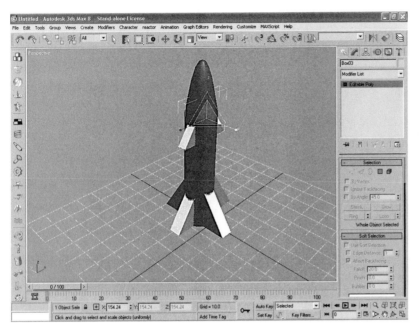

Figure 10.26
Resize the middle triangle to the approximate dimension you see here.

1. Resize, rotate, and reposition the missile to be in the middle of the grid, as shown in Figure 10.27. Remember from earlier that Blitz3D will remember the size, location, and direction of your objects when they are imported, so take the time to get them into their final position before exporting.

2. Click File > Export. The Select File to Export dialog box will appear.

3. Click the Save As Type drop-down arrow and choose 3D Studio (*.3ds). This will save your file to the .3ds format, which can be read by Blitz3D.

4. Navigate to the folder where you would like to save the file, give it the name "missile," and then click Save. You've now successfully saved the file so that it can be used in Blitz3D.

Note

Getting Models

If you're not comfortable or if you don't have the patience or time to master 3ds, you have other options for getting 3D models. Dozens of websites offer free downloads of 3D models that you can use in your games. Open Google in your Internet browser and search for "Free 3D Models" to see different websites from which you can download files.

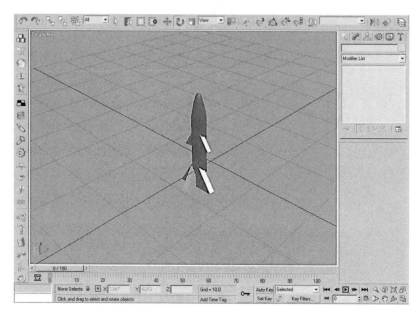

Figure 10.27
We've reduced the size of the image to get it ready for export.

Importing Models into Blitz3D

Creating your 3D models is only the first step. They won't do you any good if you can't bring them into your programs. That's what we'll take care of now by using the LoadMesh function. Once the object is imported, you can apply a texture to it like any other.

Create the following blank program, save it with any name, and make sure that the files missile.3ds and missile.jpg are in the same folder where you saved the program. Or, you can load the final version from the CD. It is titled demo10-01.bb.

We need to actually load our 3D model using the LoadMesh command. We'll also apply a texture to it, resize it, and position it at the same time by loading the following code, or running the file from the CD.

```
;demo10-01.bb - Beginning a terrain
; ------------------
Graphics3D 640,480
SetBuffer BackBuffer()

Const ESC_KEY = 1

; Create camera
camera=CreateCamera()
```

```
; Create a light
light=CreateLight()

;load missile
missile=LoadMesh ("missile.3ds")
tex=LoadTexture ("missile.jpg")
EntityTexture missile,tex
PositionEntity missile, 1,0,5
ScaleEntity missile, .07,.07,.07


; This following code deals with cameras and terrain
While Not KeyDown(ESC_KEY)
     RenderWorld
     Flip
Wend
End
```

Now run the program, and you should see the missile that you created in 3ds Max, as shown in Figure 10.28.

Figure 10.28
Import your file into Blitz3D using the `LoadMesh` command.

Let's break down the code to see how we did it:

`missile=LoadMesh ("missile.3ds")`—Using this line of code, we loaded up the 3D model. We gave the model the identifier "missile."

`tex=LoadTexture ("missile.jpg")`—This is the texture to be applied to the missile after it has been imported.

`EntityTexture missile,tex`—This applies the texture to the missile.

`ScaleEntity missile, 0.07,0.07,0.07`—Typically, the models that you import from 3ds Max will be quite large when imported. You can see here that we needed to resize the missile quite a bit in order to see it.

`PositionEntity missile, 1,0,5`—Here we simply positioned the missile in front of the camera so that we could see it.

Summary

This chapter taught you how to do 3D modeling on your own.

In this chapter, you learned how to:

- Create heightmaps

- Make a missile

- Import and export models

Chapter by chapter we are getting closer to building complete 3D games!

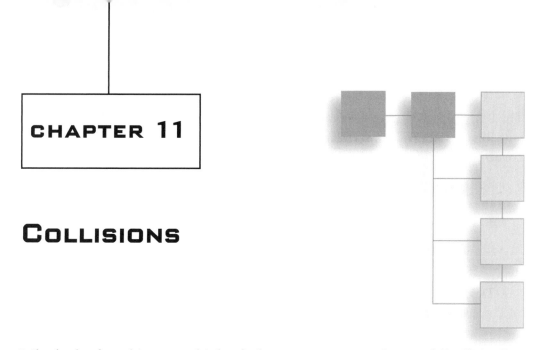

CHAPTER 11

COLLISIONS

What's the first thing you think of when someone says the word "collision"? I think of two cars hurtling down the road at one another and then smashing head-on in an impressive display of fireworks, flying metal, and screeching tires. Thankfully, in my vision nobody gets hurt! In Blitz3D, collisions control how two or more objects react with one another. Collisions are an important part of any game since they allow you to control whether your players can bump into walls or go through them. They also prevent players from falling off the edge of the screen, and they tell the computer what type of reaction should happen when two objects meet. By default, when you move one object into another using Blitz3D, the objects will pass right through each other. You have the ability to control both the method in which two objects collide and the response of the collision.

A very important concept that you must understand when defining collisions is that of *types*. Types are basically a way of grouping different objects that share similar qualities. Think of a type as a "team"—you can assign different objects to that team and then define the type of collisions for the team. For example, let's say in your 3D game you have created hundreds of different enemy invaders. Rather than having to program the collisions for each enemy invader, you can assign each invader to a team and then define the collisions for that team. The collision parameters you apply to the "team" (the type) will apply to all members of the team—in this case all the enemy invaders. When you create a type, you assign a number for your team. The number you choose isn't important; it's just important that you assign it a number.

Creating a Collision

The Collisions command is used in Blitz3D to define how objects will collide with one another. There are five different things that you must specify when creating collisions:

- **Source Type.** The source type tells Blitz3D which object it should watch for that might collide into something else. Typically, this is the player or players in your game. In the example we are going to use below, we will create a sphere that will collide with a cone. In this example, the sphere would be the source type.

- **Destination Type**. This is the object that is being collided into. In the example, the cone acting as our object to smash into will be the destination type.

Figure 11.1 illustrates the difference between a Source type and a Destination type.

- **Entity Radius.** Imagine a really skinny cat trying to walk into the open entrance of your house. The cat could probably do it with no problem at all. Now imagine an 800-pound elephant trying to get through the same door—it'd probably get stuck. In Blitz3D, you have to define how "fat" or "skinny" your objects are so that the program knows whether or not a collision should occur when two objects get close to one another. You have to define this by setting an entity radius for each source object. Keep in mind that creating a large or small entity radius doesn't actually change the shape or

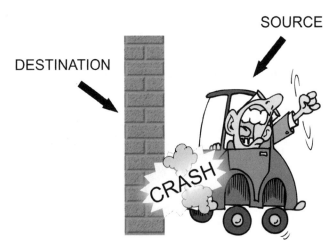

Figure 11.1
The difference between a Source and a Destination type.

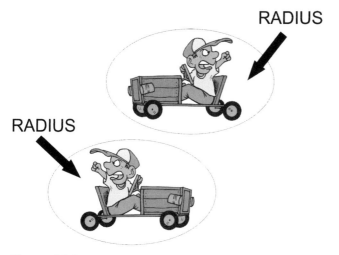

Figure 11.2
In this example, a collision wouldn't occur because the radii of the two objects don't collide.

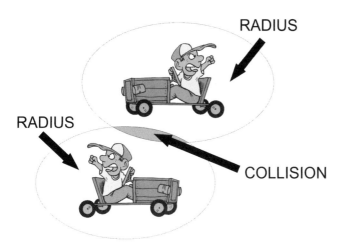

Figure 11.3
In this example, a collision occurs because the radii of the two objects collide.

size of an object; it just tells Blitz3D how close or far objects need to be to one another for a collision to be registered. Figures 11.2 and 11.3 illustrate how the radius of an object works.

- **Method**. This controls the detection method for the collisions. Your choices are:

```
ellipsoid-to-ellipsoid = 1
ellipsoid-to-polygon = 2
ellipsoid-to-box = 3
```

- ■ **Response**. This tells the program how you want an object you are moving to react when it hits another object. You can have it stop, slide sideways, or slide upwards. Different numbers indicate the type of response you want as follows:

```
Stop = 1
Slide Sideways = 2
Slide Upwards = 3
```

Collision Code

Above you learned the parts of the collision code. Let's look at the actual code you use to create a collision. We'll use this code in the next section to create our collision:

```
Collisions type_player,type_obstacle,2,2
```

Let's look at the individual parts of this code:

`Collisions`—This is the actual code that tells Blitz3D that we are about to define a collision.

`type_player`—This is the name of the source object that will be doing the colliding. In this case, we've called our type `player`, but you can give your types any names you wish. Keep in mind that the types have to be defined before this code is entered. In the next section you'll be shown how to define the types.

`,type_obstacle,`—This is the name of the object that your source will be colliding into. In this case we've called the type `obstacle`, but again, you can give your types any names you wish.

`2,2`—The first number defines the method, and the second number defines the response. The list of different methods and responses can be found in the previous section.

Colliding Objects

Now that we know what is required to define a collision, let's create one in a simple program. The following program contains two simple objects: a sphere that will be our player that we move and a cone that will be the object we smash into. Open the file demo11-01.bb or enter the following code:

```
;demo11-01.bb - Collisions
; ----------------
Graphics3D 640,480
SetBuffer BackBuffer()

Const ESC_KEY = 1
Const LEFT_KEY = 203
Const RIGHT_KEY = 205
Const UP_KEY = 200
Const DOWN_KEY = 208

camera=CreateCamera()
; Creating a light
light=CreateLight()
; Creating a sphere
sphere=CreateSphere()
ScaleEntity sphere, 0.5,0.5,0.5
PositionEntity sphere, -3,0,5
; Creating a cone
cone=CreateCone()
PositionEntity cone, 1,0,5
ScaleEntity cone, 1.5,1.5,1.5
; This following code makes our program run
While Not KeyDown(ESC_KEY)
        x#=0
        y#=0
        z#=0
        If KeyDown(LEFT_KEY)=True Then x#=-0.1
        If KeyDown(RIGHT_KEY)=True Then x#=0.1
        If KeyDown(DOWN_KEY)=True Then y#=-0.1
        If KeyDown(UP_KEY)=True Then y#=0.1
        MoveEntity sphere,x#,y#,z#
        RenderWorld
        Flip
Wend
End
```

Go ahead and run the program and use the arrow keys to move the sphere around. You can see that when the sphere gets to the cone, it goes right through. We'll now create a collision so that the sphere won't be able to go through the cone. The first thing we'll do is create the types. In this instance we'll create two types—one for the sphere, which we'll call player, and the other, which we'll call

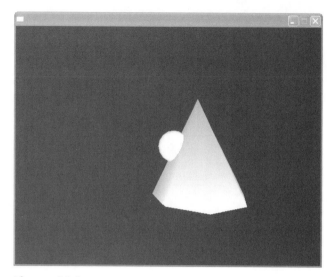

Figure 11.4
At this point the sphere can go right through the cone because no collisions have been set up in demo11-01.bb.

"obstacle." Enter the following code under the "SetBuffer" section to create the types. If you ran the program now (see Figure 11.4), the sphere could go through the cone.

```
; Creating the types
type_player=1
type_obstacle=2
```

The number that we chose for the two different types (1 and 2) don't have any importance. We could have selected any numbers; it's just important that they have a number assigned to them.

Next we have to assign the objects that we created to our types. Add the following code (in bold) to assign the two objects to the different teams (these code changes are in demo11-02.bb):

```
; Creating a sphere
sphere=CreateSphere()
ScaleEntity sphere, 0.5,0.5,0.5
PositionEntity sphere, -3,0,5
EntityType sphere,type_player
; Creating a cone
cone=CreateCone()
PositionEntity cone, 1,0,5
ScaleEntity cone, 1.5,1.5,1.5
EntityType cone,type_obstacle
```

Now we will create the collision itself. Add the code in bold below in the specified location:

```
Collisions type_player,type_obstacle,2,2
; This following code makes our program run
While Not KeyDown( 1 )
x#=0
y#=0
z#=0
If KeyDown( 203 )=True Then x#=-0.1
If KeyDown( 205 )=True Then x#=0.1
If KeyDown( 208 )=True Then y#=-0.1
If KeyDown( 200 )=True Then y#=0.1
MoveEntity sphere,x#,y#,z#
UpdateWorld
RenderWorld
Flip
Wend
End
```

Let's take a close look at the code to see what we have just done.

`Collisions type_player,type_obstacle,2,2`—This is the code that creates the collision and defines the methods and response for the collision.

`UpdateWorld`—This line is very important because it checks for collisions.

Now go ahead and run the program and you should see that your objects can't get close, as in Figure 11.5.

Collision Radius

You'll notice from the last section that the sphere couldn't get close to the cone. You can specify how close to or far from an object you can get by specifying a radius using the `EntityRadius` command. You specify the radius for the individual objects. Let's continue with the same program we were using in the last section. If you've closed it, open the file called demo11-03.bb. We simply changed the previous program a tiny bit. The change between demo11-02.bb and demo11-03.bb is highlighted in bold below.

```
; Creating a sphere
```

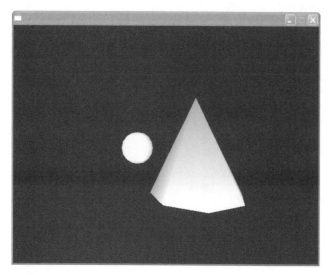

Figure 11.5
Deflector shields up! Your sphere can't get close to the cone because you created a collision in demo11-02.bb.

```
sphere=CreateSphere()
ScaleEntity sphere, 0.5,0.5,0.5
PositionEntity sphere, -3,0,5
EntityType sphere,type_player
EntityRadius sphere, 0.2
```

Go ahead and run the program now, and you'll see that you can get a lot closer to the object because you've entered a radius less than 1 (see Figure 11.6).

If you entered a radius greater than 1, you wouldn't be able to get as close to the cone.

N o t e

Now You Try

Practice entering different radius values between 0 and 1 and then greater than 1 to see how it affects how close your sphere can get to the cone.

Shields Down!—Clear Collisions

You can remove the Collisions command permanently or temporarily using the ClearCollisions command.

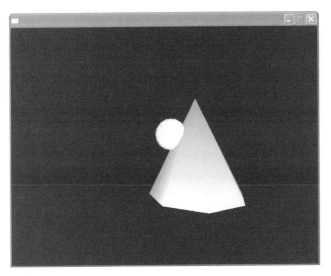

Figure 11.6
You can now get much closer to the cone in demo11-03.bb. In fact, you can get halfway through the cone before the collision occurs.

Demo11-04.bb looks like the following:

```
; This following code makes our program run
While Not KeyDown(ESC_KEY)
      x#=0
      y#=0
      z#=0
      If KeyDown(LEFT_KEY)=True Then x#=-0.1
      If KeyDown(RIGHT_KEY)=True Then x#=0.1
      If KeyDown(DOWN_KEY)=True Then y#=-0.1
      If KeyDown(UP_KEY)=True Then y#=0.1
      MoveEntity sphere,x#,y#,z#
      While KeyHit( 57 )
        ClearCollisions
      Wend

      RenderWorld
      UpdateWorld
      Flip
Wend
```

Run the program now, and when you press the space bar, the collisions are cleared, as in Figure 11.7.

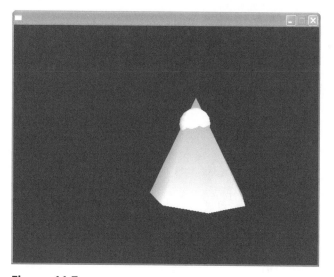

Figure 11.7
Once the space bar is pressed in demo11-04.bb, the collisions are cleared and the sphere can once
again go through the cone.

The code that we entered basically says that when the space bar is pressed, turn off
the collisions. Go ahead and run the program now. You'll see that you can still
move around the object, but as soon as you press the space bar, collisions will be
turned off. What if you wanted the ability to turn collisions on and off as you
please? Here we will add code that will turn the collisions on again when you
press the number 1.

```
If KeyDown( 200 )=True Then y#=0.1
MoveEntity sphere,x#,y#,z#
While KeyHit( 57 ) ClearCollisions
Wend
While KeyHit( 2) Collisions type_player,type_obstacle,2,2
Wend
UpdateWorld
RenderWorld
Flip
Wend
End
```

Note

Another collision you'll typically want to add is one with the terrain and one with the sky so that
your players don't fall through the terrain or over the edge.

Collision Effects

Not only can collisions prevent objects from going through one another, but you can create all sorts of effects when two objects collide with one another. When two cars collide or a bullet hits an object, you don't just want them to slide off one another; you want them to explode, leave a mark, or disappear. In this section, we will examine different collision effects that we can create when two objects collide. To create our collision effects, we'll use the CountCollisions command. This command will count how many times an object you specify has collided with another object.

Poof! Now You See It, Now You Don't

One type of collision you'll want to create often is having one object disappear when it hits another. This is perfect when you create things like bullets that hit enemies, since you'll want the enemies to disappear. We'll keep things simple in this example. We'll have one object (a cone) disappear when it is hit by a sphere. Demo11-04.bb shows how to do this. This program controls a sphere that can collide with a cone. When you run the program, you'll see that you can control the sphere, but it can't go through the cone since a collision has been created. The following code makes the disappearing occur!

```
; This following code makes our program run
While Not KeyDown( 1 )
x#=0
y#=0
z#=0
If KeyDown( 203 )=True Then x#=-0.1
If KeyDown( 205 )=True Then x#=0.1
If KeyDown( 208 )=True Then y#=-0.1
If KeyDown( 200 )=True Then y#=0.1
MoveEntity sphere,x#,y#,z#
If CountCollisions (sphere)=True Then HideEntity cone
UpdateWorld
RenderWorld
Flip
Wend
End
```

Figure 11.8
Poof! The cone disappears when it is hit by the sphere in demo11-04.bb.

Run the program now and see what happens. When the sphere hits the cone, it disappears, as seen in Figure 11.8. Let's take a close look at the one line of code we added to create this effect. The first part uses the CountCollision command. As mentioned earlier, Blitz3D counts how many times one object has collided with another. The CountCollision command will tell you how many collisions have occurred. When we add the code If CountCollisions (sphere)=True we are basically saying that if there are any collisions of the sphere at all, then do the following, HideEntity cone which will hide the cone.

Start by opening the file demo11-06.bb, and save it with a new name. This file has a sphere that you can control and two cones. Collisions are currently set up so that the sphere can't go through the cones. Let's look at the following code that will make any object that the sphere collides with disappear.

```
While Not KeyDown(ESC_KEY)

    x#=0
    y#=0
    z#=0

    If KeyDown(LEFT_KEY)=True Then x#=-0.1
    If KeyDown(RIGHT_KEY)=True Then x#=0.1
```

```
    If KeyDown(DOWN_KEY)=True Then y#=-0.1
    If KeyDown(UP_KEY)=True Then y#=0.1
```

WHAT hAPPENED ↑.
To INDENTING?.

```
    If CountCollisions (sphere)
    crash=CollisionEntity (sphere,1)
    HideEntity crash
    EndIf


    MoveEntity sphere,x#,y#,z#

    UpdateWorld
    RenderWorld

    Flip
Wend
```

Run the program now and you'll see that any object the sphere encounters will disappear. Now let's take a close look at the code we used to get this effect.

If CountCollisions (sphere)—This part of the code says that if the sphere has registered any collision at all, then do the following.

crash=CollisionEntity (sphere,1)—Here we create an entity called crash (which we could have called any name we chose) and we assign the Collision Entity command to it. The collision entity has two parameters in parentheses: the first is sphere and the second is 1. This basically tells Blitz3D to remember what the sphere has crashed into and call it crash.

HideEntity crash—This will hide the entity called crash, which is whatever the sphere has crashed into.

EndIf—This ends the If statement.

Blowing Up Stuff

Have you ever heard the saying "There are many ways to skin a cat"? That saying means that there are different methods to accomplish a specific task, and nowhere is that more true than in creating explosions in Blitz3D. I'm going to show you a simple way to create the illusion of an object blowing up. It will require quite a few lines of code, but I'll break it down into pieces in order to make it easier to understand.

Imagine a bullet (in this case the bullet will be a simple sphere) hitting an object and causing that object to shatter into a few pieces that fly away. We would accomplish this in a few different steps. The first thing that we would do is have the object (in our example the object will be a cone) disappear when it is hit by the bullet. In the last section, you learned to do this by using the HideEntity command when a collision occurred. The next thing we'll do is have three tiny spheres appear where the cone once stood and simultaneously have those fly in different directions so that it appears that they are particles from the exploding cone.

Start by opening the file called demo11-07.bb. This is the complete explosion program, with a cone that we will "blow up" and a sphere that will act as our bullet. Collision groups have already been set up for these objects. We will go over the code in this section.

We will start by making the cone disappear as soon as it is hit by the sphere. This was covered in the last section, so try doing it on your own first and then review the code below:

```
While Not KeyDown(ESC_KEY)
x#=0
y#=0
z#=0
If KeyDown(LEFT_KEY)=True Then x#=-0.1
If KeyDown(RIGHT_KEY)=True Then x#=0.1
If KeyDown(DOWN_KEY)=True Then y#=-0.1
If KeyDown(UP_KEY)=True Then y#=0.1
If CountCollisions (sphere)
HideEntity cone
UpdateWorld
MoveEntity sphere,x#,y#,z#
RenderWorld
Flip
Wend
```

The next thing we need to do is create the pieces that will make up the shattered cone. These pieces will be simple spheres. We have two options here: We can create the spheres within the If CountCollision statement, or we can create global variables. Let's say in our game we want to create many explosions. Rather than having to create particles for our exploded objects every time they are destroyed, we can create a global variable. These global variables can be included in any function. In this case we will create a global variable that creates a sphere. That way, every time an explosion occurs, we won't have to use the `CreateSphere` command; we'll only have to reference our global variable. Sound confusing? It will become quite a bit clearer in a moment when you put it in use. You can see the following three global variables at the beginning of the program just underneath the line `SetBuffer BackBuffer()`.

```
;demo11-07.bb - Explosssssionnnnns
;_____
Graphics3D 640,480
SetBuffer BackBuffer()

;Global particle variables
Global particle=CreateSphere()
Global particle1=CreateSphere()
Global particle2=CreateSphere()
```

Here we have created four spheres. The beauty of making them global variables is that whenever we need a sphere to act as part of an explosion, we don't have to create new spheres; we can just call on any of these three. As it stands, these spheres are a little big to be particles in an explosion, so in the next step we'll reduce their size and color them. Look at the following code:

```
;Handle particles
ScaleEntity particle, 0.2,0.2,0.2
EntityColor particle, 235,125,23

ScaleEntity particle1, 0.2,0.2,0.2
EntityColor particle1, 125,125,125

ScaleEntity particle2, 0.2,0.2,0.2
EntityColor particle2, 235,1,234
```

So with this code we've given each particle in the explosion a different color and we've reduced the size of the spheres. Now it's on to the code that will create the explosion. Basically, when the collision between the sphere and the cone takes place, we want to place the three spheres at the exact location of the cone, and then we will scatter those spheres. Let's take a look at the main loop:

```
While Not KeyDown( 1 )
x#=0
y#=0
z#=0
If KeyDown( 203 )=True Then x#=-0.1
If KeyDown( 205 )=True Then x#=0.1
If KeyDown( 208 )=True Then y#=-0.1
If KeyDown( 200 )=True Then y#=0.1
MoveEntity sphere,x#,y#,z#
If CountCollisions (sphere)
PositionEntity particle, EntityX(cone),EntityY(cone), EntityZ(cone)
PositionEntity particle1, EntityX(cone),EntityY(cone), EntityZ(cone)
PositionEntity particle2, EntityX(cone),EntityY(cone), EntityZ(cone)
HideEntity cone
End If
UpdateWorld
RenderWorld
Flip
Wend
End
```

INDENT? (handwritten annotation)

By adding this code, we are saying that when a collision with the sphere occurs, put the three spheres at the exact location of the cone. If we looked at the location of the cone in the code (which happens to be at 3,0,5), we could have just entered that location rather than EntityX(cone),EntityY(cone), EntityZ(cone). We entered that code because it will determine a value of the exact location of the cone, even if the cone was moving. In many games, our target will be moving, so we won't always know its exact location. Entering this code will always tell you the exact location of an object.

We need to enter one more valuable piece of code to this text. In the next section, we will send those three spheres flying. Before we do that, we need to create a variable saying that the collision has happened and that the three particles have been put in place. You can create absolutely any variable you want—it makes no difference as long as we have a variable we can call on in the next section. In this instance, we are going to create the variable called explosion and make its state ready by entering the following code in bold:

```
If CountCollisions (sphere)
PositionEntity particle, EntityX(cone),EntityY(cone), EntityZ(cone)
PositionEntity particle1, EntityX(cone),EntityY(cone), EntityZ(cone)
PositionEntity particle2, EntityX(cone),EntityY(cone), EntityZ(cone)
```

```
explosion=ready
HideEntity cone
End If
```

Adding `explosion=ready` may not make much sense right now, but in the next section you'll see why we had to add it.

Finally, we have to send our spheres flying. We'll do so by adding the following If statement in bold:

```
While Not KeyDown( 1 )
x#=0
y#=0
z#=0
If KeyDown( 203 )=True Then x#=-0.1
If KeyDown( 205 )=True Then x#=0.1
If KeyDown( 208 )=True Then y#=-0.1
If KeyDown( 200 )=True Then y#=0.1
MoveEntity sphere,x#,y#,z#
If CountCollisions (sphere)
PositionEntity particle, EntityX(cone),EntityY(cone), EntityZ(cone)
PositionEntity particle1, EntityX(cone),EntityY(cone), EntityZ(cone)
PositionEntity particle2, EntityX(cone),EntityY(cone), EntityZ(cone)
HideEntity cone
explosion=ready
End If
If explosion=ready
MoveEntity particle, -.3,.5,0
MoveEntity particle1, +.5,.5,0
MoveEntity particle2, .5,-.5,0
End If
UpdateWorld
RenderWorld
Flip
Wend
End
```

This `If` statement is quite straightforward. It says that when the variable `explosion=ready` is true, then move the spheres in the following directions. Even though this is a separate `If` statement, it is part of the main loop of the program, so it will continue over and over, meaning those particles will keep moving to infinity and beyond. If we had added it to the same loop that positioned the three spheres, then the three spheres would have only moved once by a small increment and wouldn't fly off the screen.

Here's the magic moment. Go ahead and run the program and crash the sphere into the cone. Ta da! You should have your explosion.

As I mentioned in the beginning of this section, there are many ways to skin a cat, and there are a variety of ways we could've created this type of explosion. While the code we've created here creates an explosion, there are some potential problems that may arise—for example, what about the flying debris? Does it go on forever? What if I have other objects that collide with the bullet? Will they create an explosion? Later in the book, when you learn about functions, you'll see how you can group code together to combine common tasks, which will certainly help in creating exploding objects. Another way you can solve potential problems with this collision is to use some timing.

Other Collision Commands

Before leaving collisions, there are a few other pieces of code that you should become familiar with. Throughout this chapter, we have been using the CountCollisions command to detect when a collision occurs, but there are other collision commands that you can use as well:

EntityCollided(entity,type)—This command will tell Blitz3D what other object was involved with the entity that you specified.

CollisionX(entity,index), CollisionY(entity,index), CollisionZ(entity, index)—These commands will produce the x, y, and z coordinates for the location of a collision.

CollisionEntity—This command will tell Blitz3D what other object was involved with the entity that you specified.

Summary

Collisions are pretty cool, huh! Now we can actually test for objects hitting each other—like space missiles or rockets or anything!

In this chapter, we learned how to:

- Create collisions

- Check collision radius

- Blow stuff up!

The next chapter will teach you how to deal with sounds!

CHAPTER 12

Sounds

I want you to do some homework. Don't worry; it'll be fun. Go out and rent a DVD—an action movie or a horror flick. A good movie to rent would be any in the *Star Wars* series. Turn on the closed captioning feature (which runs the dialogue across the bottom of the screen) and then turn the volume off. Now watch the movie. You'll notice that even though you can follow the story, it won't seem to have the same emotion, feel, tension, and suspense that it will have when you watch it with the sound on. Music and sounds not only play a critical role in movies, but they can make a huge difference in your games. From explosions to shooting to aliens to background music, you can add all types of sounds and music to your games using Blitz3D.

In this chapter, we'll explore most of the sound features that you can control in Blitz3D—and believe me, there are lots of controls. You can control things like the volume, the direction, the channels, the pitch, the pan, and much more.

Sounds

I remember the first time I watched the movie *Star Wars*. I recall being so amazed by the sound of the blasters firing. Later I remember watching a documentary that explained that the blaster sound was made by tapping on wires. We'll actually be using a blaster sound similar to the one used in the movie later in this section. Regardless of the sounds you decide to use, Blitz3D makes them easy to load.

Note

Audio File Formats

Digital audio files come in a variety of different formats, many of which are supported by Blitz3D. These include .raw, .mod, .s3m, .xm, .it, .mid, .rmi, .wav, .mp2, .mp3, .ogg, .wma, and .asf.

Loading and Playing Sounds

To get a sound file into your program, you first need to load it. After it is loaded, you can assign it to play at specific times. The following code will load a sound:

```
; Loading a sound
sound = LoadSound (filename)
```

Obviously, you would replace filename with the actual name of your sound file. For example, in a video game with a blast, you might write:

```
blaster = LoadSound ("blaster.wav").
```

The sound part of the code is just a name we gave our sound; you can call your sounds anything you'd like.

Open the file called demo12-01.bb and save it to a new folder. Make sure that the file called blaster.wav is in the same folder. Follow along as we go through the code.

```
blaster = LoadSound ("blaster.wav")
```

The game that we have loaded contains a sphere and a cube, where the sphere can be controlled by moving the left and right arrow keys. Now that we have a sound loaded into the game, we need to create a certain event that will trigger the sound. In the case of this game, we will play the blaster sound whenever the sphere hits the cube.

```
While Not KeyDown(ESC_KEY)
        x#=0
        y#=0
        z#=0

        If KeyDown(LEFT_KEY)=True Then x#=-0.05
        If KeyDown(RIGHT_KEY)=True Then x#=0.05
        If KeyDown(DOWN_KEY)=True Then y#=-0.05
```

```
      If KeyDown(UP_KEY)=True Then y#=0.05
      If KeyDown(Z_KEY)=True Then z#=-0.05
      If KeyDown(A_KEY)=True Then z#=0.05
      MoveEntity sphere,x#,y#,z#
      ; Collision Sound
      If CountCollisions (sphere)
            PlaySound blaster
      EndIf



      UpdateWorld
      RenderWorld
      Flip
Wend
```

Let's take a look at the code we created. We created an If statement that basically says that whenever a collision occurs involving the sphere, play the blaster sound. The code CountCollisions(sphere) says to Blitz3D, let me know if there have been any collisions involving the sphere, and tell me how many have taken place since the last UpdateWorld. The next piece of code, PlaySound blaster, tells Blitz3D to play the sound that we loaded earlier called blaster. Finally, the EndIf code ends the If statement.

Adjusting Volume

When two ships crash in your game, do you want the sound to be an earth-shattering roar? When players are talking behind enemy lines, should their voices be barely heard? You can easily adjust the volume of your sound effects by using the SoundVolume command in Blitz3D. You can even manipulate the volume of a sound so that it changes in relation to an object. For example, let's say you have an object far off in the distance. You can have the sound get louder and louder as it approaches your player. Let's start by adjusting the volume of a non-moving object and then get a bit fancier by adjusting the volume of a moving object.

Start by opening the file called demo12-02.bb. It is the same file we used in the last section that has a sphere that plays a sound when it bumps into a cube. To change the volume of a sound, you must enter a value for the volume between 0 and 1 (see Figure 12.1). Entering a value of 1 will produce the loudest sound, while entering 0 will produce no sound at all. You can enter any decimal value in

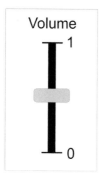

Figure 12.1
You can adjust the volume "dial" from 0 to 1 for your sounds.

between to adjust the volume level (for example, 0.3, 0.04, 0.9). In this example, we will make the volume half its current level by entering a value of 0.5.

Take a look at the following code in bold from the existing code:

```
;Collision Sound
If CountCollisions (sphere)
PlaySound blaster
SoundVolume blaster, 0.5
EndIf
```

If you run the program now, you'll notice that the volume level is half of what it was when we originally created the program. If we want to let the user change the volume, we could keep track of the volume with a variable and update Sound-Volume during each frame.

Adjusting Pitch

Do you know what the difference is between a tenor and a soprano? Tenors have voices that are low, while sopranos have voices that are higher. The level of a person's voice, high or low, is called the pitch. I'm sure you've heard sound effects in which the pitch of someone's voice is set so high that it sounds like they are talking like a chipmunk. Or, perhaps you've heard the pitch of someone's voice lowered to a point that they sound like the devil or a monster.

Pitch is measured in a unit called a Hertz (Hz). In Blitz3D, you can adjust the pitch of a sound by adjusting its Hertz. The range goes from 1 Hz to 44,000 Hz.

Adjusting the pitch is simply a matter of using the SoundPitch code. For this program, I did not create a demo on the CD—I want you to try and follow along!

Type in the following code. Before you start entering the code, save the program to a folder that contains the file hello.wav.

```
; Changing Pitch
;_____

Graphics3D 640,480
SetBuffer BackBuffer()

; Creating a light
light=CreateLight()

; Create camera
camera=CreateCamera()
PositionEntity camera, 0,1,0

;Loading the sound
hello = LoadSound ( "hello.wav" )

; Running the program
While Not KeyDown( 1 )
pitch#=12000

If KeyDown( 200 )=True Then pitch#= pitch#+500
If KeyDown( 208 )=True Then pitch#= pitch#-500
If pitch# < 1 Then pitch#=2000
If KeyDown( 57 )=True Then SoundPitch hello, pitch# PlaySound hello

RenderWorld
Flip

Wend

End
```

We'll look at the code in a moment, but for now, just run the program. Use the space bar to play the sound and then press the up or down arrows to adjust the pitch, and then press the space bar again.

Now let's look at the code we used to create the sound and adjust the pitch.

hello = LoadSound ("hello.wav")—This loads the sound into the program. We called our sound hello.

pitch#=12000—Here we created a variable and called it pitch#. We could have given the variable any name. We made the initial pitch level 12000 Hz.

If KeyDown(200)=True Then pitch#= pitch#+500—When the up arrow is pressed, the pitch will go up by 500 Hz.

If KeyDown(208)=True Then pitch#= pitch#-500—When the down arrow is pressed, the pitch will go down by 500 Hz.

If pitch# < 2000 Then pitch#=2000—If the pitch gets too low, you won't be able to hear it, so we will create a safety net that prevents the pitch from falling below 2000 Hz. The code says that if the pitch level (pitch#) falls below 2000 then just set it at 2000.

If KeyDown(57)=True Then SoundPitch hello, pitch# PlaySound hello—This code says that if the space bar is pressed, then set the pitch level and play the sound called hello.

Note

Experiment with Pitch

Unless you created the sound itself, you won't know what its pitch level is, so you'll have to experiment with different pitch levels if you want to make an adjustment.

Adjusting Pan

Most computers that have sound have two speakers, one on the left and the other on the right. You can adjust how much of a sound comes out of each speaker. If you are familiar with a car radio or home stereo, adjusting the pan is the same as moving the balance dial between left and right on your stereo (see Figure 12.2).

By adjusting the pan level, you can create some pretty cool effects because you can enhance the illusion of movement by having a sound play from one speaker to another. Imagine a ship flying across the screen. You could have the sound of the ship move from one speaker to the next as the ship moves.

Pan is applied by using the SoundPan command and setting a pan number. The pan number can be anywhere between -1 and 1. Here's how it works: A negative

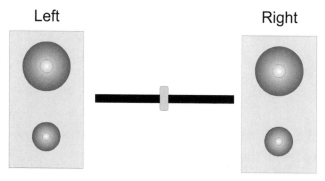

Figure 12.2
Pan allows you to adjust the level of sound coming out of each speaker.

pan number will put more of the sound out of the left speaker, while a positive pan number puts more sound out of the right speaker. Here are some examples of pan numbers and how the sound would be divided:

- **0.75**—75% of the sound would come from the right speaker, and 25% would come from the left.

- **0.25**—25% of the sound would come from the left speaker, and 75% would come from the right.

Get the idea? Let's put it to the test so that you can see how it works. Start by opening the file called demo12-03.bb. Follow along, but make sure that the sound file train.wav is in the same folder. We are now going to use the following code in bold to adjust the pan.

```
; Loading sound
train = LoadSound ( "train.wav" )
; Running the program
While Not KeyDown( 1 )
x# = 0

If KeyDown( 203 ) = True Then x# = -0.1
If KeyDown( 205 ) = True Then x# = 0.1
If x# > 0
pan# = 1
Else
pan# = -1
EndIf

MoveEntity sphere, x#,0,0

If x# <> 0
SoundPan train, pan#
PlaySound train
EndIf
UpdateWorld

RenderWorld
Flip

Wend

End
```

When you run the program and press the right or left arrow keys, you'll notice the sound "move" along with the sphere. Let's take a close look at the code we added to understand how it works.

```
train = LoadSound ( "train.wav" )
```

This loads the sound that we have called `train`.

```
If x# > 0
pan# = 1
Else
pan# = -1
EndIf -
```

This code tells Blitz3D that if the x coordinate of the sphere is greater than 0 (in other words, if it moves to the right), then the music should play out of the right speaker and vice versa for the left.

```
If x# <> 0
SoundPan train, pan#
PlaySound train
EndIf
```

This says that when the sphere moves, the music should begin playing.

Note

Looping a Sound

You can use the code `LoopSound ( "soundfile.mp3" )` if you want to have a sound loop over and over. Obviously, you'd replace `soundfile.mp3` with the actual file that you want to use.

Summary

Sounds are a really important part of a game—they really influence the user experience. This chapter taught you how to put sounds into your games.

This chapter covered the following concepts:

- Loading sounds

- Adjusting volume

- Adjusting pitch

- Adjusting pan

Hope you're ready for the next chapter, where we learn about lots of other 3D components!

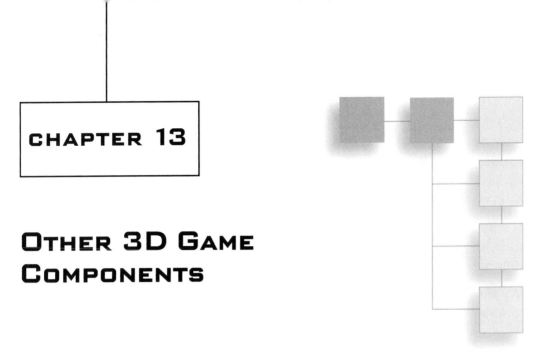

CHAPTER 13

Other 3D Game Components

So far this book has covered a lot of different components of a game, and we're almost ready to create our first fully functional game. Based on what you've learned so far, you could probably even create your first game on your own right now. There are a few key areas, however, that will help make your games look and play better, and I will cover them in this chapter. Think of this chapter as a potluck of different game elements that will improve your 3D game programming skills.

Here we will add on to some of the concepts you learned earlier by covering certain details and concepts that you weren't quite ready for until now.

In this chapter, I'm not going to provide the completed programs for you: I'm going to provide a skeleton of a program and ask you to type in specific commands to see what happens on the demos. That way, you'll actually get to program yourself!

Gravity

The concept of gravity is important to many different types of games. Unless your game takes place in space or in some alternate gravity-less universe, you'll probably want your players or objects to either stay on the ground or float back to the ground when they jump in the air. There are several ways to create the illusion of gravity, and we'll explore one of the easiest in the following example.

Start by opening the program demo13-01.bb, which includes several features that have already been covered in the book. We have a sky, created by a sphere; a terrain with a collision set up between our character (a sphere with a pattern) so that he doesn't fall through the terrain; and controls set up to move around. Run the program and use the arrow keys and the A and Z keys to navigate around our little world.

It's surprisingly easy to add code to create "gravity." Basically, what we'll do is move the object downward all of the time so that the character is always moving downward (see Figure 13.1).

We will apply just a light force of gravity so that our character will still be able to jump or move off the ground but will then float gently to the ground.

```
If KeyDown(LEFT_KEY)=True Then x#=-0.1
If KeyDown(RIGHT_KEY)=True Then x#=0.1
If KeyDown(DOWN_KEY)=True Then y#=-0.1
If KeyDown(UP_KEY)=True Then y#=0.1
If KeyDown(Z_KEY)=True Then z#=-0.1
If KeyDown(A_KEY)=True Then z#=0.1
MoveEntity sphere,x#,y#,z#
TranslateEntity sphere, 0,-.02,0
UpdateWorld
```

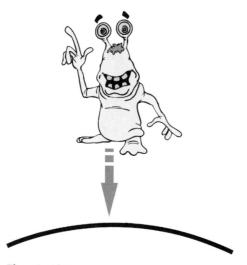

Figure 13.1
To create the illusion of gravity, we'll move an object downward continually.

```
RenderWorld
Flip
Wend
End
```

Take a look at the code that created the gravity:

```
TranslateEntity sphere, 0,-.02,0
```

We used the `TranslateEntity` command because we want the gravity to move downward on the y axis no matter what position our character is in (see Figure 13.2). The rest of the code is pretty straightforward: `sphere` is the name of the object we are applying gravity to, and `-0.02` is the force of the gravity. We use a negative value because we want the direction of the gravity to be downward along the y axis.

Use the `TranslateEntity` command rather than the `MoveEntity` command for the gravity so that no matter what direction the object is facing, it will always float downward.

Note

Not Too Much

> Don't make your force of gravity too high. Gravity levels that are too high will prevent your object from moving in any direction, as the downward force is too strong.

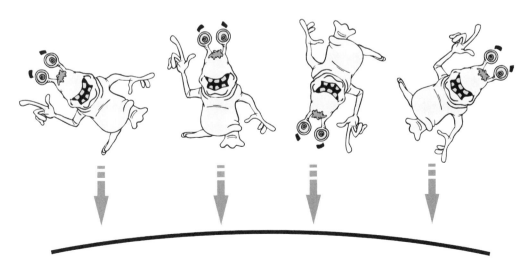

Figure 13.2
The `TranslateEntity` command in action.

Simple Jumping

Jumping is an integral part of many different types of games and can be achieved quite easily in Blitz3D. Whether it's your character jumping over obstacles, hurdles, or bad guys, the process of creating a bounce is fairly easy. I called this section "Simple Jumping" because it creates a code that will have an object jump only when a key is pressed on the keyboard. We haven't added any extra parameters. For example, the shape in this example doesn't have to be on the ground in order to jump; it can actually jump again midway through the first jump.

In order for jumping to work in this example, we need to have gravity already created on our object. Refer back to the previous section for information on creating gravity. Open the file called demo13-02.bb, which is the same file we used in the last section, with just a higher level of gravity (set at −0.1). The higher the level of gravity, the faster our object will fall back to the ground after it has jumped.

The actual process of jumping is just a matter of changing the object's position on the y axis.

```
While Not KeyDown( ESC_KEY )
x#=0
y#=0
z#=0
If KeyDown(LEFT_KEY)=True Then x#=-0.1
If KeyDown(RIGHT_KEY)=True Then x#=0.1
If KeyDown(DOWN_KEY)=True Then y#=-0.1
If KeyDown(UP_KEY)=True Then y#=0.1
If KeyDown(Z_KEY)=True Then z#=-0.1
If KeyDown(A_KEY)=True Then z#=0.1
If KeyDown (SPACE_BAR)=True Then y#=0.5
MoveEntity sphere,x#,y#,z#
TranslateEntity sphere, 0,-0.1,0
UpdateWorld
RenderWorld
Flip
Wend
End
```

Run the program now and hit the space bar once. You should notice that your ball jumps in the air and then floats back down. Now press the left and right

Figure 13.3
Pressing the space bar will make the sphere appear to "jump."

arrow keys or the A or Z keys to move the sphere, and then press the space bar to see the object jump as it moves (see Figure 13.3).

You can change how fast the object floats down by changing the gravity level. Let's take a look at the code we used to create the jump:

```
If KeyDown (SPACE_BAR)=True Then y#=0.5
```

What this says is that when the space bar is pressed, the character's position should go up by 0.5 units along the y axis. We had already set up the code for movement (MoveEntity sphere,x#,y#,z#), so we only needed to add this one line of code to create the jump.

Velocity

Creating the illusion of velocity can make your game feel more realistic. In real life, most objects don't just start and stop. Think of racers who sprint in the

Olympics. When the gun sounds they aren't going their top speed instantly; it takes several seconds for them to reach their maximum stride. The same holds true when they cross the finish line. They don't stop instantly; it takes them quite a few steps to apply the brakes and slow down. By controlling an object's velocity in your game, you can make its movement seem more realistic. In an earlier chapter, you learned how to have objects move on their own. Here you will learn to increase and decrease their speed or stop on a dime. These types of controls are great for games that contain any type of moving vehicle that the player controls.

Start by opening the program called demo13-03.bb. This program contains a textured sphere that is just sitting there. We are going to add controls that will act like a gas pedal, a brake, and an emergency brake to move and stop the sphere. To keep things simple, we will only add controls for the z axis.

```
; The following code makes the program run
While Not KeyDown(ESC_KEY)
If KeyDown(DOWN_KEY)=True Then velocity#=velocity#-0.001
If KeyDown(UP_KEY)=True Then velocity#=velocity#+0.001
If KeyDown(S_KEY) Then velocity#=0
MoveEntity sphere,0,0,velocity#
TranslateEntity sphere, 0,-0.03,0
Collisions type_player,type_ground,2,2
Collisions type_ground,type_player,2,2
UpdateWorld
RenderWorld
Flip
Wend
End
```

With these four lines of code, we've created a gas pedal, a brake (or reverse), and an emergency brake. Let's look at the breakdown of the code we added:

If KeyDown(UP_KEY)=True Then velocity#=velocity#-0.001—This code says that when the up arrow is pressed (key 208), then increase the current velocity by 0.001 units. In other words, every time you press the up arrow, the velocity will become greater and greater. By adjusting the velocity number (0.001), you can increase or decrease the speed of the acceleration. By the way, we created a variable here called velocity, but we could have called it anything we wanted—it's just a name we are assigning to this variable.

If KeyDown(DOWN_KEY)=True Then velocity#=velocity#+0.001—This code is the opposite of the code above. It says that when the down arrow is pressed, decrease the current velocity by 0.001 units.

If KeyDown (S_KEY) Then velocity#=0—This is our emergency brake. The code says that if you press the S key on your keyboard (key 31), then the velocity will become 0.

MoveEntity sphere,0,0,velocity#—This is the code that sets everything in motion. It says that while the program is running, don't move the sphere at all along the x or y axes, but move it along the z axis by the velocity number. The velocity number will change depending on whether the up arrow, down arrow, or S key is being pressed.

Now go ahead and run the program. Pressing the up arrow will increase your velocity, while pressing the down arrow will slow you down (see Figure 13.4). If you keep pressing the down arrow, you will eventually start accelerating in reverse. You can press the S key at any time to stop the acceleration.

Figure 13.4
You can use the arrow keys to zoom the ball around the playing field.

Note

Now You Try

Right now we can only accelerate and decelerate along the z axis. Add the necessary code to this program to allow for acceleration and deceleration along the x axis using the left and right arrow keys. Once you're done, compare your code to the code added below in bold.

```
; The following code makes the program run
While Not KeyDown(ESC_KEY)
If KeyDown(DOWN_KEY)=True Then velocity#=velocity#-0.001
If KeyDown(UP_KEY)=True Then velocity#=velocity#+0.001
If KeyDown (S_KEY) Then velocity#=0
If KeyDown (S_KEY) Then xvelocity#=0
If KeyDown(LEFT_KEY)=True Then xvelocity#=xvelocity#-0.001
If KeyDown( RIGHT_KEY)=True Then xvelocity#=xvelocity#+0.001
MoveEntity sphere,xvelocity#,0,velocity#
TranslateEntity sphere, 0,-0.03,0
Collisions type_player,type_ground,2,2
Collisions type_ground,type_player,2,2
UpdateWorld
RenderWorld
Flip
Wend
End
```

Chase Camera

A good percentage of 3D games use a feature called a chase camera. If you've ever played a modern-day *Mario Bros.* type of game, then you've already seen a chase camera in use. A chase camera follows the action of the player of the game. Usually the player is always just a few feet in front of the camera, and wherever the player goes, he remains in sight because the camera follows him around. There's a good likelihood that you'll want to incorporate a chase camera into your games, and the good news is that it isn't all that difficult. Don't get me wrong, though—it can be made very complicated, as there are all sorts of features and enhancements you can add to the simple chase camera that we are about to create. For now, at least, I'm going to show you a simple way to create a chase camera.

Begin by opening the file called demo13-04.bb. This file contains a cone whose acceleration can be changed by pressing the up and down arrows and can be stopped by pressing the S key. The only problem is that if you press either arrow key for more than a second or two, the cone will zoom off the screen as the camera just stays put. We can create a chase camera with just a few lines of code.

Start off by rotating the camera by 45 degrees along the x axis. Right now, this wouldn't make much sense to do, but in a moment we are going to raise the camera, so having it rotated 45 degrees will help you see the cone since it will be looking downward toward the cone.

```
; Create camera
camera=CreateCamera()
RotateEntity camera, 45,0,0
```

The next thing we are going to do is add the code that will tell Blitz3D to put the camera wherever the cone is and then position it a few units back. Add the following code in bold:

```
; The following code makes the program run
While Not KeyDown( 1 )
If KeyDown( 208 )=True Then velocity#=velocity#-0.001
If KeyDown( 200 )=True Then velocity#=velocity#+0.001
If KeyDown (31 ) Then velocity#=0
If KeyDown (31 ) Then xvelocity#=0
If KeyDown( 203 )=True Then xvelocity#=xvelocity#-0.001
If KeyDown( 205 )=True Then xvelocity#=xvelocity#+0.001
MoveEntity cone,xvelocity#,0,velocity#
TranslateEntity cone, 0,-0.03,0
PositionEntity camera,EntityX(cone),0,EntityZ(cone)
MoveEntity camera,0,0,-5
Collisions type_player,type_ground,2,2
Collisions type_ground,type_player,2,2
UpdateWorld
RenderWorld
Flip
Wend
End
```

Run the program now, and you should have a chase camera, as shown in Figure 13.5.

Figure 13.5
Chase cameras are very popular in many 3D games. The camera follows the object around the screen.

You've done it! You've created a chase camera. Let's take a close look at the code we used to create this wonderful effect:

PositionEntity camera,EntityX(cone),0,EntityZ(cone)—Here we are positioning the camera at the exact same spot of the location of the cone on the x axis and the z axis. The code EntityX(cone) enters the current location of the cone on the x axis, while EntityZ(cone) does the same for the z axis. This means that no matter where the cone is, the camera will be positioned in the exact same location on the x axis and z axis. Since we don't actually want the camera to be right on top of the cone (we want it to be a few steps back), we enter the next line of code. Note that we left the position of the camera on the y axis at 0. This is because our player doesn't really jump or move up and down, so there is no need to enter a value for the y axis position. If it did we would have replaced the 0 with EntityY(cone).

MoveEntity camera,0,0,-5—Because we don't want the camera over our cone (we want it to be a few steps back), we enter this line of code. Basically, we are saying take the current position of the camera (which at this point should be right on top of the cone) and move it back 5 units.

Go ahead and run the program now and watch as the camera follows the action.

Mirror

In previous chapters, you learned how to create planes and terrains for your game. A great effect you can add to your terrains is the illusion that there is a reflection from the ground. This can be accomplished by using the `mirror` command. When you create a mirror, it reflects everything that is either above it or below it. The `mirror` command is very simple to add:

```
; This code creates a mirror
mirror=CreateMirror()
```

Here we've created a mirror called `mirror`, but you can call it anything you'd like. You can also reposition the mirror so that it is above or below your objects (see Figure 13.6).

Figure 13.6
Notice how the cone reflects in the mirror.

Timing

Remember that your game is like a movie, going by frame by frame as seconds go by. You can use this to your advantage, not only in creating collisions and explosions, but for all types of effects in your game. Basically, you can create a countdown timer and have events take place before, during, or after a specific time. To do this, we will use the Millisecs() command. Before I start describing this command, it's important to know that 1000 milliseconds is equal to 1 second. Blitz3D is always counting the time, and the Millisecs() command will tell you what the current time is. You can use this command to create a timer and schedule events to happen based on that time. Let's use this command to create a ticking time bomb!

Start by opening the program called demo13-05.bb and save it with a new name. This file is simply five spheres. One is very big, which will be the bomb, and the other four are smaller circles hiding behind the sphere that will act as the shrapnel. What we are going to do is create a countdown timer, and after five seconds we'll make the bomb disappear and send the shrapnel flying.

We need to start by creating the timer variable, and we will do this by adding the following code in bold. Enter this code outside of the game loop, right below the section where you created the shrapnel.

```
; This code creates a variable for the timer.
timer=MilliSecs()
```

It is very important that this code remain outside of the game loop—in other words, before the line that reads While Not KeyDown (ESC_KEY); otherwise, the timer will continually reset as the game is running. So now we have a timer that has started counting every millisecond that goes by, which we have called timer. We could have given this timer any name since it is just a name we associated with the command. Now that we have a timer, we need to create some action to happen based on the timer. Add the following code:

```
; This code makes the program run
While Not KeyDown( 1 )
; This code creates the explosion

If MilliSecs() < timer + 3000 ShowEntity bomb Else HideEntity bomb
If MilliSecs() > timer + 3000 MoveEntity shrapnel, -.3,+.8,.15
If MilliSecs() > timer + 3000 MoveEntity shrapnel1, .3,-.5,.05
If MilliSecs() > timer + 3000 MoveEntity shrapnel2, -.1,+.5,-.35
If MilliSecs() > timer + 3000 MoveEntity shrapnel3, .3,0,.0
```

```
RenderWorld
Flip
Wend
End
```

Run the program now. After three seconds, the bomb will explode. Now let's look at the code that we created:

```
; This code makes the program run
While Not KeyDown( 1 )
```

If `MilliSecs() < timer + 3000 ShowEntity bomb Else HideEntity bomb`—This line basically says that after three seconds have passed, hide the sphere. Here's how it's done: If the current time (`MilliSecs()`) is less than the timer plus three seconds (`< timer + 3000`), then show the bomb (`ShowEntity bomb`). Otherwise, hide the bomb (`HideEntity bomb`).

The rest of the code deals with the particles flying. It's basically the same as the code above:

```
If MilliSecs() > timer + 3000 MoveEntity shrapnel, -.3,+.8,.15
If MilliSecs() > timer + 3000 MoveEntity shrapnel1,
.3,-.5,.05
If MilliSecs() > timer + 3000 MoveEntity shrapnel2,
-.1,+.5,-.35
If MilliSecs() > timer + 3000 MoveEntity shrapnel3, .3,0,.0
```

This code just says that after three seconds have passed, send the four spheres flying. The things you can do with timings are endless. As you've seen here, you can hide and move objects, but beyond that you can do just about anything.

Text

You may be thinking to yourself, *This is 3D game programming; why do I need text?* Text can actually play a very important role in your 3D games since it allows the game to communicate with the players. If you think about it, text is a part of almost every game that you play. Some examples of how text is used in your games include: your score, the amount of ammunition you have left, your health, your current level, the time you have left, and your position.

Adding text to your game is quite easy in Blitz3D. You simply have to indicate where on the screen you want the text to appear and what you want the text to say. You can also add variables to your text so that changing information can also be displayed.

Adding and Positioning Text

Adding and positioning text in your games can all be done with one line of code, simply called the Text command. When you enter the Text command, you specify what text is to be included, where it is to be positioned, and how it should be justified. Here is an example of a line of code that will create a line of text that says "Your Score Is:":

```
Text 100,20, "Your Score Is: ",True,False
```

If you positioned this text in the right location and then ran the program, you should get the same result as seen in Figure 13.7.

Now let's dissect the code we created to see how we created this text:

Text 100,20,—The word Text starts the command and is followed by two numbers separated by commas. The first number represents the x coordinate for

Figure 13.7
Entering the code to create the text above is simply a matter of using the Text command.

the position of the text, and the second number represents the y coordinate. In this example, the 100 represents how far in from the left the text should appear, and the 20 represents how far down from the top the text should appear. Figuring out the exact positioning of your text will take some trial and error, so experiment with different values. Figure 13.8 shows text positioned at different coordinates throughout the screen.

"Your Score Is:"—The actual text that you want to have appear on the screen should be entered between quotation marks. In this case, the text that is within the quotation marks, Your Score Is:, will appear onscreen.

,True,False—These next parts of the code are optional, but they allow you to justify the text within a line. Either one can be made True or False. The first word, in this case True, either turns off or turns on horizontal centering. When horizontal centering is turned on, the text is centered around the x position you have set; otherwise, it is left justified starting at the x coordinate. The best way to understand this is to look at an example. Following are four lines of code, each positioned at the 280 mark for the x coordinate (the 280 mark is actually marked with an x in the last line of text). Notice how the two lines of code that were set to

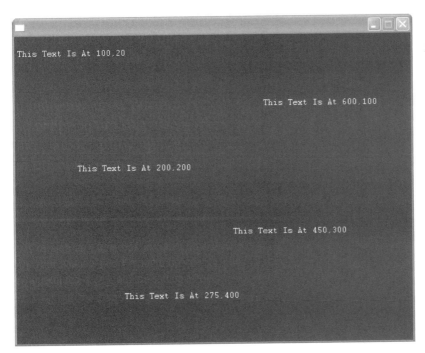

Figure 13.8
Figuring out the positioning of text on the screen will take some trial and error.

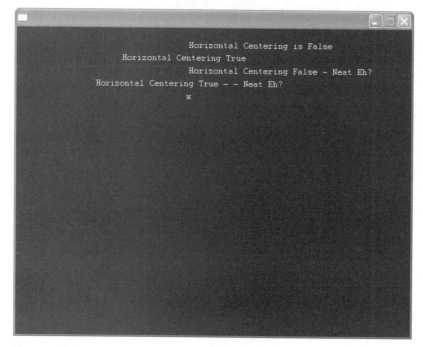

Figure 13.9
You can adjust the horizontal settings for your text. The x in this image represents the center point.

True for horizontal centering are centered around the 280 point, while the ones that were set to False are left justified at the 280 mark. See the results of the following in Figure 13.9.

```
Text 280 ,20, "Horizontal Centering is False ",False,False
Text 280,40, "Horizontal Centering True ",True,False
Text 280,60, "Horizontal Centering False - Neat Eh?",False,False
Text 280,80, "Horizontal Centering True - - Neat Eh?",True,False
Text 280,100 ,"x", True,False
```

The code with the horizontal centering set to True is centered around the x coordinate.

The second word of the code, in this case set to False, deals with the vertical centering around the y coordinate that you specify. True centers the text vertically, while False does not.

Now that you've seen the code, it's time to put it into action. The only hard part about adding the Text line of code is entering it in the right location. The Text code needs to be placed within the game loop, between the RenderWorld line and the Flip line. Open the file called demo13-06.bb, which is a program that contains a sphere and a cone and that has some collisions set up.

Add the following line of code (in bold) between the `RenderWorld` and `Flip` commands:

```
; This following code makes our program run
While Not KeyDown(ESC_KEY)

x#=0
y#=0
z#=0
If KeyDown(LEFT_KEY)=True Then x#=-0.1
If KeyDown(RIGHT_KEY)=True Then x#=0.1
If KeyDown(DOWN_KEY)=True Then y#=-0.1
If KeyDown(UP_KEY)=True Then y#=0.1
MoveEntity sphere,x#,y#,z#
UpdateWorld
RenderWorld
Text 10 ,20, "Score: ", False, False
Flip
Wend
End
```

Take a look at Figure 13.10 to see the results.

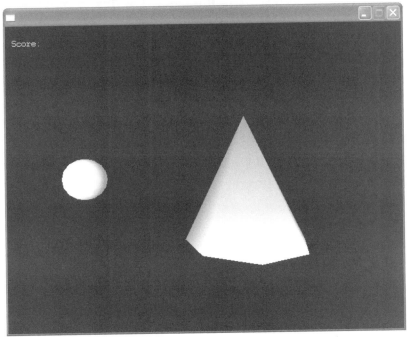

Figure 13.10
If you ran the program now, you would see the word "Score" in the top-left corner.

Note

Positioning

The location where you enter code is very important when it comes to the Text command. It needs to be inserted between the RenderWorld and Flip commands. Don't believe me? Try placing the Text code anywhere else. Either the program won't run, or you won't be able to see the text on the screen.

Adding Text Variables

As you can see by the example in the last section, having text without some sort of variable just isn't that effective. In that example, we have the word "Score," but more importantly, what we don't have is the actual score. This can be added by expanding our Text command. Think of the Text command as an equation; if you want to add something, just use the + sign.

Now we'll continue on with the example we used in the last section, so if for some reason you thought it would be a good idea to skip that section and jump to here, think again. Go back and add the "Score" line to the demo13-06.bb program.

Before we add the code necessary to display the score on the screen, we have to determine how we are going to keep score in this game. For this example, we'll say that every time the sphere touches the cone, a point will be earned. You learned in Chapter 11, "Collisions," that the CountCollisions command will count the number of times an object collides with another within each frame. We'll use this to act as our score. To actually add the score variable to the text onscreen, we simply use a + sign. Let's add the following code in bold to our program:

```
; The following code makes the program run
While Not KeyDown(ESC_KEY)
x#=0
y#=0
z#=0
If KeyDown(LEFT_KEY)=True Then x#=-0.1
If KeyDown(RIGHT_KEY)=True Then x#=0.1
If KeyDown(DOWN_KEY)=True Then y#=-0.1
If KeyDown(UP_KEY)=True Then y#=0.1
If CountCollisions (sphere) Then score#=score#+1
MoveEntity sphere,x#,y#,z#
UpdateWorld
```

```
RenderWorld
Text 10 ,20, "Score: " + score# , False, False
Flip
Wend
End
```

Run the program now, and using the arrow keys, move the sphere into the cone. As soon as the sphere touches the cone, the score will start registering, as in Figure 13.11.

We added only two little snippets of code to create the score. Let's see how we did it:

If CountCollisions (sphere) Then score#=score#+1—Here we are saying that if a collision occurs between the sphere and the cone, then the variable we created called score# will become score# + 1. In other words, the score starts out at 0. If a collision occurs, then the score becomes 0 + 1, which would make the score 1. If another collision occurs, the score (which is now at 1) becomes 1+1, in other words, 2. This continues on, and we see the score getting higher and higher as long as the two objects are colliding.

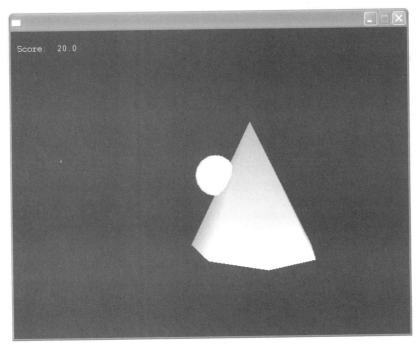

Figure 13.11
When the sphere touches the cone, the score will appear on the screen.

Text 10 ,20, "Score: " + score# , False,False—Here we added the score variable to the existing text by using a + sign before adding the variable. You can add a variety of variables to your text strings simply by adding a + sign.

Let's now add some other variables to our text string. The only other variables we have in the program we are using are the x and y locations of the sphere, so let's add a line of text that displays the position of the sphere at all times. Add the following code to the program:

```
; The following code makes the program run
While Not KeyDown(ESC_KEY)
x#=0
y#=0
z#=0
If KeyDown (LEFT_KEY)=True Then x#=-0.1
If KeyDown (RIGHT_KEY)=True Then x#=0.1
If KeyDown (DOWN_KEY)=True Then y#=-0.1
If KeyDown (UP_KEY)=True Then y#=0.1
If CountCollisions (sphere) Then score#=score#+1
MoveEntity sphere,x#,y#,z#
UpdateWorld
RenderWorld
Text 10 ,20, "Score: "+ score#,False,False
Text 10 ,60, "Sphere x-coordinate: " + EntityX(sphere) + " Sphere y-coordinate: "
+ EntityY(sphere) , False,False
Flip
Wend
End
```

Run the program now, and move the sphere around using the arrow keys. Your screen should look similar to Figure 13.12.

Let's take a closer look at the code we entered to see how we accomplished this:

Text 10 ,60,—This specifies that the text needs to be placed 10 units from the left of the screen and 60 units down.

"Sphere x-coordinate: "—As you learned earlier, we need to add text in between quotation marks.

+ EntityX(sphere)—By adding a + sign, we are able to add additional variables or text. In this case, we used the variable EntityX(sphere), which displays the x coordinate of the sphere.

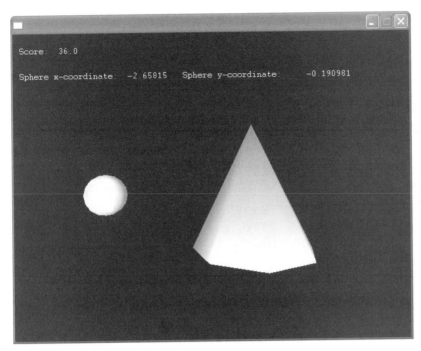

Figure 13.12
The code you added will display the x and y coordinates of the sphere.

+ " Sphere y-coordinate: "—Notice the spaces that were left between the ends of the text and the quotation marks, allowing space for the numbers.

+ EntityY(sphere)—This produces the y coordinate of the sphere.

, False,False—We turned off horizontal and vertical centering. We actually didn't need this part of the code at all, since these are the defaults.

Setting Font Size and Appearance

As you can see by the previous examples, the appearance of the text didn't look too spectacular. It was plain white, was relatively small, and used a standard font. You can change all that by loading fonts, specifying their attributes, and then applying those fonts and attributes to your string of text.

In Blitz3D, you use the LoadFont command to bring fonts into the program and specify their attributes. You can create different font variables so that applying different styles to your text becomes quite easy. Once your fonts are loaded, you can use the SetFont command to apply your font to a specific line of text.

Let's look at a typical line of code used to load a font:

```
FntArial14U=LoadFont("Arial",14,False,False,True)
```

This code may look a little long and involved, but it's actually pretty straight-forward. There are seven parts to the LoadFont command:

```
Identifier = LoadFont (fontname$[,height][,bold][,italic][,underlined])
```

Let's break down the code used as an example to see how it works:

FntArial14U =—This is the identifier, or name, that we've given to the font we're loading. It's a good idea to give it a descriptive name that you'll understand. Typically, the identifier for a font should start with Fnt so that you can quickly recognize what it is. In this case I called the font FntArial14U, which to me indicates that the font is Arial, its size is 14, and it is underlined. Keep in mind that the identifier can be any name you choose.

LoadFont—This is the command that will initiate the font loading. Everything after this command will be within parentheses.

("Arial",—This is the font you are loading. You have to put the font name in quotation marks.

14,—This is the size of the font you are creating. The default size for fonts is 12.

False,—The first of three True or False parameters. This parameter controls whether or not the font is bold. True indicates that the font will be bold, while False will not be bold.

False,—This parameter controls whether or not the font is italicized. True indicates that the font will be in italics, while False will not be italicized.

True)—This parameter controls whether or not the font is underlined. True indicates that the font will be underlined, while False will not be underlined.

Note

Now You Try

Test your understanding of loading fonts. Take a look at the following code and try to determine how the font will appear:

```
F=LoadFont("Times",28,True,True,False)
```

If you guessed that it would be Times, size 28, bold, italic, and not underlined, then you'd be right!

It's a good idea to use only one or two different fonts in your games to avoid distracting players from your game. It's also a good idea to load all of your fonts in various configurations all at once so that accessing them is easy. For example, if you are going to be creating some text in the font Times, you probably should load a few different sizes and some different configurations of attributes all at once so that you don't have to create them as you go along while programming your game. Here's a typical example of how you would create several different "flavors" of the same font so that you would have a library to choose from while programming:

```
fntTunga14=LoadFont("Tunga",14,False,False,False)
fntTunga 14B=LoadFont("Tunga",14,True,False,False)
fntTunga14I=LoadFont("Tunga",14,False,True,False)
fntTunga14U=LoadFont("Tunga",14,False,False,True)
```

Above I've created four different versions of the font Tunga. The first is simply size 14, the second is size 14 and bold, the third is size 14 and italicized, and the last one is size 14 and underlined. You can create any combination of fonts that you want; just keep in mind that every font you load takes up space in memory.

Note

Font Defaults

By default, fonts are set to size 12 with bold, italics, and underline set to False. This means that you do not need to include them as part of your code if you are accepting the defaults. For example, if we wanted to load the font Tunga at size 12, with no bold, italics, or underline, then rather than having to enter `fntTunga12=LoadFont("Tunga",12,False,False,False)`, we would only have to enter `fntTunga12=LoadFont("Tunga")` because all the other defaults are accepted.

Now that you know how to load a font, it's time to learn how to actually apply the font. You do this by using the `SetFont` command right before the line of text you are applying. For example, let's say you've loaded a font as follows:

```
FntArial14BI=LoadFont("Arial",14,True,True,False)
```

You would then apply this font using the following code right before your line of text.

```
SetFont Fntarial14BI
```

All the text that is created after the font is set will take on those attributes (in this case, Arial, size 14, bold, and italicized) until either a new font is set or the font is turned off.

Let's practice applying a font. Create a new program with the following code:

```
; Changing Fonts
;_____
Graphics3D 640,480
SetBuffer BackBuffer()
; Create camera
camera=CreateCamera()
;Create light
light=CreateLight()
;The following code makes the program run
While Not KeyDown( 1 )
RenderWorld
Text 300,20, "This is Arial 24", True
Text 300,120, "This is Arial 24 Bold", True
Text 300,220, "This is Arial 24 Italics",True
Text 300,320, "This is Arial 24 Underlined", True
Text 300,420, "This is Arial 24 Bold, Italics and Underlined", True
Flip
Wend
End
```

Now enter the following code in bold to load the fonts and then apply them:

```
; Changing Fonts
;_____
Graphics3D 640,480
SetBuffer BackBuffer()
; Create camera
camera=CreateCamera()
;Create light
light=CreateLight()
; Loading the fonts
fntArial=LoadFont("Arial",24)
fntArialB=LoadFont("Arial",24,True)
fntArialI=LoadFont("Arial",24,False,True,False)
fntArialU=LoadFont("Arial",24,False,False,True)
fntArialBIU=LoadFont("Arial",24,True,True,True)
;The following code makes the program run
While Not KeyDown(1)
RenderWorld
SetFont fntArial
Text 300,20, "This is Arial 24", True
SetFont fntArialB
```

```
Text 300,120, "This is Arial 24 Bold", True
SetFont fntArialI
Text 300,220, "This is Arial 24 Italics",True
SetFont fntArialU
Text 300,320, "This is Arial 24 Underlined", True
SetFont fntArialBIU
Text 300,420, "This is Arial 24 Bold, Italics and Underlined", True
Flip
Wend
End
```

Take a look at Figure 13.13, which shows how the program should look when you run it now.

Note

Font Color

You can change the color of your font by using the `Color` command before entering the `Text` line. To apply the `Color` command, you simply type `Color` followed by the red, green, and blue values of the color you want to apply. For example, if you wanted to create some red text, you'd enter the code as follows:

```
Color 255,0,0
Text 200,300, "This text will be red because it is preceded by the Color command"
```

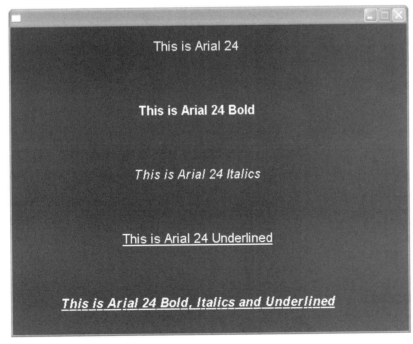

Figure 13.13
When you run the program now, you should see the different fonts applied.

Freeing Fonts

Fonts take up room in memory while they are loaded and therefore could potentially slow down your game. For this reason you should remove your fonts from memory using the FreeFont command after they have been applied. FreeFont works the same way that SetFont does in that you simply name the font that you want to free. You can free the fonts outside of the main loop of the program. Using the example from the previous section, free the fonts by adding the following code in bold:

```
While Not KeyDown( 1 )
RenderWorld
SetFont fntArial
Text 300,20, "This is Arial 24", True
SetFont fntArialB
Text 300,120, "This is Arial 24 Bold", True
SetFont fntArialI
Text 300,220, "This is Arial 24 Italics",True
SetFont fntArialU
Text 300,320, "This is Arial 24 Underlined", True
SetFont fntArialBIU
Text 300,420, "This is Arial 24 Bold, Italics and Underlined", True
Flip
Wend
FreeFont fntArial
FreeFont fntArialB
FreeFont fntArialI
FreeFont fntArialU
FreeFont fntArialBIU
End
```

Math

Don't skip this section just because of the title! I know that math can be fairly intimidating for many people, but I promise that this will be easy. Math actually plays a huge role in all types of video games, but luckily for us, most of the calculations are done behind the scenes by the computer. That being said, there will be various instances where you will have to do some calculations in your programs. The truth is that throughout the examples in the book so far, we've actually done a bit a math, and you probably didn't even notice.

Let's start with a simple example of how you would use math. Earlier in this chapter, we used math when we were determining the score when a sphere bumped into a sphere. Do you remember the code we entered? It was score#=score#+1. See? Just simple addition. The beauty of doing math in Blitz3D is that not only can you work with numbers, but you can also include variables in your equations. The following chart shows you the commands you can use in Blitz3D to write equations:

+   Addition

—   Subtraction

×   Multiplication

/   Division

=   Equals

Let's put our math skills to use by writing a small program that does some math (by the way, all programs you create use math). We are going to write a program that does a simple conversion for us. I happen to live in Argentina, where everyone uses the metric system, which makes things difficult when driving through the States because our speed limits are in kilometers per hour and the U.S. speed limits are in miles per hour. So, as an example, let's start by creating a program that converts kilometers to miles. Start by creating a blank program that contains the following code:

```
; Km conversion
;_____
Graphics3D 640,480
SetBuffer BackBuffer()
; Create camera
camera=CreateCamera()
;Create light
light=CreateLight()
;The following code makes our program run
While Not KeyDown( 1 )
RenderWorld
Flip
Wend
End
```

In order for this program to work, players will first need to enter the number of kilometers they want converted. To do this, we will add something called a *string variable.*

```
;Create light
light=CreateLight()
;Inputting the text
Km = Input (''Please enter the number of km you want to convert to miles '') ;
The following code makes our program run
While Not KeyDown( 1 )
```

Now it's time for the math. At this point, the player has entered in a number for the number of kilometers he wants converted. This number becomes the variable called Km#. Since there are about 0.62137 miles for every kilometer, we need to do some multiplication to figure out the number of miles. To do this, we are going to have Blitz3D calculate the answer to Km#* 0.62137 and then display it onscreen. Remember that * is multiplication in Blitz3D. Enter the following code:

```
;Create light
light=CreateLight()
;Inputting the text
Km = Input (''Please enter the number of km you want to convert to miles '')
;The following code makes the program run
While Not KeyDown( 1 )
RenderWorld
Text 100,50, ''There are '' +km*0.62137 + '' miles in ''
+ km + '' kilometers''
Flip
Wend
End
```

Run the program now, and you'll see your math skills in action. You enter a number in kilometers, and you get your answer in miles (see Figure 13.14). Pretty cool, eh? (That's Canadian talk for "Pretty cool, isn't it?")

While this is just one simple example of how math can be used, you can see that we didn't create any special variables for our equation; we just multiplied our variable (km#) by an amount to get our answer.

Random

Random is your best friend. Well, maybe not your best friend, but a really, really, really good friend. You can do a lot of cool stuff with the Random command in Blitz3D. Okay, enough already, what is Random? The Random command ... well ... makes things random. So far in this book, whenever we've wanted to specify an attribute for an object—for example, the color or size or position of a shape—we

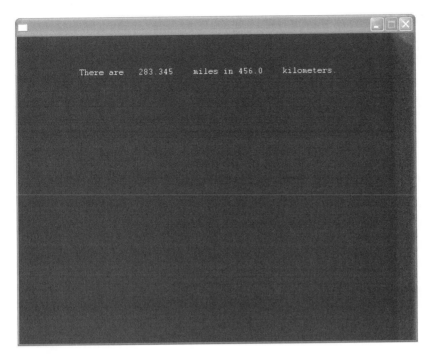

There are   283.345   miles in 456.0   kilometers.

Figure 13.14
Your math skills have created a conversion calculator.

would actually tell Blitz3D what that attribute should be. Using the `Random` command, you can have Blitz3D randomly set the attributes for your object.

Why would you want to use `random`? Let me count the ways. There are literally thousands of different applications for the `Random` command, but I'll give you just a few. Typically, the `Random` command is used when you are dealing with more than one object. Here are a few examples of scenarios where you would use it:

■ Imagine you had a game with 100 different aliens. Rather than having to provide a color to each alien, you could have Blitz3D randomly give them each a color.

■ Let's say you are creating a series of objects like an asteroid field. You'd probably want each asteroid to be a little different in shape. Rather than having to shape each asteroid individually, you could use the `Random` command to randomly create different shapes for your asteroid.

■ In a game with different enemies, you want the enemies to be in a different location each time the game is played. Using the `Random` command, you could have the enemies positioned randomly around the playing field.

So far we've been calling it the `Random` command, but the actual command you use when coding looks something like this:

```
Rand (-10,50)
```

The two numbers that you put in parentheses after the `Rand` command are very important because they allow you to control the range. The number on the left is the lowermost limit for the number, and the number on the right is the uppermost number. In other words, if we were to run this code right now, Blitz3D would randomly choose a number between −10 and 50.

Let's create some code using the `Rand` command so that you can get a better understanding as to what it does. In the following example, we will create a sphere and then randomly give it a color. Start by entering the code for the following program that just creates the sphere:

```
; Random color
;_____
Graphics3D 640,480
SetBuffer BackBuffer()
; Create camera
camera=CreateCamera()
;Create light
light=CreateLight()
;Create a sphere
sphere=CreateSphere()
PositionEntity sphere, 0,0,6
;The following code makes our program run
While Not KeyDown( 1 )
RenderWorld
Flip
Wend
End
```

Now let's add the code to color the sphere. As you should recall, when we color an object we provide a number for the Red, Green, and Blue values. This number is anywhere between 0 and 255 for each color. In this case, we will have Blitz3D randomly select the number for each color by entering the following code in bold:

```
;Create a sphere
sphere=CreateSphere()
PositionEntity sphere, 0,0,6
EntityColor sphere, Rand(0,255),Rand(0,255),Rand(0,255)
```

If you run the program now, you'll see that the sphere has been given a random color. We set the lowest possible number for each color value to be 0 and the highest to be 255 with the code Rand(0,255).

Now let's try something really interesting. I want you to cut the line you just added and paste it into the game loop. The code for the program should now look like this:

```
; Random color
;_____
Graphics3D 640,480
SetBuffer BackBuffer()
; Create camera
camera=CreateCamera()
;Create light
light=CreateLight()
;Create a sphere
sphere=CreateSphere()
PositionEntity sphere, 0,0,6
;The following code makes our program run
While Not KeyDown( 1 )
EntityColor sphere, Rand(0,255),Rand(0,255),Rand(0,255)
RenderWorld
Flip
Wend
End
```

Go ahead and run the program now. Because we added the command to randomly assign a color to the sphere inside the game loop, the color of the sphere changes with each loop of the game. By the way, you are seeing 30 different color changes per second! Here we have randomly changed the color of an object, but you could have just as easily randomly changed its shape or location or any other attribute.

Note

Rand, Rnd, and SeedRnd

There are actually three different commands you can use for generating a random value. The Rand command will result in an integer value, while the Rnd command will produce a floating-point value. You'll learn more about floating-point values and integers in the next chapter, but in a nutshell, an integer cannot have decimal places while a floating-point value can. The Rand and Rnd numbers don't *really* create random numbers; they choose a random number based on a starting point called a *seed value.* The seed value is always the same, so if you ran a Rnd or Rand command, you'd get the same number every time you ran the program. The SeedRnd command changes the seed value so that the numbers it generates are truly random.

As I mentioned earlier, using the Rand command comes in very handy when working with multiple objects. In the next example, we will code a program that creates multiple spheres. We are then going to use the Random command to change the shape of the sphere.

The code used to create the multiple spheres is a For...Next statement. I'll discuss this type of statement further in the next chapter. For now we are just concerned with the Random command that will be used to change the shape of the spheres.

Enter the following code to create the program:

```
; Random Sphere Shapes
;_____
Graphics3D 640,480
SetBuffer BackBuffer()
; Create camera
camera=CreateCamera()
PositionEntity camera, 25,28,-40
;Create light
light=CreateLight()
;Creating Many Spheres
For x = 1 To 10
For y = 1 To 10
sphere=CreateSphere()
PositionEntity sphere, x*5,y*5,6
Next
Next
;The following code makes the program run
While Not KeyDown( 1 )
RenderWorld
Flip
Wend
End
```

Run the program now, and you should see 100 spheres as in Figure 13.15.

Now we will use a Random command to randomly change the shape of each sphere. We are going to add a ScaleEntity command to change the size and shape of the spheres, and we will set the range to be any integer between −3 and 3.

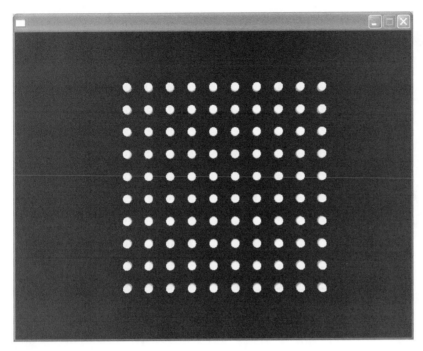

Figure 13.15
We've created 100 spheres using a `For...Next` statement.

Do this by adding the following code in bold:

```
;Creating Many Spheres
For x = 1 To 10
For y = 1 To 10
sphere=CreateSphere()
PositionEntity sphere, x*5,y*5,6
ScaleEntity sphere, Rand(-3,3), Rand(-3,3), Rand(-3,3)
Next
Next
```

When you run the program now, you should have randomly shaped spheres as in Figure 13.16.

Note

Now You Try

I want you to try to create a traffic light that is out of order. It should be a cube stretched to look like a rectangular shape. Within the rectangle, there should be three spheres that will act as lights: one red on the top, one yellow in the middle, and one green on the bottom. Make each of the three lights flicker between different shades of their color. Take a look at Figure 13.17 to get a reference for what the shape should look like. When you are finished, compare your code with the following code. You can also open the file called demo13-07.bb to preview the program.

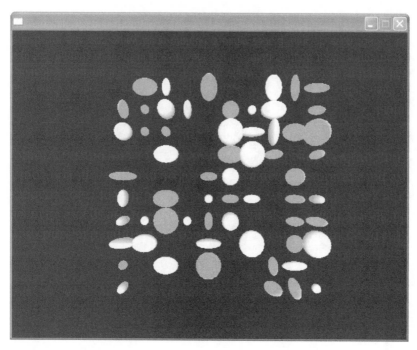

Figure 13.16
Using the Rand command, we created randomly shaped spheres.

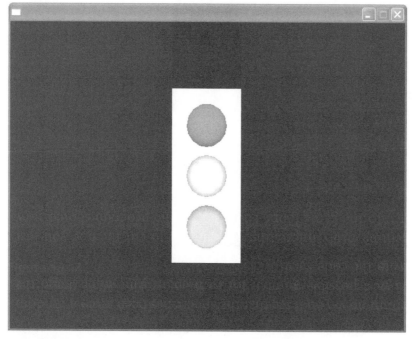

Figure 13.17
Your traffic light should look something like this.

```
;demo13-07.bb - Out of Order Traffic Light
;_____
Graphics3D 640,480
SetBuffer BackBuffer()
; Create camera
camera=CreateCamera()
;Create light
light=CreateLight()
;Create a cube
cube=CreateCube()
ScaleEntity cube, 0.7,1.7,1
PositionEntity cube, 0,0,5
EntityColor cube, 234,234,23
;Create red light
red=CreateSphere()
PositionEntity red, 0,1.2,4.9
ScaleEntity red, 0.5,0.5,0.5
EntityOrder red,-1
;Create yellow light
yellow=CreateSphere()
PositionEntity yellow, 0,0,4.9
ScaleEntity yellow, 0.5,0.5,0.5
EntityOrder yellow,-1
;Create green light
green=CreateSphere()
PositionEntity green, 0,-1.2,4.9
ScaleEntity green, 0.5,0.5,0.5
EntityOrder green,-1
;The following code makes our program run
While Not KeyDown( 1 )
EntityColor red, Rand(177,255),Rand(0,110),Rand(0,87)
EntityColor yellow, Rand(236,255),Rand(193,255),Rand(0,85)
EntityColor green, Rand(0,113),Rand(193,255),Rand(0,120)
RenderWorld
Flip
Wend
End
```

Guns and Bullets

A major component to almost every game is guns and bullets. You have several
options when it comes to creating your weapons. You can design and create them

from scratch using a 3D modeling program, you can download existing weapons that other people have created and are willing to share, or you can create them from basic shapes directly within Blitz3D. Whichever method you choose, there are a few little tricks that you should be aware of when inserting these weapons into your game. This section will cover some of these hints that will make it easier for you to position and use the weapons in your game.

Positioning a First–Person Shooter Gun

In most first-person shooter games, the player's weapon stays in the middle of the screen throughout the entire game. The easiest way to accomplish this is to move the weapon along with the camera. Let's create a simple game that has a small cylinder as our weapon. Our goal is to have the cylinder positioned at the bottom of the screen that moves along with the movement of the player. Start by opening the program called demo13-08.bb. Save the file with a new name and make sure that the files sky.jpg and grass1.jpg are copied to the same folder as the program.

The first thing we'll do is create a weapon for our game. In this case, our weapon will be a simple cylinder that is slightly stretched to give it the look of a cannon. Add the following code:

```
sky_tex = LoadTexture ( "sky.jpg" )
EntityTexture sky,sky_tex
;Creating the Weapon
gun=CreateCylinder(12)
EntityColor gun, 100,100,100
ScaleEntity gun ,0.1,0.6,0.1
PositionEntity gun ,48,1,52
; This following code makes our program run
While Not KeyDown( 1 )
```

Run the program now to see what you've created. We've created a cylinder, given it a gray color, and slightly stretched it. Your screen should look the same as Figure 13.18.

We've created a cylinder that will act as our gun, but it still needs to be rotated and positioned properly.

Our next step is to rotate and position the "gun" so that it is sticking out from the bottom of our screen. To do this, we will change the PositionEntity gun coordinates

Figure 13.18
At this point your gun should look like this cylinder.

and add a `RotateEntity gun` command. Let's start rotating our gun by adding the following line in bold:

```
;Creating the Weapon
gun=CreateCylinder(12)
EntityColor gun, 100,100,100
ScaleEntity gun ,0.1,0.6,0.1
PositionEntity gun ,48,1,52
RotateEntity gun, 55,0,45
```

When you run the program now, your gun should be rotated as in Figure 13.19.

Now that we have our gun rotated, we need to reposition it so that it appears at the bottom of our screen. To do this, simply change the coordinates of the `PositionEntity gun` line as seen in bold:

```
;Creating the Weapon
gun=CreateCylinder(12)
EntityColor gun, 100,100,100
ScaleEntity gun ,0.1,0.8,0.1
```

Figure 13.19
We've rotated the gun along the x and z axes to make it appear like it's pointing outward and upward.

```
PositionEntity gun ,49.2,0.02,50.3
RotateEntity gun, 55,0,45
```

Run the program now. The gun should be positioned as you see in Figure 13.20.

As the program is running, use the left and right arrow keys to move. See the problem? While the camera moves, the gun stays still and therefore quickly moves off the screen. To resolve this problem, we will associate the gun with the camera by making the camera the parent entity of the gun. I touched on parent entities earlier in the book, but to recap: by making an entity a parent of another object, you are in essence "gluing" them together. Whenever you move the parent item, the child item will move along with it. In this instance, the gun will be the child, and the camera will be the parent. The following code in bold is how we create a parent for the gun:

```
;Creating the Weapon
gun=CreateCylinder(12)
EntityColor gun, 100,100,100
ScaleEntity gun ,0.1,0.8,0.1
PositionEntity gun ,49.2,0.02,50.3
RotateEntity gun, 55,0,45
EntityParent gun,camera
```

Figure 13.20
We've positioned the gun at the bottom of the screen. It's almost ready to start blowing away enemies!

Run the program now, and you'll see that wherever you move, the gun follows along because we have attached the camera and the gun using the EntityParent command. When using the EntityParent command, the first element after EntityParent is the object you want to be the child (in this case, gun), which is followed by a comma and the next element, the parent itself (in this case, camera).

Bullets

Creating a bullet itself is really quite simple. You can use an image from a 3D modeling program, but in most cases, spheres or cylinders work just fine. You can fancy up your bullet by applying a bright texture or giving it a color. One idea would be to have the bullet flash by randomly changing its color as it flies. Regardless of how you create your bullet, the tricky part is to make it fly, create multiple bullets, and have them go in the right direction. That's what I'll be covering in this section. The method I describe here is not the only way to create and fire bullets, but it's one of the easiest. We'll explore different options for bullets, including setting a maximum number of bullets, reloading, and changing the direction of the bullets.

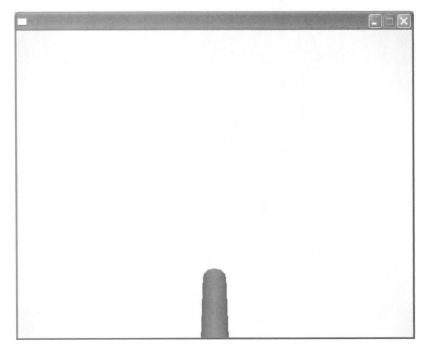

Figure 13.21
You can move this gun around by pressing the left and right arrow keys.

For this example, we'll use a program similar to the one we created in the previous section, with just a few positioning differences. Start by opening the file called demo13-09.bb. Once you have the file open, save it with a new name. If you ran the program now, you'd see a gun made from a cylinder with controls that move the camera (which the gun is attached to), as seen in Figure 13.21.

The goal of our program is to create a bullet that flies out of our gun when the mouse button is pressed. We want the bullet to fly for a few seconds and then disappear. It sounds fairly simple, but there are a few steps involved. We are going to put the code for the bullet firing in the main game loop. Whenever the space bar is pressed, a bullet will fire. Let's start by adding the following code in bold to execute this command:

```
MoveEntity camera, 0,cy#,cz#
RotateEntity camera, 0,rx#,0
;Firing bullets
If KeyDown(SPACE_BAR) Then
EndIf
```

What we have done here is said that whenever the space bar is pressed, then run the following code, until the EndIf is reached. We haven't added the code to actually fire any bullets yet; we'll do that shortly and place the code in between those two lines. To do this, we will create an *array*. Arrays were discussed in Part I. Remember that arrays are used to create multiple variables with just a few lines of code. The bullets themselves are simply spheres that are slightly stretched out. Enter the following code in bold to create the bullets, and then I'll explain:

```
EntityOrder gun, -1
EntityParent gun,camera
EntityColor gun, 100,100,100
;Creating the bullets
fullcart=100
Dim bullet(fullcart)
For i=0 To fullcart
bullet(i)=CreateSphere()
EntityColor bullet(i), 100,100,100
ScaleEntity bullet(i),0.2,0.4,0.2
HideEntity bullet(i)
Next
```

Let's take a look at the code we just entered.

fullcart=100—Here we are creating a variable called fullcart to represent a full cartridge of bullets. In this case, we are saying that the cartridge has 100 bullets available.

Dim bullet(fullcart)—This is how we create an array. This array, which is started with the code Dim, will help create and control the 100 available bullets.

For i=0 To fullcart—This is the start of a For...Next statement. These statements will also be discussed in full detail in the next chapter. Here we are telling Blitz3D to loop the next statements 100 times.

```
bullet(i)=CreateSphere()
EntityColor bullet(i), 100,100,100
ScaleEntity bullet(i),0.2,0.4,0.2
```

These three lines of code create the bullets. Notice the letter i in parentheses beside each bullet name. This i corresponds with the i in the statement For i=0 To fullcart, which allows us to create 100 individual bullets.

HideEntity bullet(i)—This will hide the bullets until we are ready to fire them.

Next—This ends the For...Next loop.

So now that we've got 100 bullets loaded, we need to create the code to fire them. We will add this code in between the code we created earlier that starts an action whenever the space bar is pressed. So let's add the following code in bold that will fire our bullets:

```
MoveEntity camera, 0,cy#,cz#
RotateEntity camera, 0,rx#,0
;Firing bullets
If KeyDown(SPACE_BAR) Then
ShowEntity bullet(t)
PositionEntity bullet(t),EntityX(gun,1),EntityY(gun,1),EntityZ(gun,1)
EntityColor bullet(t),Rand(0,255),Rand(0,255),Rand(0,255)
t=t+1
EndIf
```

Let's take a look at the four lines of code to see what we've done:

`ShowEntity bullet(t)`—When the bullets were first created we hid them. This command will show the bullets. Notice the letter t in parentheses after the word `bullet`. This is a variable that we made up for each individual bullet, and we'll need to use this variable in a moment. We used the letter t, but you can use any variable name.

`PositionEntity bullet(t),EntityX(gun,1),EntityY(gun,1),EntityZ(gun,1)`— This places the bullet right at the position of the gun.

`EntityColor bullet(t),Rand(0,255),Rand(0,255),Rand(0,255)`—For a neat little effect, we'll have each bullet be a different color as it comes out of the gun.

`t=t+1`—This bumps up the variable t by one so that a new bullet is created whenever the space bar is pressed. If this code wasn't there, each time you pressed the space bar, the same bullet would be fired, replacing the existing one. We'll experiment with this code in a moment.

So far, when the space bar is pressed, a bullet will appear at the location of the gun. The bullet will be behind the gun, so you won't be able to see it. In order to make the bullet move, we are going to add another `For...Next` statement. This time, we'll create a new variable, the letter q, that will move each of our 100 bullets as they are fired. Add the following code in bold:

```
;Firing bullets
If KeyDown(SPACE_BAR) Then
ShowEntity bullet(t)
```

```
PositionEntity bullet(t),EntityX(gun,1),EntityY(gun,1),EntityZ(gun,1)
EntityColor bullet(t),Rand(0,255),Rand(0,255),Rand(0,255)
t=t+1
EndIf
For q = 0 To fullcart
MoveEntity bullet(q), 0,1,3
Next
```

So the code we created here will move the bullets whenever they are fired. It's time to run our program. When you press the space bar, you should see bullets fly, as in Figure 13.22.

Our code isn't quite done for a couple of reasons. If you move the left or right arrow keys as you fire, you'll notice a problem. The bullets won't follow the direction of the gun. The gun has moved, but the bullets continue to fly in their original direction, as shown in Figure 13.23.

We need to alter the direction of the bullet to follow the gun by rotating the bullet based on the rotation angle of the gun. Here's how:

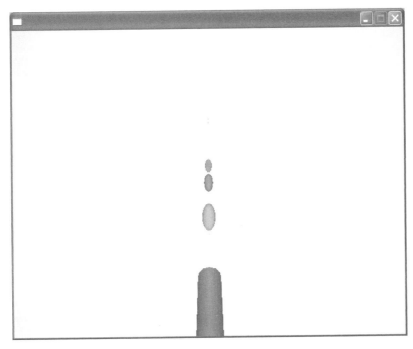

Figure 13.22
When you press the space bar, different color bullets will fly out of the gun.

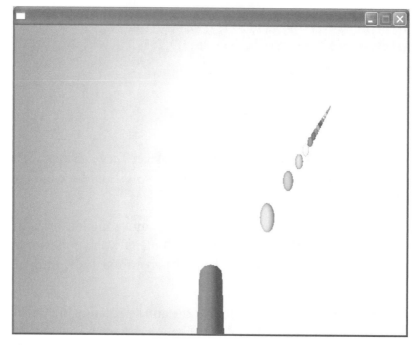

Figure 13.23
When you move the gun, the bullets still fly in their original direction.

```
If KeyDown(SPACE_BAR) Then
ShowEntity bullet(t)
PositionEntity bullet(t) ,EntityX(gun,1),EntityY(gun,1),EntityZ(gun,1)
RotateEntity bullet(t),EntityPitch#(gun,1)-
35,EntityYaw#(gun,1),EntityRoll#(gun,1)
EntityColor bullet(t),Rand(0,255),Rand(0,255),Rand(0,255)
t=t+1
EndIf
```

Run the program now, and you'll see that the bullets follow the direction of the gun, as seen in Figure 13.24.

If you continue to fire, you will notice that after 100 bullets have been fired, an error message appears, as shown in Figure 13.25.

The reason for this is that the cartridge we created has only 100 bullets (fullcart=100). We can either increase this number to be incredibly high so that the player will never run out of bullets, or we can have our cartridge reload. I'll cover reloading in a moment, but for now, let's experiment a little with the code we've already created. Remember earlier that we added the code t=t+1. I want you to temporarily delete this code and then run the program. Notice now that you can fire only one bullet at a time (as seen in Figure 13.26)

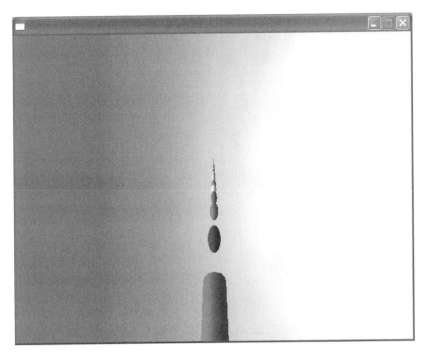

Figure 13.24
After adding the `RotateEntity bullet(t)` code, the bullets now follow the direction of the gun.

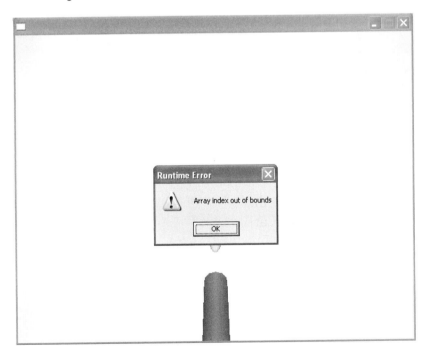

Figure 13.25
When you run out of bullets, a Runtime Error dialog box appears.

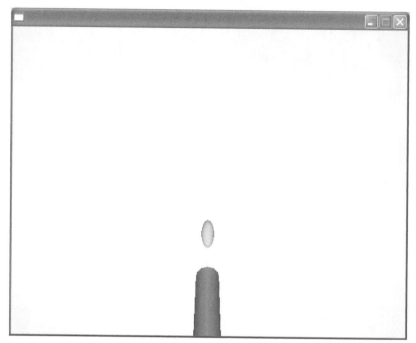

Figure 13.26
You'll only be able to fire one bullet when you remove the t=t+1 code.

because the same bullet is being reused. Go ahead and put that code back into the program.

You can also experiment with the direction of the bullets. You can have them fly higher or lower by changing the y variable in the code MoveEntity bullet(q), 0,1,3. You can also make the bullets fly faster or slower by changing the z variable—in this case, changing the number 3.

Reloading

As just discussed, once you hit 100 bullets, an error will occur because you go beyond the cartridge total. Let's start by getting a better idea of how many bullets we have fired, which we'll do by adding the following code in bold:

```
bulletcount=100-t
RenderWorld
Color 0,0,0
Text 0,15,"Bullets Remaining: "+ bulletcount
```

Here we create a variable called bulletcount, which is created by subtracting the value of t (the variable we associated with each bullet) from the total number of

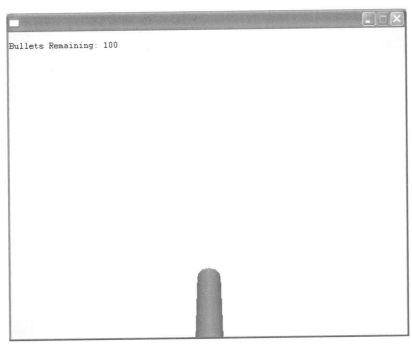

Figure 13.27
The text you entered (Bullets Remaining:) will appear on the screen.

bullets in our cartridge, 100. We then added a line of text that will display the value of the bulletcount. When you run the program now, you'll see the bullets that you have remaining listed at the top left of the screen, as seen in Figure 13.27. Although this is nice, it doesn't solve our problem of the error that appears when we run out of bullets.

The variable t that we created represents each individual bullet. By adding an If statement, we can say that whenever t reaches 100 bullets fired, it should revert back to 1; this way we won't run out of bullets and the error won't appear. Enter the following code in bold:

```
bulletcount=100-t
If t=100 Then
t=1
Endif
RenderWorld
```

Run the program now, and you'll see that whenever the bullet count gets down to 1, it will revert back to 100. We purposely put this If . . . Then statement on three different lines so that we can add to it in the next section. So we've now gotten rid of the error, but it's not really an authentic reload. Usually a player will have to press a button in order to have his weapon reload. In this case, we'll make it so that when the player presses the letter R on the keyboard, his cartridge will be reloaded. We can accomplish this by adding a condition to the firing process and creating a new variable. The new variable we are going to create is called `reload`. We'll change the code so that in order to be able to fire a bullet, `reload` has to be equal to 0; otherwise, we can't fire. Start by adding this line in bold to the "Firing bullets" area of the code:

```
If KeyDown(SPACE_BAR) And reload=0 Then
```

By adding the code `And reload=0 Then` we've made it so that two conditions have to be true in order for a bullet to be fired. First, the space bar needs to be pressed, and secondly, the variable we just created called `reload` needs to equal 0. By default, all variables equal zero unless something changes them, so the program will run just the same at this point.

Now we need to change the value of the `reload` variable once we run out of bullets. Remember that we run out of bullets when the variable t equals 100. Since we already have an `If` statement with the variable `t=100`, we'll just add to it by entering the following code in bold:

```
If t=100 Then
t=1
reload=1
Endif
```

What we've said here is that once 100 bullets have been fired, the `reload` variable will equal 1. Since the `reload` variable needs to equal 0 in order to fire, you will no longer be able to fire. Go ahead and run the program now and press the space bar until you run out of bullets. You'll notice that once the counter reaches 0, you'll no longer be able to fire.

Let's now incorporate a message to the player, letting him know that he has run out of bullets and that he needs to press the letter R in order to reload. We do this by adding the following `Text` code in bold:

```
UpdateWorld
RenderWorld
Color 0,0,0
Text 10,15,"Bullets Remaining: "+bulletcount
If reload=1 Then Text GraphicsWidth()/2, GraphicsHeight()/2,"Press R to
```

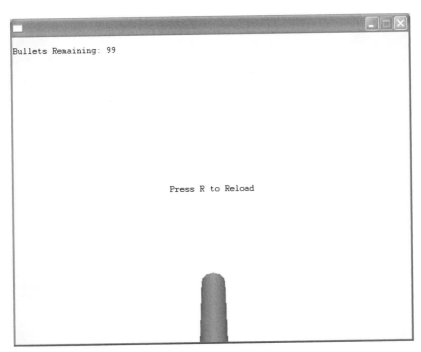

Figure 13.28
The player will see this message as he's reloading.

```
Reload",1,1
Flip
Wend
End
```

This code tells Blitz3D to display the text "Press R to Reload" when the reload variable is equal to 1. Rather than putting in coordinates for where to place the text, we entered the code GraphicsWidth()/2, GraphicsHeight()/2, which places the text halfway on the screen both vertically and horizontally, or, in other words, we put the text in the center of the screen. When you run the program now, a message will appear on the screen, as shown in Figure 13.28, when you run out of bullets.

Now we need to add the code that will reload our cartridge back to 100 bullets and let us fire again. We can accomplish this with a simple If statement:

```
If KeyDown (R_KEY) = True then
t=1
reload=0
EndIf
RenderWorld
```

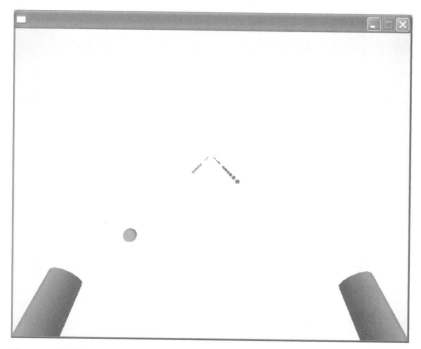

Figure 13.29
Try to create these two guns that fire different color bullets.

Here we are telling Blitz3D that when the letter R is pressed, the variable t should equal 1, or in other words, load 100 bullets. We also change the variable called reload so that it will equal 0 and we can fire again.

Note

Bullet Timing

The bullets that we've created so far in this program come out at rapid fire. As the space bar is pressed, bullets seem to flow out of the gun at Mach speed, and after a moment you are out of bullets. The easiest way around this is to change the code for firing bullets from If KeyDown(SPACE_BAR) to If KeyHit(SPACE_BAR). This will require the player to actually press and let go of the space bar in order to fire another bullet. In other words, holding down the space bar will fire only one bullet.

Note

Now You Try

Take a look at Figure 13.29. Try to create two different guns that appear out of the bottom corners of the screen. Make it so that the gun on the left fires red bullets when the left mouse button is pressed, and the gun on the right fires blue bullets when the right mouse button is pressed. Once you are done, compare your program to the following code:

```
;Double Gun Fire
;_____
Graphics3D 640,480
SetBuffer BackBuffer()
; Create camera
camera=CreateCamera()
;Create light
light=CreateLight()
; Creating the background
background=CreateSphere(32)
ScaleEntity background, 200,200,200
FlipMesh background
EntityColor background, 255,214,100
;Creating the gun
gun=CreateCylinder(12)
ScaleEntity gun,0.2,0.6,0.4
RotateEntity gun,45,0,0
PositionEntity gun, EntityX(camera)+2.5,EntityY(camera)-2, EntityZ(camera)+3
EntityOrder gun, -1
EntityParent gun,camera
EntityColor gun, 100,100,100
maxbull=100
;Creating the gun
gun1=CreateCylinder(12)
ScaleEntity gun1,0.2,0.6,0.4
RotateEntity gun1,45,0,0
PositionEntity gun1, EntityX(camera)-2.5,EntityY(camera)-2, EntityZ (camera)+3
EntityOrder gun1, -1
EntityParent gun1,camera
EntityColor gun1, 100,100,100
;Creating the bullets
Dim bullet(maxbull)
For i=0 To maxbull
bullet(i)=CreateSphere()
EntityColor bullet(i), 100,100,100
ScaleEntity bullet(i),0.2,0.2,0.2
HideEntity bullet(i)
Next
Function Fire()
End Function
```

```
While Not KeyDown( 1 )
;Camera Controls
If KeyDown(200)= True Then cz#=cz#+.01
If KeyDown (208)= True Then cz#=cz#-.01
If KeyDown(205)= True Then rx#=rx#-1
If KeyDown (203)= True Then rx#=rx#+1
If KeyDown(30)= True Then cy#=cy#+.01
If KeyDown (44)= True Then cy#=cy#-.01
If KeyDown (48) Then cy#=0 cz#=0
;Control camera turning radius
If rx# > 180 Then rx#=-180
If rx# < -180 Then rx# = 180
MoveEntity camera, 0,cy#,cz#
RotateEntity camera, 0,rx#,0
;Firing bullets
If MouseDown(1)
ShowEntity bullet(t)
PositionEntity bullet(t),EntityX(gun,1),EntityY(gun,1),EntityZ(gun,1)
RotateEntity bullet(t),EntityPitch#(gun,1)-
35,EntityYaw#(gun,1),EntityRoll#(gun,1)
EntityColor bullet(t),0,0,255
t=t+1
EndIf
If MouseDown(2)
ShowEntity bullet(t)
PositionEntity bullet(t),EntityX(gun1,1),EntityY(gun1,1),EntityZ(gun1,1)
RotateEntity bullet(t),EntityPitch#(gun1,1)-
35,EntityYaw#(gun1,1),EntityRoll#(gun1,1)
EntityColor bullet(t),255,0,0
t=t+1
EndIf
For q = 0 To maxbull
MoveEntity bullet(q), 0,1,3
Next
If t=100 Then
t=1
EndIf
RenderWorld
Flip
Wend
End
```

Pausing

Imagine that you are in the middle of playing the game of your life. Everything is coming together, all cylinders are firing, and the high score is in sight. Just then the telephone rings, the dog starts barking, the doorbell goes off, your mother starts yelling, and nature calls. You don't want to ruin your chances at getting that high score, but what do you do? Easy: You pause the game. Thankfully, programming a pause into your game is easy because Blitz3D has a command that will pause all the action in your game until you press a key. The command for pausing is WaitKey(), which will pause the game until any key is pressed. Let's incorporate it into a game. Open the file called demo13-10.bb, which contains several spheres flying around a nucleus. Save this file to a new location on your computer and make sure the files sunskin.jpg and orbit.jpg are saved in the same location. We'll add a command that initiates the pause whenever the letter P is pressed. Add the following code in bold to the program:

```
While Not KeyDown(ESC_KEY)
If KeyDown(P_KEY) Then WaitKey()
; Turn pivots, making atom orbit around the nucleus.
TurnEntity pivot,0,3,0
TurnEntity pivot2, 3,0,0
TurnEntity pivot3, 0,0,3
```

Now run the program and press the letter P. The action on the screen will stop. Press any other key on the keyboard and the action will resume.

Note

WaitJoy() and WaitMouse()

In addition to using the WaitKey() command, you can also use WaitJoy(), which will pause the program until a joystick button is pressed, or WaitMouse(), which will pause the program until a mouse button is pressed.

Typically, when you pause a program, you'll want something on the screen to indicate that the game has been paused—for example, the words "Game Paused." Earlier in this chapter you added text using the Text command, which is how we'll indicate that the game is paused.

Replace the code If KeyDown(P_KEY) Then WaitKey() with this:

```
If KeyDown(P_KEY) Then
Text 100,150, 'Game Paused - Press any key (except P) to continue'
Flip
```

```
WaitKey()
EndIf
```

Run the program now, and press the letter P. The game should pause, and you should see the same text that appears in Figure 13.30. Notice in the code that we added the command called `Flip`. We need this command because the text is drawn on the back buffer, and we wouldn't be able to see it otherwise. To bring it to the front buffer (directly onscreen), we need to use the `Flip` command.

Note

Pause Function

Rather than putting the pause code in the main game loop, you should create a function for it. It's always the best practice to put as little code in the main game loop as possible. Look back to Part I for instructions on how to use functions.

One other option you might want to use when creating a pause in your program is to clear the screen of action while the game is paused. To do this, you can use the `Cls` command. This command will clear the front buffer (everything on the screen) until the game is resumed. Simply add the `Cls` command as seen here in

Figure 13.30
When the game is paused, this text should appear. It will disappear as soon as the game is resumed.

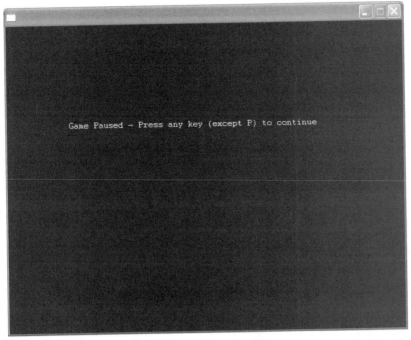

Figure 13.31
Using the Cls command clears the front buffer so that all you will see is the text we created until the game is resumed.

bold. After you've added the code, run the program and then press the P key. The screen should be clear, except for the text shown in Figure 13.31.

```
If KeyDown(P_KEY) Then
Cls
Text 100,150, "Game Paused - Press any key (except P) to continue"
Flip
WaitKey()
EndIf
```

Earlier in the book we created a fancy looking Pause screen that we can incorporate when the game is paused rather than just having boring text. Make sure that the image pause.bmp is saved to the same location as the program. Replace the existing pause code with the following to load your pause image whenever the letter P is pressed:

```
If KeyDown(P_KEY) Then
Cls
pause=LoadImage ("pause.bmp")
```

```
DrawImage pause,0,0
Flip
WaitKey()
EndIf
```

You can see that all of the code created here is almost identical to the pause code that just contained text. The difference is that we used the command `pause=LoadImage ("pause.bmp")` to load the image into the program. We then drew it, starting at point 0,0 (the top-left corner of the screen) by using the code `DrawImage pause,0,0`. Once again, notice how we used the `Flip` command to bring the image to the front buffer. Since our image is exactly the same size as the screen of our program, when we placed it starting at point 0,0, it took up the entire screen. When you run the program now and press P, you should see the Pause screen image appear.

Note

Exit Screen

You can use the same technique covered here to create an Exit screen, asking users if they are sure they want to quit before exiting.

Welcome Screens

Almost every game should have a Welcome screen that provides the player with information on how to start the game, how to control the game, and how to end it. Earlier in the book, we designed a Welcome screen that we will now incorporate into our program. The code we are going to use to load our Welcome screen will be a function (I'll cover functions in greater detail in the next chapter) that we'll include at the very beginning of our program. Start by opening demo13-11.bb, which is a program with several spheres pivoting around each other. Save the file with a new name in another location on your computer, and make sure the files sunskin.jpg, and orbit.jpg are saved in the same location. Make sure that the image welcome.bmp is also located in the same location.

The key to the Welcome screen code is to put the function right at the beginning of our program, before all other code. After the function is executed, the main program will start at the point where the function ended. Enter the following code right at the beginning of the program:

```
; demo13-11.bb - welcome screen
```

```
; --------------------------------
welcome()
Function welcome()
Graphics 640,480
screen=LoadImage ("welcome.bmp")
DrawImage screen,0,0
While Not KeyDown(1)
If KeyDown(31) Then Return
Wend
End Function

Graphics3D 640,480
SetBuffer BackBuffer()
```

Let's take a look at the code line by line to see what we've just done:

`welcome()`—This launches the function called `welcome()`.

`Function welcome()`—This is the start of the definition of the function we have called welcome.

`Graphics 640,480`—This line sets the screen resolution.

`screen=LoadImage ("welcome.bmp")`—This will load the image called "welcome.bmp" into the program but will not display it.

`DrawImage screen,0,0`—This will display the image we have loaded, starting at the 0,0 point on the screen.

`While Not KeyDown(1)`—This starts a loop within the function.

`If KeyDown(31) Then Return`—If the letter S is pressed, the function will end, and we will be returned to the main program.

`Wend`—This ends the loop.

`End Function`—This ends the function.

Run the program now, and you should see the Welcome screen appear. When you press the letter S, the Welcome screen should disappear and the game should begin.

Summary

We learned a heck of a lot in this chapter! We went over tons of different 3D game components—everything you need to make your own game!

This chapter covered the following concepts:

- Gravity

- Jumping

- Velocity

- Chase cameras

- Text

- First-person-styled shooter games

Finally, in the last chapter, we are going to build our own game!

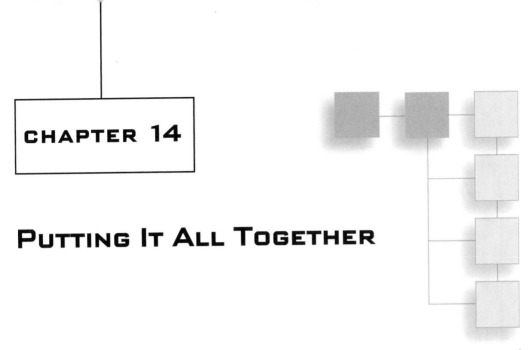

CHAPTER 14

PUTTING IT ALL TOGETHER

Think of everything that you've learned so far in this book as a semester of learning leading up to your final exam. This chapter is the final exam, in which you'll put together many of the concepts that you've learned so far and apply them while creating an actual video game. The game won't be like *Doom*, *Halo*, *Half-Life*, or any of the other commercial games that you see on the market. It will actually be quite simple. That being said, it will apply many of the concepts you've learned, and you should be proud of the work that you've done to bring you to this point.

Rather than just copying the code you see in this chapter, try to actually think of it as an exam. Before each block of code, I'll create a section describing what we are trying to accomplish. Read these sections and try to create the game on your own. If you get stuck, refer to the code and see where you went wrong.

Planning the Game—"3D Gallery"

Here is the breakdown of the game that we will now create called "3D Gallery." The game will be a 3D version of a shooting gallery at a local fair. The player will shoot at different objects moving around the game environment. The goal of the game is to find and shoot all of the moving objects. Here are the key points of the game:

- The game will be a first-person shooter, meaning that the player won't actually be seen.

- The player will have a gun that will be seen at the bottom of the screen wherever the player is moved.

- When the player fires the gun (by pressing the space bar), a missile will fly out of the gun, moving forward and slightly upward.

- There will be five different types of items in the gallery.

- The targets will be grouped in five and will be constantly moving.

- If the target hits the ground, it will randomly be placed at another position in the sky.

- The world will have gravity and all objects will float to the ground.

- The world of the game will contain water and hills.

- The player will earn one point for every target hit.

- The targets will disappear when a bullet hits them.

- The game ends when all the targets have been destroyed or when three minutes have elapsed.

- Using the up and down arrow keys, you can move the player forward and back.

- Using the left and right arrow keys, you can rotate the player horizontally.

- The player will have 100 missiles but can reload by pressing the R key.

- The game can be paused by pressing the P key.

- When the game ends, the player will be presented with a screen instructing him how to restart or exit.

- When the game starts, the player will be presented with a Welcome screen showing instructions for controlling the player and the game.

- When the game is paused, a screen will appear indicating to the player that pressing the mouse button will restart the game.

- The score, time remaining, and bullets remaining will be displayed on the screen.

Files for the Game

Most of the files that we will use in this game we either have created earlier in the book or will create specifically for this game. That being said, we are going to use some existing 3D models for the targets. Special thanks to Adam Kruvand at Studio2a for providing the models. Make sure that you create a new folder on your computer and copy the following files from the CD into the folder:

duck.3ds

seahorse.3ds

donkey.3ds

flamingo.3ds

dolphin.3ds

snake.3ds

bullet.3ds

welcome.bmp

pause.bmp

end.bmp

ground.jpg

explode.wav

phaser.wav

Creating the Water Texture

The only file that we are going to create from scratch is that of the water. Using Corel PHOTO-PAINT, we'll create a texture that looks like water. One problem with the textures that we've created so far is that they weren't seamless. We need to create textures that look identical where they start and end so that there are no "seams." I'll show you a technique you can use in PHOTO-PAINT so that your textures are seamless.

1. Launch PHOTO-PAINT and click the New button in the Welcome screen that appears. In the dialog box that appears (see Figure 14.1), change the

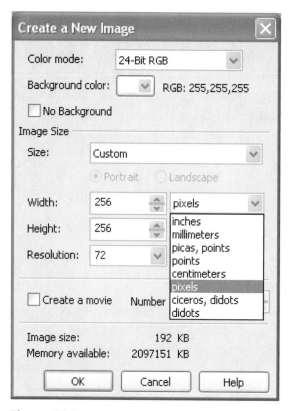

Figure 14.1
Enter the dimensions in this dialog box to create a texture document.

units of measurement to pixels. Make the height and width of the document 256 pixels, and change the resolution to 72 dpi. Also change the Color mode to 24-bit RGB and click OK.

2. Click Edit > Fill to bring up the Fill dialog box (see Figure 14.2). Click the Texture Fill button (the last large colored button) and then click the Edit button. You can now select and modify the fill.

3. Click on the Texture Library drop-down menu and select Samples from the list (see Figure 14.3). Now scroll through the list of different textures and choose Swimming pool2. Click OK, and you will be returned to the main dialog box. Click OK to close the dialog box. The fill will now be applied to your document, and you should see an image of some clouds.

4. We are now going to make the texture "seamless" by making sure that when copies of the texture are placed side by side, the player won't be able to tell where the texture begins or ends. Click Effects > Distort > Offset.

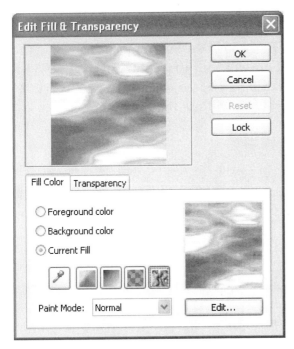

Figure 14.2
Click the Texture Fill button and then the Edit button.

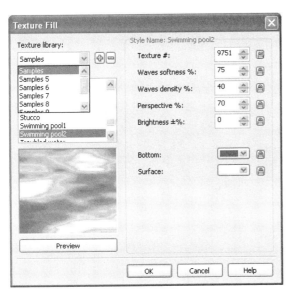

Figure 14.3
Choose the Swimming pool2 fill to create a water-like texture.

This will bring up a dialog box (see Figure 14.4), from which we can shift texture horizontally or vertically. Enter 50 in the horizontal box and 0 in the vertical box and then click OK. This will shift the texture over by 50% so that you can see the "seam" that will be created when the textures are placed side by side. To remove this, we will use the Clone tool.

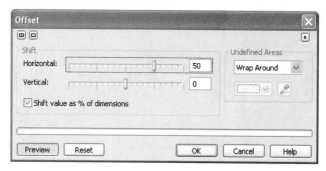

Figure 14.4
Shift the texture vertically and you'll see the seam.

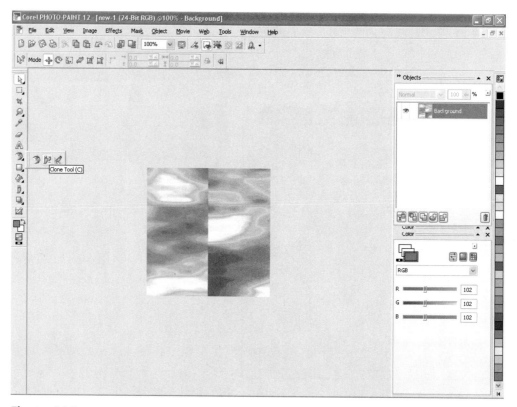

Figure 14.5
Choose the Clone tool from the flyout.

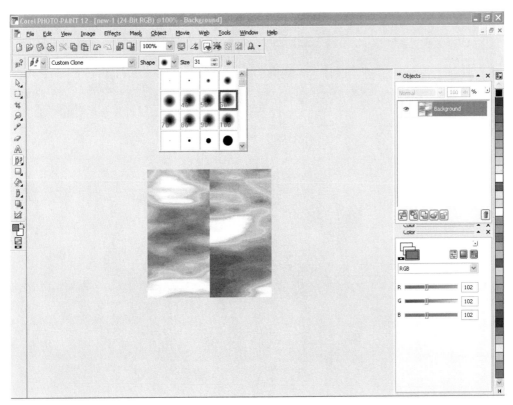

Figure 14.6
Choose the size 60 brush from the drop-down menu.

5. Click and hold the tool right under the letter A in the toolbox. A flyout of tools will appear. From that flyout (see Figure 14.5), click the Clone tool (which is the button with two little brushes).

6. Click on the Shape drop-down button from the toolbar. From the menu that appears, select the feathered option with a 60 on it (see Figure 14.6).

7. Right-click on an area beside the stitch but not including the stitch. This area will now be the source. Now click on the stitch and you'll see the stitch area disappear. Repeat this step for other areas until the stitch is completely removed, as shown in Figure 14.7.

8. Click Effects > Distort > Offset. This will bring up a dialog box from which we can shift texture horizontally or vertically. This time we will change the vertical offset. Enter 0 in the horizontal box and 50 in the vertical box and then click OK. You will now see a preview of how the texture will appear when the segments are lined up one on top of the other.

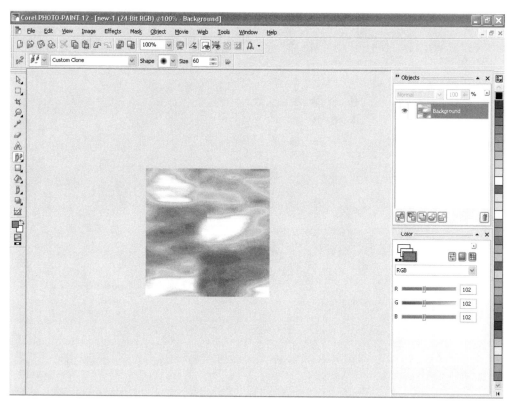

Figure 14.7
Clone the area beside the stitch onto the stitch so that it will disappear.

9. Repeat Step 7 to remove the vertical stitch (see Figure 14.8). You will now have a seamless texture.

10. Click Effects > Distort > Offset. Enter a 0 in both the horizontal and vertical boxes and then click OK. You'll be left with your final texture, which is now seamless.

11. Click File > Save As to bring up the Save As dialog box. Click the drop-down menu, choose the file type called JPG, and give the file the name water.jpg. Save the file into the folder where you saved the other game files.

Welcome Screen

In almost every game, you'll find a Welcome screen that gives the player instructions on the controls needed to play the game. Our game will be no different. We'll use the Welcome screen that we created in Chapter 8, "Getting

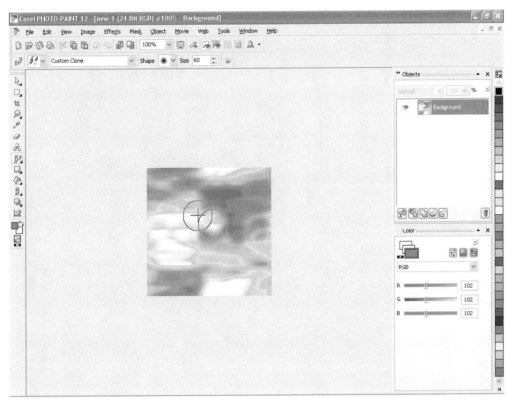

Figure 14.8
Remove the vertical stitch using the Clone tool.

Graphic." If you happen to have skipped that chapter, now would be a good time to go over the process of creating your Welcome screen since you'll need it for this section of code. Start off by creating a new program in Blitz3D and saving it with any name to the folder where you stored all of the files necessary for this game. The first thing that we are going to do is create a function that will initiate the Welcome screen. While creating our program, we'll use lots of comments so that keeping track of where things are will be a breeze. Let's start by adding the following code to create our function:

```
;Shooting Gallery
;_____
;Key constants
Const ENTER_KEY = 28
Const R_KEY = 19
Const V_KEY = 47
```

```
Const P_KEY = 25
Const LEFT_KEY = 203
Const RIGHT_KEY = 205
Const UP_KEY = 200
Const DOWN_KEY = 208
Const SPACE_BAR = 57
Const ESC_KEY = 1
;This line launches the welcome function
    welcome()
;Creating the welcome function
Function welcome()
    Graphics 1024,768
    screen=LoadImage ("welcome.bmp")
    DrawImage screen,0,0
    While Not KeyDown(ESC_KEY)
        If KeyDown(ENTER_KEY) Then Return
    Wend
    End Function
```

Note

Tabs

Notice how there are different tab indentations for different lines. Since our program is going to contain many lines of code, indenting groups of code will make it easier to identify.

Most of this function should already make sense to you. If it doesn't, refer back to Chapter 3 to review functions. That being said, the process of loading an image was only briefly covered, so let's look at the following two lines of that code in particular:

```
screen=LoadImage ("welcome.bmp")
DrawImage screen,0,0
```

These two lines of code start by creating an identifier called screen, and then the LoadImage command loads the image called welcome.bmp into the program. The code DrawImage screen will draw the image starting from the top-left corner of the screen (position 0,0). Go ahead and run the program now, and, with any luck, you should see the Welcome screen appear. When you press the Enter or Return key, the program should end. Notice that the display was set at 1024 × 768, which means the game should take up the entire screen

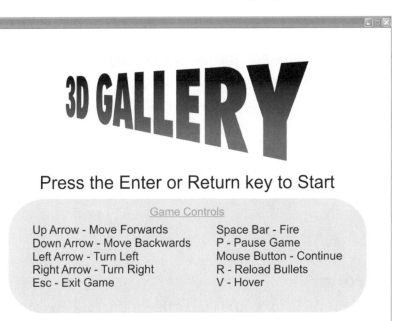

Figure 14.9
The Welcome screen is generated in the function run at the beginning of the program.

on most monitors. If you run the program now, you should see the Welcome screen, as in Figure 14.9.

Setting Up the Graphic Elements and Camera

As done for all our programs, we'll need to set the resolution and the buffer. Even though we set the resolution for earlier in the function, we need to set it for the rest of the program. To do this, we'll enter the following code:

```
EndIf
Wend
End Function
;Setting the graphics for the program
    Graphics3D 1024,768
    SetBuffer BackBuffer()
; Creating the camera
    camera=CreateCamera()
; Creating a light
    light=CreateLight()
```

Setting Up the Game Elements

Now we'll create the game loop for the program using the same code we've used throughout the book. Add the code below:

```
; Creating a light
   light=CreateLight()
; The following code makes our program run
While Not KeyDown(ESC_KEY)
Renderworld
Flip
Wend
End
```

Creating the World

The world for our game is going to be made up of three different elements. The water in the lakes will be a plane on which we will apply the texture we created earlier. For the hills, we will use a heightmap on which we will apply another texture. The sky won't actually be an object—instead, we'll change the color of the camera, which will make everything that is black appear the color that we specify.

To do this, we'll use the `CameraClsColor` command. Let's start by applying that command in bold:

```
; Create camera
camera=CreateCamera()
CameraClsColor camera, 0,125,255
```

If you run the program now, you'll notice that everything on the screen is the light blue color that we specified in the `CameraClsColor` command. Now we are going to create the water, which, as mentioned earlier, is just a plane with a texture applied to it. Let's add this code in bold:

```
; Creating a light
light=CreateLight()
;Creating the water plane
water=CreatePlane()
PositionEntity water, 0,-15,0
watertexture=LoadTexture ("water.jpg")
EntityTexture water, watertexture
ScaleTexture watertexture,15,15
```

At this point, every part of that code should make sense to you. It's simply a plane with the water texture that we created earlier applied to it. We scaled the texture to make it look more spread out, and we positioned the plane 15 units below the 0 level on the y plane.

Now we will create the terrain for the game. It will be a heightmap with a texture applied to it, scaled and positioned.

```
ScaleTexture watertexture,15,15
; Loading the heightmap
terrain=LoadTerrain ( "ground.jpg" )
    ScaleEntity terrain,5,50,5
    PositionEntity terrain,-500,-20,-500
    tex=LoadTexture( "greenery.jpg" )
    ScaleTexture tex, 50,50
    EntityTexture terrain,tex
    EntityType terrain, type_scenery
```

Run the program now and you should see the sky, mountains, and water, as shown in Figure 14.10.

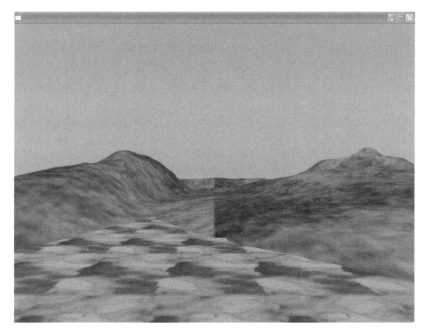

Figure 14.10
Create the sky, mountains, and water.

Gallery Items

The gallery items that will serve as targets for our game will be made up of seven different animals. There will be five copies of each animal for a total of 35 animals. For each animal, we'll create an array of five of the animals and position them, scale them, and color them. Each of the animals will be a .3ds file that we will load. Let's start by creating the ducks, and then we'll create the other animals. Add the following code:

```
EntityTexture terrain,tex
EntityType terrain, type_scenery
;Creating the gallery items

Dim ducks(5)

For x = 1 To 5
ducks(x)= LoadMesh ("duck.3ds")
PositionEntity ducks(x), x*15,0,90
EntityColor ducks(x), 255,255,0
ScaleEntity ducks(x), 0.2,0.2,0.2
Next
```

Run the program now, and with any luck you should have five ducks across the screen, as in Figure 14.11.

Figure 14.11
The array you created should produce five yellow ducks.

Now we need to re-create this array for the other animals. The code will look almost exactly the same with the exception that we'll change the animal name and adjust their position and size.

```
;Creating the gallery items

Dim ducks(5)
        For x= 1 To 5
ducks(x)= LoadMesh ("duck.3ds")
PositionEntity ducks(x), x*15,0,90
EntityColor ducks(x), 255,255,0
ScaleEntity ducks(x), 0.2,0.2,0.2
    Next

Dim seahorse(5)
For x = 1 To 5
seahorse(x)= LoadMesh ("seahorse.3ds")
PositionEntity seahorse(x), x*6,10,45
EntityColor seahorse(x), 255,102,0
ScaleEntity seahorse(x), 0.03,0.03,0.03
Next

Dim donkey(5)
For x = 1 To 5
donkey(x)= LoadMesh ("donkey.3ds")
PositionEntity donkey(x), x*5,35,85
EntityColor donkey(x), 204,204,204
ScaleEntity donkey(x), 0.3,0.3,0.3
Next

Dim flamingo(5)
For y = 1 To 5
flamingo(y)= LoadMesh ("flamingo.3ds")
PositionEntity flamingo(y), y*6,8,25
EntityColor flamingo(y), 102,51,51
ScaleEntity flamingo(y), 0.003,0.003,0.003
Next

Dim dolphin(5)
For x = 1 To 5
dolphin(x)= LoadMesh ("dolphin.3ds")
PositionEntity dolphin(x), x*6,45,0
EntityColor dolphin(x), 102,153,255
```

```
ScaleEntity dolphin(x), 0.3,0.3,0.3
Next

Dim snake(5)
For x = 1 To 5
snake(x)= LoadMesh ("snake.3ds")
PositionEntity snake(x), x*16,10,10
EntityColor snake(x), 153,255,153
ScaleEntity snake(x), 0.06,0.06,0.06
Next
```

Run the program now, and you should see many of the animals, as in Figure 14.12.

Note

Changing the Animals

Feel free to import the animal models into 3ds Max and alter them using some of the techniques you learned earlier in the book.

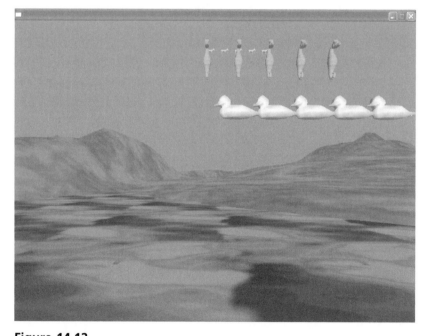

Figure 14.12
You'll see some of the animals at this point, but not all because they are spread out in different locations around the playing field.

Creating the Guns and Bullets

The gun for our game will simply be a cylinder that we will "attach" to the camera so that wherever we move the camera, the gun will follow. The bullets will be copies of the missile that we created in 3ds Max earlier in the book. If you happened to skip Chapter 10, "3D Modeling," you have these options: you can go back and create the missile or grab the file from the CD or download it from our website. Let's start by creating the code in bold for the gun:

```
EntityType snake(x), type_gallery
        EntityRadius snake(x), 5
    Next
;Creating the gun
gun=CreateCylinder(12)
   ScaleEntity gun,0.2,0.6,0.4
   RotateEntity gun,45,0,0
   PositionEntity gun, EntityX(camera),EntityY(camera)-2,
EntityZ(camera)+3
   EntityOrder gun, -1
   EntityParent gun,camera
EntityColor gun, 100,100,100
```

The code that we've used to create the gun simply creates a cylinder, colors it, positions it at the bottom of our screen, and then assigns the camera as its parent so that wherever the camera goes, it goes. The code we'll use for the bullets is very similar to that which we used in Chapter 13, "Other 3D Game Components." It will be an array that contains 100 bullets and loads the missile we created earlier. We'll also create a variable called maxbull that will limit the number of bullets in our cartridge to 100 before having to reload. We'll deal with reloading later; for now, let's create the bullets by adding the following code in bold:

```
EntityParent gun,camera
EntityColor gun, 100,100,100
;Creating the bullets
maxbull = 100
   Dim bullet(maxbull)
     For i=0 To maxbull
        bullet(i)=LoadMesh ("bullet.3ds")
        EntityColor bullet(i), 100,100,100
     Next
```

Run the program now, and you should see the gun at the bottom of the screen. You won't see any bullets because we haven't positioned them; we'll do that during the firing process a little later on in the program.

Game Control and Gravity

The controls for the game are actually quite simple. The arrow keys will move the player back and forth or rotate the view from side to side. In this section, we'll also create the illusion of gravity by constantly moving the player downward, and we'll allow the player to jump by moving the camera upward every time the letter V is pressed. I chose the letter V because it is close to the space bar (which is what will be used for firing bullets later) so that the player can jump and fire using the same hand. Add the following code in bold to add controls and gravity for the game:

```
; The following code makes our program run
    While Not KeyDown(ESC_KEY)
If KeyDown(RIGHT_KEY)=True Then TurnEntity camera,0,-1,0
If KeyDown(LEFT_KEY)=True Then TurnEntity camera,0,1,0
If KeyDown(DOWN_KEY)=True Then MoveEntity camera,0,0,-1
If KeyDown(UP_KEY)=True Then MoveEntity camera,0,0,1
If KeyDown(V_KEY)=True Then TranslateEntity camera,0,3,0
MoveEntity camera, 0,-0.8,0
```

If you run the program now, you may be in for a little shock. Because we created gravity, the camera will move downward and fall right through the ground because we have yet to set up collisions. If you hold down the letter V, you can hover above the plane to get a good look at your playing field, as in Figure 14.13.

Moving Targets

Right now, the targets in the game would be really easy to hit because they aren't moving. We'll change that by adding the code to move the different objects at different speeds. We'll create different speeds and different directions for each of the types of targets so that it will be difficult to hit them with the bullets. We'll use a For. . . Next statement to move each of the five copies of each animal. Add the following code in bold:

```
If KeyDown(V_KEY)=True Then TranslateEntity camera,0,3,0
MoveEntity camera, 0,-0.8,0
; Moving the targets
For a = 1 To 5
```

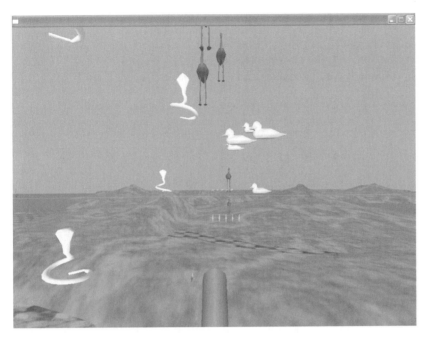

Figure 14.13
If you hold down the letter V and press the arrow keys, you can get a good view of your playing field.

```
MoveEntity ducks(a), 0.1,-.02,0
MoveEntity seahorse(a), 0,-.02,0
MoveEntity donkey(a), 0,-.02,0
MoveEntity flamingo(a), 0.1,-0.2,0
MoveEntity snake(a), -0.2,-0.2,0
MoveEntity dolphin(a), 0,-0.2,-0.3
Next
```

Firing Bullets

The ability to fire bullets is one of the most important aspects of our game and will involve quite a bit of code. As stated earlier, we have a cartridge of 100 bullets, and we want the player to have to reload when he runs out of bullets. We'll also need to create collisions so that when a bullet strikes a target, the target disappears and the score goes up by one. We'll take care of that in a bit; for now, we'll just create the code that fires the bullets.

```
MoveEntity dolphin(a), 0,-0.2,-0.3
Next
;Firing bullets
If KeyHit (SPACE_BAR)
```

```
PositionEntity bullet(t)
,EntityX(gun,1),EntityY(gun,1),EntityZ(gun,1)
        RotateEntity bullet(t),EntityPitch#(gun,1)-
35,EntityYaw#(gun,1),EntityRoll#(gun,1)
        EntityColor bullet(t),0,0,255
    EndIf
For q = 0 To maxbull
    MoveEntity bullet(q), 0,0.8,3
Next
```

If you ran the program now, you could fire by pressing the space bar—the only problem being that you are still falling through the ground because the gravity isn't offset by a collision. In a moment, we'll create our collisions, but before that, let's cover pausing the game.

Pausing the Game

If the player needs to take a break, he can always pause the game by pressing the letter P. When the letter P is pressed, a new image will appear on the screen, informing the player that he can press the mouse button to resume the game. Add the following code in bold to create the pause code:

```
For q=0 To maxbull
        MoveEntity bullet(q), 0,0.8,3
    Next
;Pausing the game
If KeyDown(P_KEY) Then
    Cls
    pause=LoadImage ("pause.bmp")
    DrawImage pause,0,0
    Flip
    WaitMouse()
EndIf
```

Creating Collisions

Collisions are of utmost importance to our game for several reasons. Using collisions, we'll have the bullets destroy the targets, we'll prevent the player from falling through the ground, and we'll randomly reposition the targets when they hit the ground. We need to identify our collisions, assign a collision type to each object, and then define the collisions. We'll start with the easy part, identifying the collision types. There are four different groups of collision objects that we will create for this game: the scenery, the bullets, the player, and the gallery items. To define these groups, add the following code in bold:

```
Graphics3D 1024,768
SetBuffer BackBuffer()

;Setting the type values
type_player=1
type_scenery=2
type_gallery=3
type_bullet=4
```

Now that we have the types identified, we need to assign each object in our game to one of these types by using the `EntityType` command. Since many of the objects, such as the targets and the bullets, are part of an array, we need to enter this code within the actual array scattered throughout the program. There are actually eleven different lines of code you need to add in different locations. Here is a list that you can use as a checklist as you go through your program:

```
EntityType camera, type_player
EntityType water, type_scenery
EntityType terrain, type_scenery
EntityType ducks(x), type_gallery
EntityType seahorse(x), type_gallery
EntityType donkey(x), type_gallery
EntityType flamingo(y), type_gallery
EntityType dolphin(x), type_gallery
EntityType snake(x), type_gallery
EntityType bullet(i), type_bullet
```

While we're at it, we're also going to set the radius size for each of the objects using the `EntityRadius` command. Here are the `EntityType` commands in bold, within the actual text of the program along with the corresponding `EntityRadius` commands.

```
;Shooting Gallery
;_____
;Key constants
Const ENTER_KEY = 28
Const R_KEY = 19
Const V_KEY = 47
Const P_KEY = 25
```

```
Const LEFT_KEY = 203
Const RIGHT_KEY = 205
Const UP_KEY = 200
Const DOWN_KEY = 208
Const SPACE_BAR = 57
Const ESC_KEY = 1

welcome()
Function welcome()
    Graphics 1024,768
    screen=LoadImage ("welcome.bmp")
    DrawImage screen,0,0
    While Not KeyDown(ESC_KEY)
       If KeyDown(ENTER_KEY) Then
           Return
       EndIf
    Wend
End Function

;Setting the graphics for the program
    Graphics3D 1024,768
    SetBuffer BackBuffer()

;Setting the type values
    type_player=1
    type_scenery=2
    type_gallery=3
    type_bullet=4; Creating the camera
    camera=CreateCamera()
    CameraClsColor camera ,0,125,255
    EntityType camera, type_player
    EntityRadius camera, 5

; Creating a light
    light=CreateLight()

; Creating the water plane
water=CreatePlane()
PositionEntity water, 0,-15,0
watertexture=LoadTexture ("water.jpg")
EntityTexture water, watertexture
ScaleTexture watertexture,15,15
EntityType water, type_scenery
```

```
; Loading the heightmap
terrain=LoadTerrain ( "ground.jpg" )
ScaleEntity terrain,5,50,5
PositionEntity terrain,-500,-20,-500
tex=LoadTexture( "greenery.jpg" )
ScaleTexture tex, 50,50
EntityTexture terrain,tex
EntityType terrain, type_scenery
;Creating the gallery items
    Dim ducks(5)
        For x = 1 To 5
            ducks(x)= LoadMesh ("duck.3ds")
            PositionEntity ducks(x), x*15,0,90
            EntityColor ducks(x), 255,255,0
            ScaleEntity ducks(x), 0.2,0.2,0.2
            EntityType ducks(x), type_gallery
            EntityRadius ducks(x), 3
        Next

Dim seahorse(5)
    For x = 1 To 5
        seahorse(x)= LoadMesh ("seahorse.3ds")
        PositionEntity seahorse(x), x*6,10,45
        EntityColor seahorse(x), 255,102,0
        ScaleEntity seahorse(x), 0.03,0.03,0.03
        EntityType seahorse(x), type_gallery
        EntityRadius seahorse(x), 3
    Next

Dim donkey(5)
    For x=1 To 5 donkey(x)= LoadMesh ("donkey.3ds")
        PositionEntity donkey(x), x*5,35,85
        EntityColor donkey(x), 204,204,204
        ScaleEntity donkey(x), 0.3,0.3,0.3
        EntityType donkey(x), type_gallery
        EntityRadius donkey(x), 3
    Next

Dim flamingo(5)
    For y=1 To 5
        flamingo(y)= LoadMesh ("flamingo.3ds")
        PositionEntity flamingo(y), y*6,8,25
        EntityColor flamingo(y), 102,51,51
        ScaleEntity flamingo(y), 0.003,0.003,0.003
```

```
            EntityType flamingo(y), type_gallery
            EntityRadius flamingo(y), 3
        Next

Dim dolphin(5)
    For x=1 To 5
        dolphin(x)= LoadMesh ("dolphin.3ds")
        PositionEntity dolphin(x), x*6,45,0
        EntityColor dolphin(x), 102,153,255
        ScaleEntity dolphin(x), 0.3,0.3,0.3
        EntityType dolphin(x), type_gallery
        EntityRadius dolphin(x), 3
    Next

Dim snake(5)
    For x=1 To 5
        snake(x)= LoadMesh ("snake.3ds")
        PositionEntity snake(x), x*16,10,10
        EntityColor snake(x), 153,255,153
        ScaleEntity snake(x), 0.06,0.06,0.06
        EntityType snake(x), type_gallery
        EntityRadius snake(x), 5
    Next

;Creating the gun
gun=CreateCylinder(12)
ScaleEntity gun,0.2,0.6,0.4
RotateEntity gun,45,0,0
PositionEntity gun, EntityX(camera),EntityY(camera)-2, EntityZ(camera)+3
EntityOrder gun, -1
EntityParent gun,camera
EntityColor gun, 100,100,100

;Creating the bullets
maxbull = 100
Dim bullet(maxbull)
    For i=0 To maxbull
        bullet(i)=LoadMesh ("bullet.3ds")
        EntityColor bullet(i), 100,100,100
        EntityType bullet(i), type_bullet
    Next
```

Wow, that was a lot of fishing through our code, but we got it done! Now that we have our objects assigned to different collision types, we must create the collisions themselves. We want to set the collisions for the gallery items and the scenery, the bullets and the gallery items, and the player and the scenery. All will be set to slide (a collision value of 2) except for the collision between the player and the scenery, in which case we want the collision to stop, so we assign it a collision value of 1. Enter the following code in bold:

```
bullet(i)=LoadMesh ("bullet.3ds")
   EntityColor bullet(i), 100,100,100
   EntityType bullet(i), type_bullet
Next
; Defining the Collisions
Collisions type_gallery,type_scenery,2,2
Collisions type_bullet,type_gallery,2,1
Collisions type_player,type_scenery,2,2
Collisions type_scenery, type_gallery, 2,2
```

Before we can run our program and test to see if our collisions work, there is one important line of code we need to enter: UpdateWorld. UpdateWorld checks for collisions and takes the appropriate actions, and we need to enter it before RenderWorld near the end of the program:

```
Updateworld
   RenderWorld
   Flip
Wend
End
```

Now run the program, and, with any luck, what you see on your screen should look similar to Figure 14.14. Notice how your player no longer falls through the ground, because of the collisions we've created.

Changing the Gallery

Because we have our collisions set up, we can now control how different objects in our game interact with one another. To add an additional element of difficulty to our game, we'll have the gallery items change their location whenever they hit the ground. We'll use a For . . . Next statement that will check every gallery item to see if it has collided with the ground. If a collision has occurred, we'll reposition the item that has collided with the ground to a random location on the

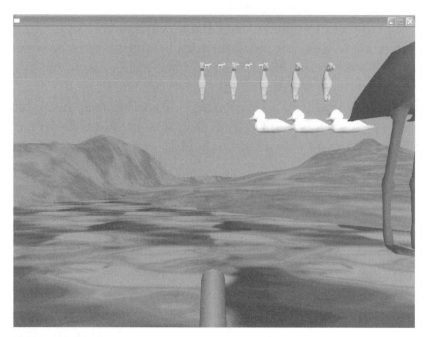

Figure 14.14
After creating collisions, the game should start to come together.

playing field. If you are unclear on the code used here, review Chapter 11, "Collisions." Enter the following code in bold:

```
MoveEntity dolphin(a), 0,-0.2,-0.3
   Next
;Changing the position of gallery items
   For q = 0 To maxbull
      If CountCollisions (terrain)
         smash=CollisionEntity (terrain,1)
         PositionEntity smash, 0,Rand(10,100),Rand
           (-100,100)
      EndIf
   Next
```

Destroying Gallery Items

The goal of the game is to destroy the gallery items by hitting them with the bullets that you fire from your gun. To accomplish this, we need to check to see whether a bullet has collided with a gallery item and, if so, hide the gallery item that has been hit.

```
For q = 0 To maxbull
   MoveEntity bullet(q), 0,0.8,3
   If CountCollisions (bullet(q))
      crash=CollisionEntity (bullet(q),1)
      HideEntity crash
   EndIf
Next
```

Run the program now and start firing away. You should notice that whenever a gallery item is hit, it disappears.

Reloading Bullets

We only want our players to have 100 bullets before they reload. In order to accomplish this, we will need to add another condition to our If statement that controls the firing of the bullets. We'll then use the R key (19) to reload the bullets. We created code similar to this in Chapter 13 so if any of the following code doesn't make sense, then go back and review that chapter.

```
;Firing bullets
   If KeyHit (SPACE_BAR) And reload = 0
      PositionEntity bullet(t)
,EntityX(gun,1),EntityY(gun,1),EntityZ(gun,1)
      RotateEntity bullet(t),EntityPitch#(gun,1)-
35,EntityYaw#(gun,1),EntityRoll#(gun,1)
      EntityColor bullet(t),0,0,255
      t=t+1
   EndIf
   For q = 0 To maxbull
      MoveEntity bullet(q), 0,0.8,3
      If CountCollisions (bullet(q))
         crash=CollisionEntity (bullet(q),1)
         HideEntity crash
      EndIf
   Next
bulletcount=100-t
If t=100 Then
   reload=1
EndIf
If KeyDown (R_KEY) = True Then
   t=0
```

```
        reload=0
    EndIf
    ;Firing bullets
        If KeyHit (SPACE_BAR) And reload = 0
            PositionEntity bullet(t)
    ,EntityX(gun,1),EntityY(gun,1),EntityZ(gun,1)
            RotateEntity bullet(t),EntityPitch#(gun,1)-
    35,EntityYaw#(gun,1),EntityRoll#(gun,1)
            EntityColor bullet(t),0,0,255
            t=t+1
        EndIf
        For q = 0 To maxbull
            MoveEntity bullet(q), 0,0.8,3
            If CountCollisions (bullet(q))
                crash=CollisionEntity (bullet(q),1)
                HideEntity crash
            EndIf
        Next
    bulletcount=100-t
    If t=100 Then
        reload=1
    EndIf
    If KeyDown (R_KEY) = True Then
        t=0
        reload=0
    EndIf
```

Score

Every time a bullet collides with a gallery object, we want the score to go up by one. This is easy to accomplish. We'll create a variable called score# and have it go up by one whenever a bullet-to-gallery object collision occurs. Enter the following code in the "Firing bullets" section:

```
For q = 0 To maxbull
MoveEntity bullet(q), 0,0.8,3
If CountCollisions (bullet(q))
crash=CollisionEntity (bullet(q),1)
HideEntity crash
score#=score#+1
EndIf
Next
```

Time Remaining

As discussed earlier in this chapter, the game will end when one of two things happen: either all the gallery items have been destroyed or three minutes have elapsed. In order to time the game, we need to create two timers—one outside the game loop that will start the timer and one inside the game loop that will indicate the current time in the game. When we subtract the current time from the start time, we'll end up with how much time has elapsed. Start by creating a variable called starttime just before the game loop:

```
;Defining the starting time of the game
starttime=MilliSecs()
;The following code makes our program run
While Not KeyDown(ESC_KEY)
```

Now we'll create two more variables within the game loop: one called currenttime that will indicate the current time in the game and will change with every loop of the game and then another one called timeleft.

```
UpdateWorld
RenderWorld
currenttime = MilliSecs()
timeleft= 180000 - ((currenttime - starttime))
```

Let's take a closer look at the timeleft variable. Keep in mind that we want our game to be three minutes long, which is 180,000 milliseconds. So we subtract the starttime from the currenttime to see how many milliseconds have passed. We then subtract this from 180,000 to see how many milliseconds are left in the game.

Ending the Game

For the game to end, all of the gallery items need to be destroyed (in other words, the score has to equal 35) or the time elapsed will need to equal zero. Whenever one of those two conditions is met, a graphic will appear allowing the user to exit the game or start over. If he elects to start over, we need to have the program jump back to the beginning. We'll accomplish this by using a Goto command. Remember that with Goto commands we need to create a bookmark so the computer knows where to jump to. In this case, we'll create a bookmark at the beginning of the program. Add the following bookmark in bold to the game code:

```
;Creating a bookmark
    .start
;Setting the graphics for the program
```

```
Graphics3D 1024,768
SetBuffer BackBuffer()
```

Now we need to create the code that will load the graphic and jump to the starting point if the space bar is pressed when the game is over or will end the program if the Esc key is pressed. Enter the following code in bold.

```
;Ending the game
If score# = 35 Or timeleft < 0 Then
Cls
End=LoadImage ("end.bmp")
DrawImage End,0,0
Flip
WaitKey()
If KeyDown(ESC_KEY) Then End
If KeyDown (SPACE_BAR) Then Goto start
EndIf
UpdateWorld
RenderWorld
```

Play the game now and wait three minutes. At the end, the end.bmp image should appear, as in Figure 14.15

Figure 14.15
When all the gallery items are destroyed or three minutes have elapsed, the end.bmp image will appear.

Text

We need to add three different text elements to the screen: the score, the time remaining, and the bullets remaining. Since we already have variables created for all three, we'll just have to add a line of code to display each of them. Notice how we divide the `timeleft` variable by 1000 so that the player will see the time remaining in seconds. We'll also add a line of text to appear when the player has run out of bullets. Add the following code in bold:

```
Text 100,10,"Score: " +score#,True,False
Text 400,10,"Bullets Remaining: "+bulletcount
Text 800,10,"Time Remaining: "+TimeLeft /1000
If reload=1 Then Text GraphicsWidth()/2, GraphicsHeight()/2,"Press R to
Reload",1,1
Flip
Wend
End
```

Run the game now, fire 100 bullets, and you should see text appear on your screen, as in Figure 14.16.

Sounds

Before we're ready to sit down and play our game for hours, let's add just a few sound effects. In particular, we'll create sounds when a bullet is fired and when a gallery target is hit. If you remember Chapter 12, "Sounds," you'll know that we need to start by loading our sounds, which we'll do right after the Welcome function at the beginning of the game:

```
Return
EndIf
Wend
End Function
; Loading the sounds phaser=LoadSound("phaser.wav")
explosion=LoadSound("explode.wav")
```

Next we need to associate the sound whenever a bullet is fired:

```
;Firing bullets
   If KeyHit (SPACE_BAR) And reload=0
      PlaySound phaser
      PositionEntity bullet(t),EntityX(gun,1),EntityY(gun,1),EntityZ(gun,1)
```

Figure 14.16
You should see the text indicating the time and bullets remaining, along with the score. When you run out of bullets, the reload message will appear.

We also need to add a sound whenever a gallery item is destroyed, also in the "Firing bullets" section:

```
For q = 0 To maxbull
   MoveEntity bullet(q), 0,0.8,3
   If CountCollisions (bullet(q))
      crash=CollisionEntity (bullet(q),1)
      HideEntity crash
      score#=score#+1
      PlaySound explosion
   EndIf
```

That's it! Your game is complete. Congratulations. Now . . . enjoy!

Note

Not Working?

If for any reason your game isn't working, open the file called shootinggallery.bb, which contains a working version of the final game. Compare your code to the code in the final version to see where things went wrong.

Epilogue

The game is over and the book is done. I've had a lot of fun traveling down this path with you, and I hope that what I have taught you will help you reach new limits in game programming and in life. I know this sounds cliché, but really, I want you to use your new knowledge to make some new games!

Let's talk about the future of game programming—namely, yours. If you enjoyed what we have done with this book, you should know that there is a heck of a lot more out there to learn. Play around with the compiler and the Blitz3D language and create your own games. Believe me, the best way to get better is to practice.

Blitz3D is an excellent language for learning programming. Now that you have the necessary skills for basic programming, you will understand a lot more if you choose to move on to other languages. Some concepts, such as loops and functions, have been hammered into your head in this book, and it won't be nearly as hard to understand them when doing the same in a different language.

As you well know, life is simply a maze of paths, and each choice you make leads you down a path you have to follow. Choose to continue programming, choose to continue making games, choose to enjoy what you are doing, or don't. It's that simple.

Anyway, my tirade is over. I want to hear from you, however! I will gladly help with any games or programs that you create. Simply e-mail me the program at:

maneesh@maneeshsethi.com

I want you to go to my website and join the community! You can find forums that talk about this book also.

http://www.maneeshsethi.com

Lastly, if you liked this book, make sure you review it on amazon.com! It really helps sales! (Tell your friends also.)

Oh yeah, one more thing. Make sure you check out my other books. *Web Design for Teens* teaches you how to make websites, and *How to Succeed as a Lazy Student* will help you learn how to succeed in school without doing any work. *Game Programming for Teens 3rd Edition*, also written by yours truly, allows you to make 2D games for all platforms: PC, Mac, and Linux. Keep your eye out for other things I will be putting out.

I would love to hear from you, so don't hesitate to e-mail me. Heck, just e-mail me and say hi, if you want.

"The greatest trick the devil ever pulled was convincing the world he didn't exist. And like that, *whoosh*, he's gone."

That's it from me. Maneesh Sethi, signing out.

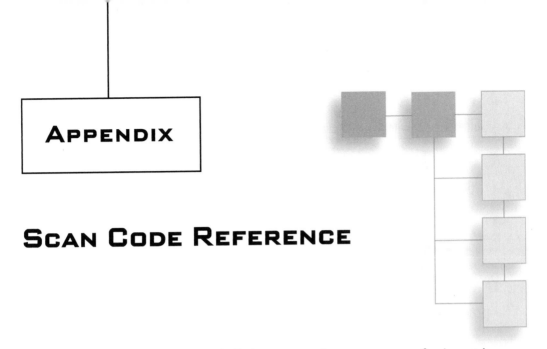

APPENDIX

SCAN CODE REFERENCE

This appendix contains a list of all the scan codes you can use for input in your programs. Scan codes are used in functions such as KeyHit() or KeyDown() like this:

```
KeyDown(scancode)
```

Input the scan code for the key you want to test, and this function will return 1 if the key was pressed.

Many of the following keys won't appear on your keyboard; some of them are international keys (like the symbol for the Yen) and some of them only exist on advanced keyboards that have extra keys (like the Calculator key). Anyway, you can find any key that you would ever think of using on this list, shown in Table A.1

Table A.1 The Scan Code Reference

Keyboard Key	Scan Code	Comments
ESCAPE	1	
1	2	
2	3	
3	4	
4	5	
5	6	
6	7	
7	8	
8	9	
9	10	
0	11	
Minus (−)	12	On main keyboard
Equals sign (=)	13	
Backspace	14	Backspace key
Tab	15	
Q	16	
W	17	
E	18	
R	19	
T	20	
Y	21	
U	22	
I	23	
O	24	
P	25	
Left bracket ([)	26	
Right bracket (])	27	
Return/Enter	28	Return/Enter on main keyboard
Left control	29	
A	30	
S	31	
D	32	
F	33	
G	34	
H	35	
J	36	
K	37	
L	38	

Table A.1 (continued)

Keyboard Key	Scan Code	Comments
Semicolon (;)	39	
Apostrophe (')	40	
Grave	41	Accent grave
Left shift	42	
Backslash (\)	43	
Z	44	
X	45	
C	46	
V	47	
B	48	
N	49	
M	50	
Comma (,)	51	
Period (.)	52	On main keyboard
Slash (/)	53	On main keyboard
Right shift	54	
Multiply (*)	55	On numeric keypad
Left Alt/menu	56	
Space	57	
Capital	58	
F1	59	
F2	60	
F3	61	
F4	62	
F5	63	
F6	64	
F7	65	
F8	66	
F9	67	
F10	68	
NumLock	69	
Scroll Lock	70	
NumPad 7	71	
NumPad 8	72	
NumPad 9	73	
Subtract (−)	74	On numeric keypad
NumPad 4	75	
NumPad 5	76	
NumPad 6	77	

(continued)

Table A.1 (continued)

Keyboard Key	Scan Code	Comments
Add (+)	78	On numeric keypad
NumPad 1	79	
NumPad 2	80	
NumPad 3	81	
NumPad 0	82	
Decimal (.)	86	On numeric keypad
OEM_102	87	On UK and German keyboards
F11	87	
F12	88	
F13	100	(NEC PC98)
F14	101	(NEC PC98)
F15	102	(NEC PC98)
Kana	112	On Japanese keyboards
ABNT_C1	115	/? On Portuguese (Brazilian) keyboards
Convert	121	On Japanese keyboards
NoConvert	123	On Japanese keyboards
Yen	125	On Japanese keyboards
ABNT_C2	126	Numpad on Portuguese (Brazilian) keyboards
Equals	141	Equals (=) on numeric keypad (NEC PC98)
PrevTrack	144	Previous Track (DIK_CIRCUMFLEX) on Japanese keyboards
AT	145	(NEC PC98)
Colon (:)	146	(NEC PC98)
Underline	147	(NEC PC98)
Kanji	148	On Japanese keyboards
Stop	149	(NEC PC98)
AX	150	Japan AX
Unlabeled	151	(J3100)
Next track	153	Next Track
Enter	156	Enter on numeric keypad
Right control	157	
Mute	160	Mute
Calculator	161	Calculator
Play/Pause	162	Play/pause
Media stop	164	Media stop
Volume down	174	Volume −
Volume up	176	Volume +
Web home	178	Web home
Comma (,)	179	On numeric keypad (NEC PC98)
Divide (/)	181	On numeric keypad

Table A.1 (continued)

Keyboard Key	Scan Code	Comments
SysReq	183	
Right Alt/menu	184	Right Alt
Pause	197	Pause
Home	199	Home on Arrow keypad
Up	200	Up Arrow on Arrow keypad
Page Up/Prior	201	Page Up on Arrow keypad
Left	203	Left Arrow on Arrow keypad
Right	205	Right Arrow on Arrow keypad
End	207	End Key on Arrow keypad
Down	208	Down Arrow on Arrow keypad
Next	209	Next Key on Arrow keypad
Insert	210	Insert Key on Arrow keypad
Delete	211	Delete Key on Arrow keypad
Left Windows	219	Left Windows key
Right Windows	220	Right Windows key
Apps	221	Apps Menu key
Power	222	System power
Sleep	223	System sleep
Wake	227	System wake
Web search	229	
Web favorites	230	
Web refresh	231	
Web stop	232	
Web forward	233	
Web back	234	
My Computer	235	
Mail	236	
Media select	237	

INDEX

You're a teen with a great imagination...

Written specifically for teens in a language you understand, on topics you're interested in! Each book in the *For Teens* series features step-by-step instructions to help you conquer the tools and techniques presented. Hands-on projects help you put your new skills into action. And the accompanying CD-ROM or web downloads provide tutorials, instructional videos, software programs, and more!

...unleash your creativity with the series!

Computer Programming for Teens
ISBN: 1-59863-446-1 • $29.99

Web Comics for Teens
ISBN: 1-59863-467-4 • $29.99

Game Programming for Teens
Third Edition
ISBN: 1-59863-518-2 • $29.99

Game Creation for Teens
ISBN: 1-59863-500-X • $29.99

Torque for Teens
ISBN: 1-59863-409-7 • $29.99

Web Design for Teens
ISBN: 1-59200-607-8 • $19.99

Microsoft Visual Basic
Game Programming for Teens
Second Edition
ISBN: 1-59863-390-2 • $29.99

Game Art for Teens
Second Edition
ISBN: 1-59200-959-X • $34.99

COURSE TECHNOLOGY
CENGAGE Learning
Professional • Technical • Reference

Check out all of the *For Teens* books
and order online at **www.courseptr.com** or call **1 800 354 9706**

License Agreement/Notice of Limited Warranty

By opening the sealed disc container in this book, you agree to the following terms and conditions. If, upon reading the following license agreement and notice of limited warranty, you cannot agree to the terms and conditions set forth, return the unused book with unopened disc to the place where you purchased it for a refund.

License

The enclosed software is copyrighted by the copyright holder(s) indicated on the software disc. You are licensed to copy the software onto a single computer for use by a single user and to a backup disc. You may not reproduce, make copies, or distribute copies or rent or lease the software in whole or in part, except with written permission of the copyright holder(s). You may transfer the enclosed disc only together with this license, and only if you destroy all other copies of the software and the transferee agrees to the terms of the license. You may not decompile, reverse assemble, or reverse engineer the software.

Notice of Limited Warranty

The enclosed disc is warranted by Course Technology to be free of physical defects in materials and workmanship for a period of sixty (60) days from end user's purchase of the book/disc combination. During the sixty-day term of the limited warranty, Course Technology will provide a replacement disc upon the return of a defective disc.

Limited Liability

THE SOLE REMEDY FOR BREACH OF THIS LIMITED WARRANTY SHALL CONSIST ENTIRELY OF REPLACEMENT OF THE DEFECTIVE DISC. IN NO EVENT SHALL COURSE TECHNOLOGY OR THE AUTHOR BE LIABLE FOR ANY OTHER DAMAGES, INCLUDING LOSS OR CORRUPTION OF DATA, CHANGES IN THE FUNCTIONAL CHARACTERISTICS OF THE HARDWARE OR OPERATING SYSTEM, DELETERIOUS INTERACTION WITH OTHER SOFTWARE, OR ANY OTHER SPECIAL, INCIDENTAL, OR CONSEQUENTIAL DAMAGES THAT MAY ARISE, EVEN IF COURSE TECHNOLOGY AND/OR THE AUTHOR HAS PREVIOUSLY BEEN NOTIFIED THAT THE POSSIBILITY OF SUCH DAMAGES EXISTS.

Disclaimer of Warranties

COURSE TECHNOLOGY AND THE AUTHOR SPECIFICALLY DISCLAIM ANY AND ALL OTHER WARRANTIES, EITHER EXPRESS OR IMPLIED, INCLUDING WARRANTIES OF MERCHANTABILITY, SUITABILITY TO A PARTICULAR TASK OR PURPOSE, OR FREEDOM FROM ERRORS. SOME STATES DO NOT ALLOW FOR EXCLUSION OF IMPLIED WARRANTIES OR LIMITATION OF INCIDENTAL OR CONSEQUENTIAL DAMAGES, SO THESE LIMITATIONS MIGHT NOT APPLY TO YOU.

Other

This Agreement is governed by the laws of the State of Massachusetts without regard to choice of law principles. The United Convention of Contracts for the International Sale of Goods is specifically disclaimed. This Agreement constitutes the entire agreement between you and Course Technology regarding use of the software.